A
Short History
OF
Ontario

ROBERT BOTHWELL

A Short History OF Ontario

Hurtig Publishers Ltd.

EDMONTON

Hurtig Publishers Ltd.
10560 – 105 Street
Edmonton, Alberta
Canada T5H 2W7

Canadian Cataloguing in Publication Data

Bothwell, Robert, 1944–
    A short history of Ontario

Bibliography: p. 198
Includes index.
ISBN 0-88830-287-8 (bound). — ISBN
0-88830-288-6 (pbk.)

1. Ontario — History. I. Title.
FC3061.B68 1986 /   971.3   C85-091512-0
F1058.B68 1986

54,512

Printed and bound in Canada

To the memory of
my grandfather,
John Rutherford of Simcoe

Contents

Introduction:
The Unknown Province *ix*

1 The Forest Primeval *3*

2 Upper Canada, 1784–1841 *18*

3 The Province United —
and Divided *47*

4 Prosperity and
Provincial Rights *71*

5 Empire Ontario *97*

6 Two Steps Forward,
and Two Back: 1919–39 *120*

7 The Search for Security *149*

8 The Golden Horseshoe
and Beyond *174*

Further Reading *198*

Appendix *201*

Index *207*

Maps

Counties of Southern Ontario *204*

Cities of Southern Ontario *205*

Northern Ontario *206*

Introduction:
The Unknown Province

This book is a first outline of the history of Canada's most populous, richest, most varied, and least known province. When I was first asked to undertake this book, the request gave me pause. Born in Ontario, trained in its universities, and teaching at one, I had had a great deal of exposure to what might be called "the Ontario experience," in its mid-twentieth-century variety. Ontarians wandering outside their province, visiting other parts of Canada, find that other Canadians have no doubt of their own identity, and find, too, that they are prepared to explain to their Ontario visitors what they think their home province is really like. The effect is seldom flattering, but it is also seldom contradicted, because Ontarians often have little sense of what their own province is like, how much there is of it, and how it got the way it is. Nor are Ontarians certain that it is *not* the way others depict it — central and centralizing, self-absorbed, self-congratulatory, and dedicated to a narrow version of provincial self-interest.

The fuzziness of the Ontario self-image is a paradox. No province has had more written about it. Local history is an honourable and ancient profession in Ontario. People living in Renfrew County or in Elgin or the Lakehead can trundle off to their libraries and return with bags full of literature on the history of their locality. But, unless they are prepared to devote months of study to the task, they are unlikely to come away with a book, or collection of books, that can introduce them to the common experience of the province. That is what this book attempts.

It will not take long for the reader to guess that the author is a political historian. Ontario's political experience is the thread that links the various periods and chapters examined in this book. Moreover, what I have tried to stress is the common experience of Ontarians as opposed to the regional. The regional background to Ontario history is already well represented in historical literature; and it is the common past, and the political past, that convey best the sense of what it has been like to live, work, and shape what has now been an identifiable, separate political unit for almost two hundred years. But while the shape of this book is a generalization, it cannot be denied that the regional backgrounds of the province make it exceptionally difficult to establish an "Ontario character" or even a consistent "Ontario political tradition" or political identity. This short history will argue that there have been several such traditions, varying by locality and by ideology — and, in eastern and northern Ontario, by language as well.

This book is a beginning. It is intended for people with little or no background in the common history of Ontario. If it leads on to an interest in the many aspects of the province's history that have already been written about, so much the better. And if it leads on to further attempts to expand our knowledge of the story of the province as a whole, better still. For much, far too much, remains to be done.

Robert Bothwell
Toronto, July 1985

A Short History of Ontario

The Forest Primeval

1   The province of Ontario occupies 412,582 square miles in the centre of North America. It extends from the 74th to the 95th parallels of longitude, and from the 42nd parallel of latitude to the 56th. Its boundaries run through the middle of the Great Lakes and the Saint Lawrence River, on the south, and hug the shores of James and Hudson bays to the north. On the east, the boundary is the Ottawa River for most of its length, and to the west and northeast Ontario is squared off by straight surveyors' lines running in a variety of geometrical patterns.

The boundaries we see on a map are artificial. The countryside is much the same north or south, east or west of a given border. The borders are also relatively recent. The oldest date from 1783, when the future Canada was sundered from the present United States; the most recent date from 1912, when the Canadian government carved off parts of its Northwest Territories to feed the appetites of Ontario, Quebec, and Manitoba. In none of the boundary settlements were the wishes of the inhabitants consulted. But then, Ontario has always been part of a larger political entity, and seldom has had the freedom, or the influence, to have its own way precisely when, and how, it wanted it.

To begin with, there was no Ontario at all. If we go back far enough we find a great brackish inland sea covering Paleozoic mud-beds. Periodically, paleontologists dig up the fossilized remains of Ontario's earliest inhabitants: humble creatures who crawled, flew, or swam through the sea. The earth eventually rose, in various stages. The Canadian Shield became the oldest part of the province. In succeeding years the Shield, and the land to the south, were submerged by Pleistocene glaciers, which came not once but four times to scour the landscape, dredge out future lakebeds, and leave behind deposits of rocks and sand on the landscape. The last glaciation, the Wisconsin, covered all of the province. When it melted, about 10,000 years ago, it created great glacier-fed lakes. The first to reach its present level and shape was Lake Erie. The lakes discharged through a variety of outlets: first, the Mississippi, then the Ottawa River via Lake Nipissing, and finally the St Lawrence River, which assumed its present form and function about 6000 years ago.

During this period the climate was warming up. At the time the first men appeared in what is now Ontario, it was distinctly unpleasant — sub-Arctic to be precise — and supported little more than great game animals whom the early hunters pursued with stone-tipped spears. The climate, and the hunting culture it supported, moved slowly north as the glaciers melted. In the southern Great Lakes basin ice and scrub gave way to forests until, finally, the vegetation of the south assumed roughly the character it has today.

The dominant feature of the landscape is forest. In the extreme north, beside Hudson and James bays, the climate is still sub-Arctic, and beside Ontario's ocean (the only point at which the province connects with salt water) there is a stretch of bog, rock, and swamp that does not support trees. But not much further south the tree-line occurs. The forest of northern Ontario is mostly coniferous, spruce and fir mixed with the ever-present swamp and muskeg of the north. The flora becomes more varied closer to the Great Lakes and, along the north shore of Lake Superior, there is mixed forest, containing both deciduous and coniferous trees: spruce, beech, maple, and other northern hardwoods. Most important of all, there is the pine, red and white. The red pine (*Pinus resinosa*) is the smaller of the two; the white pine (*Pinus strobus*), however, has been known to attain a height of 250 feet, and to measure 6 feet in diameter or even more. (The red pine, an historian of the lumber trade notes, can be just as thick but never as tall.) And, providentially, where the white pine grew there was a great lake and river system to carry it away to future markets.

The markets, at the time we are considering, were a few thousand years in the future, and the pines stayed unmolested in the ground. The early explorers wrote of the great gloomy forests of the Great Lakes region, shading in the south, near Toronto, into walnut, chestnut, magnolia, and sycamore — the southern hardwoods that populate the forests south to the Gulf of Mexico. The Great Lakes, the explorer Cadillac wrote in 1702, were "so temperate, so good and so beautiful that one can justly call it the earthly paradise of North America."

To the paradise came a succession of prehistoric immigrants. In the north, life was nomadic, dependent on hunting and fishing. Further south there grew a dependence on agriculture. By 900 AD there were three main groupings of inhabitants. In the north were Algonkian-speaking tribes, groupings of hunters who would later be subdivided into Algonkin, Cree, and Ojibwa. Further south there were two groups of Iroquoian-speaking tribes, one along the St Lawrence and one in southwestern Ontario. The Iroquoian tribes included not only the Five (later Six) Nations of the Iroquois, but the Huron, Petun, Neutral, Erie, and Susquehannock. Their culture was based on corn agriculture; they lived in large villages, which were frequently surrounded by palisades; and inside the walls there were longhouses. In historic times, after 1600, the dominant peoples living in Ontario were the Huron, south of Georgian Bay; the Petun, further west along Lake Huron; and the Neutral, southwards towards Lake Erie. To the north, where the Canadian Shield fringes the Great Lakes, lived the Algonkian tribes, the Ottawa and the Ojibwa.

The first white men to penetrate the Great Lakes region were the French, who came up the St Lawrence to its junction with the Ottawa at what would later become Montreal. The explorer Jacques

Cartier had reached that point in 1535 but, dependent on his ship, he could not pass the rapids on either the Ottawa or the St Lawrence. Further penetration would depend on the establishment of permanent settlements that could support exploration of the interior. Finally, in 1608, Samuel de Champlain founded Quebec and not long afterwards the French were found canoeing up the Ottawa into the unexplored west.

The first Frenchman actually to set foot in the future Ontario appears to have been Étienne Brûlé in 1612. Sent by Champlain to get to know the tribes of the interior, he ended up as the main course of a feast. But before Brûlé passed to his reward he was able to guide his mentor into the Great Lakes to meet the Huron of Georgian Bay. Champlain came twice, once in 1613, when he got no further than the upper Ottawa, around Chalk River, and again in 1615 when he wintered with the Huron.

This tribe, or rather collection of tribes, lived just to the south of Georgian Bay, in what is now the northern half of Simcoe County. They were divided by tribe and by village, and lived by sowing and harvesting corn. The total number of Huron is a matter for controversy, and estimates range from 18,000 to 32,000; the best guess seems to be about 21,000. Some Huron villages, with more than 2000 inhabitants, were far larger than the feeble white settlements that clung to the Atlantic seaboard. In the recent past, the Huron had been successful in war, expelling some of their Iroquoian cousins across the Great Lakes, and they wished to expand their range. The prize was not mere territorial aggrandizement but the possibility of wealth through trade, for the white man had discovered North America's rich harvest of fur-bearing animals, in particular the beaver.

The beaver exists both in Europe and North America. A rodent, it lives in waterlogged colonies housed in mud lodges. It has a talent for proliferation, and when it moves it takes its aquatic environment with it, building dams on streams and living on the waterlogged trees it helps to exterminate. It naturally flourished in the lakes and streams of the Canadian Shield, as well as in the heavily wooded and well-watered country to the south. But it was the beaver's fur, as well as its numbers, that stimulated interest. Beaver fur was well adapted to making felt, and felt hats with wide brims were in fashion in Europe from the sixteenth to the nineteenth century. Furs were transportable, for they were relatively light once their occupants had been removed from them. They could fit in a canoe, and could therefore pass the rapids on the St Lawrence and the Ottawa.

Huronia — the country of the Huron — was no longer good fur country; the density of population and the prevalence of agriculture had driven the fur-bearing animals out. But the Canadian Shield was nearby, and so were other tribes well-equipped to hunt and to bring furs to the natural middlemen — the Huron. So at least the Huron reasoned, and the French accepted their arguments. From the 1620s until 1650 the Huron acted as intermediaries in the fur trade. Montreal (founded as Ville Marie in 1643) became the entrepot for the trade, and from large cargoes of furs there derived large profits. Meanwhile, as the French cultivated Mammon, the Huron were being told about God.

Colonization involves many strands of policy. It can and often does mean the transplantation of people, settlers seeking to better themselves in another land. It certainly involves the application of policy, the transference of the strategic interests of the mother country to the fledgling colony across the seas. And it can mean the politics of culture: the influence of a metropolitan civilization on the indigenous culture of the colony. To their subjects and associates in the New World, therefore, the French brought Roman Catholicism.

This was entirely natural. Religion bulked large at home. Europe had been convulsed for a century by religious wars between Catholic and Protestant, and France had experienced (and was still going through) turmoils between rebellious Protestant subjects and Catholic monarchs. The variety of religion exported by those monarchs to the forests of the Great Lakes was Catholic, and it was to be inculcated by the great missionary order of the day, the Society of Jesus or Jesuits.

What the French sought was nothing less than a cultural revolution. Out would go the Huron religion, or most of it, and in would come Christian precepts. The early Jesuits made few converts, and many of the few were to be found among the dying. Since the latter, naturally, then died, some Huron ascribed a connection between Christianity and instant mortality. Sometimes, to assert the superiority of their ways over those of the Huron religion, the Jesuits deployed the technology of the seventeenth century, a very secular way of reinforcing faith. The Jesuits' position continued precarious until a series of calamities broke down traditional resistance, and with it the whole Huron nation.

The first and most deadly was disease. In an epidemic in 1638 more than half the Huron perished. Society was disrupted, and the tribe fatally weakened. Then, in the late 1640s, there came the Iroquois. The confederation of the Five Nations, as they then were — the Mohawk, Cayuga, Oneida, Onondaga, and Seneca — were rivals for the position of middleman in the fur trade. Armed with muskets procured from the Dutch at Fort Orange (the modern Albany, New York), the Iroquois sent war parties into Huronia. In 1648 and 1649 one village after another fell to the invaders, who massacred their inhabitants. The principal Jesuit mission of Ste Marie repelled an attack, but it was then abandoned and burned. After a miserable winter on an inhospitable island in Georgian Bay, the Huron dispersed. Some sought refuge far to the south, with the Susquehannock. Others fled west where, using their own term for themselves, *Wendat*, they became known as the Wyandotte. Others accompanied the French back to New France and formed a small settlement under Jesuit auspices.

The Iroquois followed up the destruction of the Huron by the annihilation of the Erie, Neutral, and Petun. Southern Ontario thereby became depopulated, since the Iroquois objective was not conquest but the control of trade and the elimination of a strategic threat. Although they remained south of the lakes, the Iroquois continued to influence life to the north by forming a barrier between the Dutch and later English colonies along the Atlantic coast and the interior. Controlling the Mohawk River, the only access besides the St Lawrence from the coast to the Great Lakes, the Iroquois guaranteed that the St Lawrence rather than the Mohawk would serve as the principal artery of navigation for the next hundred years and more.

Although the Iroquois threatened New France's westward connections at least until the early 1680s, the colony nevertheless managed to extend its trade links along the Ottawa, across Lake Nipissing and the French River, to Lakes Huron and Michigan and finally Superior. The *coureurs de bois*, among them the great explorers and entrepreneurs Pierre Radisson and Médard Chouart des Groseilliers, roamed the woods, bringing back furs to Montreal and profit to themselves.

Where economic power extended, politics was not far behind. In 1670 the governor of New France, Rémi de Courcelle, paddled up the St Lawrence to Lake Ontario, and in 1673 his successor, the comte de Frontenac, followed suit. Frontenac left a permanent memorial in the shape of Fort Cataraqui (subsequently Fort Frontenac) in a fine harbour at the foot of Lake Ontario, where Kingston now stands. Workmen were conscripted from Montreal, and it became the first permanent (or almost permanent) European settlement in the Great Lakes region.

"Settlement" may somewhat overstate the case. The French sought control and profit, but the profit came from the fur trade, while the control was designed to exclude the hated English from New York and to serve France's greater strategic interest. That interest extrapolated itself over the next few decades, as French explorers voyaged along, beside, and over the Great Lakes to reach the Mississippi River and the great fur-bearing lands of present-day Wisconsin, Minnesota, and the Canadian northwest. To protect the trade routes and repel the English, the French government sent officially licensed traders, established posts, and garrisoned them with troops. Along the lakes and rivers new names appeared, though usually on what is now the American side of the border: Fort Niagara (1720), Fort Detroit (1701), and Fort Michilimackinac, which had started off as a mission and only later became a focus for trade. The English (now the British, because of changes in their constitution at home) responded by building Fort Oswego at the southeast corner of Lake Ontario, opposite Fort Frontenac. The French completed their encirclement of the British colonies in 1718 by founding the city of New Orleans in their new colony of Louisiana.

Between the British and French posts there were usually hundreds of miles of trackless wilderness. In the early wars of the eighteenth century (1702–13 and 1744–48) few soldiers ventured to cross this space, but this reluctance disappeared in the Seven Years' War (1756–63), which finally put an end to France's North American empire. By then, British settlements were pressing up against the Appalachians. Land speculators hungered to cross the mountains, and when the French resisted British claims on French-occupied territory, hostilities broke out. War in fact started in North America before it began in Europe, and when it did the British were determined to break the French lines of communications on the river-and-lake route that linked Quebec with New Orleans. The Great Lake region lay squarely athwart their path.

At first the British were unsuccessful. The French defeated an attempt to take Fort Duquesne (Pittsburgh) in 1755. In 1756 the French military commander, the marquis de Montcalm, brought a small army up the St Lawrence and captured the British Fort Oswego. Further frontier fighting in 1757 left the French firmly on the offensive. In 1758 the balance shifted. The British, enjoying virtual command of the sea, and drawing on a large pool of reinforcements and supplies, went over to the attack. On the Atlantic coast the fortress of Louisbourg fell. A new attack on Fort Duquesne succeeded. The most unexpected blow fell on Fort Frontenac.

Colonel John Bradstreet, Nova Scotia-raised but a regular British officer, led a collection of American provincial troops from the Mohawk valley across to Lake Ontario. Bradstreet had some 3000 men, including a few warriors from the Six Nations (they had been six since the addition of the Tuscarora). The defending French had 110 men, and the issue was not long in doubt. Although the French had the benefit of a stone fort, the British had artillery as well as numbers, and on August 27, 1758, Fort Frontenac surrendered. With it went one of the main French transshipment points, seven ships, and a great booty of furs and other stores.

The British did not stay at Fort Frontenac, but the next year they came again, this time heading for Fort Niagara, at the mouth of the Niagara River. Once again the British forces moved up the Mohawk valley, but this time they moved through the heart of the Iroquois country and about 1000 warriors accompanied the British army, which was commanded by General John Prideaux and the British superintendent of Indian affairs, Sir William Johnson. Fort Niagara was a large fort and a strong one, and its commander was determined to resist. It took a regular siege and a futile attempt at relief by a French force to bring about surrender, on July 26, 1759.

There followed the siege and capture of Quebec in September. The French still held out in Montreal, and a British army descended the St Lawrence from Lake Ontario in 1760. In August the last French stronghold on the St Lawrence surrendered and in September, Montreal capitulated. The French forts in the distant interior followed suit, and the war was over in North America.

The war had followed the pattern of the French forts that protected communications and the fur trade. Most of the actual fighting was done outside the boundaries of present-day Ontario, but the consequences for the Great Lakes country were tremendous. The Great Lakes passed from one empire to another. They passed as a whole, so that the old French lines of communications remained intact and nearly unaltered. It was now, of course, possible to reach that line overland from the Atlantic seaboard rather than pass through Montreal, and that is precisely what thousands of settlers began to do, far to the south.

Flooding over the mountains, American settlers came into contact with the native peoples of the interior. The British government, mindful of the explosiveness of the situation, which had been brought home by a rebellion of the tribes of the northwest under Pontiac in 1763, tried to contain and, if possible, halt the colonists' expansion. The interior became an imperial concern, ruled by British rather than colonial officials, and regulated by a series of garrisons in the old French forts of Niagara, Detroit, and Michilimackinac.

Questions of Indian policy came under Sir William Johnson, whose headquarters were at Johnstown on the Mohawk River, in Iroquois country. Johnson had a powerful influence over the Iroquois, and as political troubles mounted in the British seaboard colonies the superintendent strove to keep the Iroquois well-disposed to the king and suspicious of the land-hungry colonists. The Iroquois formed a buffer between the British garrisons and lines of communication in the interior and the troublesome colonies; they were intermediaries, as well, between the British-occupied territories and the interior tribes in the upper lakes and Ohio regions.

Dissension in the colonies centred in Massachusetts and its capital, Boston. Colonial politicians demanded a progressively greater measure of autonomy from British jurisdiction during the 1760s and 1770s. "Patriotic" Americans believed that the British government was plotting to take away their liberties and property, with the result that by 1774 Massachusetts had become virtually ungovernable. A series of parliamentary enactments endeavoured to provide for the government of the colony as well as the punishment of unruly Boston, but their effect was to inflame rather than intimidate opinion, not only in Massachusetts but in other colonies as well.

In the middle of the quarrel with Massachusetts the British government decided to regularize the administration of some of its newly acquired territory in North America. By the Quebec Act of 1774 the British Parliament settled the frontiers of the province of Quebec, formerly New France. These were extended to include the whole Great Lakes basin and stretched as far west as the Mississippi River and as far south as the Ohio. What would later become Ontario was now included, as a matter of convenience, in Quebec. Quebec, unlike other colonies, would have no elected assembly; Catholics would be tolerated, and admitted to office, an unheard-of act in a fiercely Protestant country; and the civil law of Quebec would be the law of the old French regime in New France. Government was entrusted to a governor in Quebec City, Sir Guy Carleton.

There was still not enough settlement in Ontario to justify locating civil officials in the area north of the lakes; the administration, such as it was, lay in the hands of the commanders of the British forts, and at Detroit, where there was sufficient population left over from the French regime to support a resident magistrate.

Events were, however, beginning to overtake Ontario. In July 1774 Sir William Johnson died. In September delegates of most of the American colonies met in a continental congress in Philadelphia to organize opposition to British measures. During the winter opposition was transmuted gradually into resistance, culminating in pitched battle between British regulars and American rebels at Lexington and Concord on April 18, 1775. The British were besieged in Boston, while up and down the Atlantic seaboard rebel governments were set up in the colonies. Those who supported the crown, "Tories" according to the rebels, "Loyalists" according to themselves, fled to the protection of British garrisons or ships, or subsided into uneasy, intimidated silence when they could not flee.

In the fall of 1775 the rebels invaded the province of Quebec and in November took Montreal. The posts on the lakes were cut off from Governor Carleton, who barely managed to hang on at Quebec City in the face of a rebel army. The French Canadians, whose loyalty Carleton thought he had purchased through the concessions of the Quebec Act, held back, favouring, for the most part, neither one side nor the other. Fortunately for the British, rash generalship, lack of supplies, and the severe winter decimated the besieging Americans. When spring came, the Royal Navy came too, and Quebec was saved. The American army ran for the border, and communication with the west was restored.

The west still counted as a strategic asset for the British. Using the Great Lakes, the British could encircle the revolted colonies. Using the Iroquois and the western Indians, the British could terrorize the frontier and drain American resources, both military and financial. And, using the Great Lakes as a base, it might be possible to support a larger plan to reconquer America. Neither the Iroquois nor the other Indian nations were enthusiastic about the role that British strategy had devised for them, but support was not entirely lacking. Certain Iroquois, such as the Mohawk war chief Joseph Brant, placed their whole trust in the crown. Believing that a nation as rich and powerful as Great Britain could not fail, they willingly backed what they believed would be the winning side, and they gradually involved others in support of the king.

Frontier warfare depended on stealth and mobility. To no small degree it also depended on terror, inspired by a hundred years of tales (many true) of Indian atrocities. This time the Indians were joined by increasing numbers of Loyalists, driven from their homes and property by rebel mobs. Now they were driven by revenge to return and mete out to their former neighbours what had been meted out to them. At first the Loyalists, and their Iroquois allies, believed that they would return as part of a conquering army sent by the king to discipline his unruly subjects. That dream vanished when a dual invasion, up the Richelieu and down the Mohawk, was turned back at Oriskany and defeated at Saratoga. The invaders at Saratoga surrendered and a whole British army and its general passed into captivity. What had been a short and certain war became a long and doubtful one.

The Americans had declared their independence in 1776. A few months after Saratoga, in February 1778, the new United States signed an alliance with its old enemy France. Around the Great Lakes worried British commanders looked askance at their French neighbours. They worried even more about the possibility of an American invasion, and in their anxiety handed out thousands of pounds worth of gifts to the Indians of the interior. Many Indians were already on the move along the frontier, burning and killing in concert with the Loyalists and the few British regular troops who could be spared, or who could survive the arduous trip across the wilderness to the nearest American settlements.

At Fort Niagara John Butler, one of Sir William Johnson's assistants, organized his own corps, known as Butler's Rangers, to harass the rebels. At Montreal Sir John Johnson, Sir William's only legitimate son, raised a regiment, generally called Johnson's Greens from the colour of their uniform. Joseph Brant had his own following, mostly white men; but recognition was slow in coming to Brant, and he could feed but not pay his soldiers. Moving sometimes independently, sometimes in combination, these frontier forces ranged up and down the Alleghany mountains of Pennsylvania and New York, driving off the local militia and burning settlements. Sometimes matters got out of hand, as at Wyoming valley, Pennsylvania, in July 1778, or at Cherry valley, New York, four months later. Men, women, and children, Loyalists or rebels, were indiscriminately slain. Those who survived faced starvation or flight, since there was nothing left to live on.

The refugees descended on Schenectady or Albany to become a burden on the rebel governments, which had to feed them at great cost from diminishing resources. Terror, however, was a double-edged weapon, as the Americans determined to prove. In the summer of 1779 a punitive expedition under General John Sullivan set out to punish Britain's principal Indian allies, the Iroquois. The expedition, from the American point of view, was a complete success; from that of the Iroquois it was a disaster. Iroquois villages were burnt and crops destroyed. Unable to resist the force the Americans brought to bear, the Iroquois fled westward, across the Genesee, until they came to a halt under the ramparts of Fort Niagara. There they became the immediate clients of the British government, utterly dependent on what the British could dole out by way of food, blankets, and shelter.

Sullivan's expedition did not end the war along the frontier. Colonel John Butler and his Rangers, Colonel Sir John Johnson and his Greens, and Captain Joseph Brant and his irregulars continued to roam and strike where they wished. The bitterest warfare, in which attacks on civilians were a principal tactic, continued until July 1782. The Americans suffered great loss. Many farms were burnt, families disrupted, people killed. These losses, though severe, could be replaced on the American side. Those on the British and Iroquois side could not. Politically, the Iroquois confederacy was disrupted by the war. Some Iroquois, principally the Oneidas, sympathized with the Americans. Others, the majority, joined with the British, and suffered for it. The society of the Iroquois was broken and with it their military power. The end of hostilities meant the disappearance of the Indian barrier between the Great Lakes and the American frontier, and the end of the possibility that the Indian nations by themselves, or in alliance with the French and then later the British, could keep white settlement at bay.

By the time war ceased along the frontier, it was all but over elsewhere in the world. The British government came to terms with its enemies, old and new, and at Versailles in 1783 signed a peace treaty with the United States. The United States became independent. Its frontier would run up the middle of the St Lawrence, and likewise through Lakes Ontario, Erie, Huron, and Superior, and their connecting rivers. Further west the border became a trifle fanciful, since the limits of geographical knowledge were reached and surpassed by the peacemakers, but it would eventually approach the 49th parallel at the Lake of the Woods, and that would serve to bisect the rest of the continent.

By the terms of the treaty the American Congress agreed that it would earnestly recommend to the individual states to do justice to those who had lost the war, the Loyalists. In theory Loyalists should recover their rights, including the right to sue for damages or lost property. Nothing was said about the Indians, and those Indians who had suffered as a result of the war had no legal right to recoup their losses as a result of the peace.

There was in fact less difference between the Loyalists and the Indians than these terms suggest. Congress had no power to compel the states to do its bidding, and the terms that affected the Loyalists promptly became a dead letter. Loyalists who returned home were encouraged to leave. One Loyalist, for example, was met by a midnight reception committee, tied to a tree and whipped; as the whipping proceeded his tormentors reminded him of the atrocities he was supposed to have committed during the war; surviving the beating, he left the next morning.

Thousands of Americans had supported the king. Many had supported him in arms, and in the process communities split, families quarrelled, and old allegiances fell apart. As the war proceeded, many Loyalists concentrated where British troops could protect them, first at Boston and later at New York and Charleston, South Carolina. Others, closer to Quebec, made it to Fort Niagara or Montreal or the great refugee camp at Sorel, where the Richelieu flows into the St Lawrence. Of those who fled, some chose to go to the West Indies or Bermuda, where the British flag still waved. Others proceeded to England to pursue their careers and rebuild their lives and families. The largest group, however, looked northward. They would stay in North America, in a country they knew. They would remain under King George III. To such men and women, the Great Lakes region, unspoiled by war and still far from American guns, looked very tempting. That was where they would go.

Upper Canada, 1784–1841

The American war left King George III a much shrunken domain in North America. On the Atlantic seaboard were the Maritimes: Nova Scotia, swollen with 28,000 Loyalist settlers; New Brunswick, newly created as a Loyalist province; Prince Edward Island, small, fertile, and isolated in the Gulf of St Lawrence; and Newfoundland, a fishing rather than a settling colony. There were also the vast and indefinite possessions of the Hudson's Bay Company around the great frozen inland ocean of Hudson Bay; and, finally, the province of Quebec, home to 130,000 French-speaking subjects and about 7000 English-speaking refugees. All these remaining North American possessions had their good points. All, except for Newfoundland, had pockets of fertility in valleys and alluvial plains. But only Quebec had fertile land in quantity, and with it the potential for growth. And land, with what grew upon it, was to be the centre of policy and politics for the next half century.

Land was British North America's greatest resource. It had the power to attract settlers and confer wealth, though not always in proportion to effort expended. Its forests sustained life by furnishing fuel and shelter and an immediate cash crop for those who could get wood to market. Land speculation was an avenue to wealth, and land hunger a lever to discontent. For governments, land meant revenue either indirect or direct: indirect from the settlers it enticed to British America and the wealth they produced; direct from land rents and sales. Land could be used instead of cash to endow the great engines of society—the churches, schools, and hospitals of the future.

The lower St Lawrence was already largely filled up, its best lands divided among seigneuries from Rivière-du-Loup to Longueuil, just west of Montreal. The best and biggest tracks of land lay to the west, in the region between the Great Lakes and the Ottawa River. It was an area almost as large as Pennsylvania, well-watered (though wetter and colder to the east and drier and warmer to the west) and easily accessible, once a few rapids and waterfalls were left out of account.

It was often described as empty, but the description was not quite accurate. To the north, as there had always been, there were the Algonkian tribes. To the south, besides the remnants of France's former Iroquoian allies, there were recently arrived Algonkian tribes, the Missisauga (the spelling varies, but this is the most common) and the Chippewa. The Missisauga, like most other tribes in the area, had come under the influence of the Iroquois and particularly under that of the active and able Joseph Brant. There were also a few white farmers, at Cataraqui, at Niagara, and across from Detroit, whose duty it was to supply the British garrisons at those places. To accommodate them, the British had bought the requisite tracts of land from the Missisauga. These farmers, however, did not own their land and had no choice of market for their produce. If asked, they might have said that their situation was better than nothing but far from what they desired.

What they desired, after it became obvious that they were never going to go back to their former homes in the United States, was to reproduce their former life in a new land. The British side of the Great Lakes was not unpromising or unappetizing. The forests along the northern side of Lake Erie resembled those they had left behind: and a hardwood forest promised fertile land and good crops, as they knew from experience back in New York and Pennsylvania. It was not difficult for Loyalist leaders to turn their eyes westward from Montreal and to covet the forests of western Quebec.

The British authorities were taken somewhat by surprise. In their plans the interior would continue as it had been, a refuge for Indian tribes and a barrier against the Americans. The emigrants they wished to export there were loyal, it was true, but they were the remnants of the Six Nations, huddling in camps under the guns of Fort Niagara. Land was purchased from the Missisaugas for this purpose, some around the Bay of Quinte (or Quinté, as it was called), and some along the Grand River about fifty miles west of Niagara. The Six Nations went to this land in two batches. The eastern branch, under Chief John Deseronto, refused to move along to the Grand River, which thereby became a field for the dominance of Joseph Brant. It was not Brant alone, as whites usually failed to recognize, who stood out among the Grand River Iroquois; Brant exercised his influence largely through his relatives and connections by marriage rather than in his own right.

Brant gave freely of Iroquois land to those whites who had served alongside him during the war; and he had no great objection to the arrival of other refugees who had suffered in the cause of the king. And so, in 1783, General Frederick Haldimand, the governor of Quebec, sent his surveyors to the west to delineate townships for settlement. They marked out lands along the front, by the shores of the main rivers and Great Lakes. As winter closed in a few Loyalists arrived to winter near the British posts on the king's rations; the next spring there would be many more.

There were, all told, 6000 Loyalists who came to settle in western Quebec in 1784. They were of two main kinds. Some were soldiers disbanded from Loyalist regiments, with their families. Some were civilian Loyalists who had followed the king's armies. They settled in three main clumps: the easternmost were just to the west of the last French seigneury, Longueuil, along the St Lawrence River; the next group chose the north shore of the Bay of Quinte, and the remainder the Niagara region. These groups, and their followers, totalled 10,000 by the end of the decade.

While the Loyalists increased in numbers, the Indian population of the Great Lakes region was declining. The Missisaugas, who sold off land along the lakefront to the British government, suffered from repeated epidemics which reduced their numbers, already small, to the point of insignificance. The Missisaugas may have sensed that they were outnumbered and that their way of life could not long be maintained. They had become highly dependent on British gifts and subsidies, and the income derived from the land sales was probably necessary as well as welcome to them. The sale of lakefront was completed in 1805, when the British bought out the area of Burlington Bay to what is now Etobicoke. Further sales in 1818 and 1819 moved the Missisaugas even further back from the lake; reservations in the Peterborough area would eventually receive the remnants of the tribe.

The effect of British-Indian interaction north of the lakes was, with rare exceptions, peaceful if not entirely happy. South of the lakes it was a different story. American troops clashed repeatedly with the tribes of the Ohio valley. These tribes in turn relied on the British for material aid and political advice. (Gifts to Indians south of the border did not cease until 1843.) The result was contradictory and unhappy. The Indians expected help that never came, in the form of military support; and the Americans suspected the Indians were getting help the British did not give. Events north and south of the lakes, in British and American territory, continued therefore to be closely linked, and the possibility of another great Indian war lurked in the minds of British soldiers and officials. If such a war came, and Britain and the United States came to blows, was it yet possible that the revolution could be reversed and the two countries reunited?

British long-term policy nevertheless had to take account of the reality of settlement, and the necessity of organizing the thousands of new settlers who had come to live in the province of

Quebec. Quebec was a predominantly French and overwhelmingly Catholic colony. Its laws were French, and its land tenure seigneurial. The British settlers along the lakes found the situation disquieting. They were not used to seigneurial dues and they wished for a familiar legal system. Starting in 1785 they asked for both English laws and land tenure and, by the end of the decade, the British government had decided, in principle, to give them what they wanted.

In London William Grenville, the secretary of state, determined to regulate the government of the king's remaining North American colonies so as to appease discontent and provide a reliable structure for the future. Grenville's solution, the Constitutional Act, passed through the British Parliament in the spring of 1791. It divided the old province of Quebec into two parts. The border would run along the Ottawa River until it reached the already settled seigneuries west of Montreal. It jogged along their western limit down to the St Lawrence. West of the line there would be English law and English land tenure in the new province of Upper Canada. To the east there would be both the French and English languages, French civil law, and seigneurial tenure. In both Upper and Lower Canada (as the two provinces were called) there would be an elected assembly, an appointed legislative council to serve as an upper house, and an executive council to assist the governor in his acts.

Generations of Canadian students have been bored and distracted by the niceties of Grenville's constitution: the piling of councils on assembly in a province whose population did not exceed the present population of Kenora may seem to have been excessive then, and pointless now. But the system of government created in 1791 was at the heart of Canadian politics for the next fifty years: it was not merely a forum for debate, but a subject of debate, and so it becomes necessary to pause and examine the details of Grenville's system. The idea of an appointive upper house, the Legislative Council, and an elective lower house, the Legislative Assembly, was not new. It had existed in some of the prerevolutionary American colonies, and it reflected, in modified form, what contemporaries called ''the glories of the British constitution.'' This was of course no accident. Believing in the inherent superiority of British institutions, statesmen of the 1790s searched the recent past — the American Revolution — to discover ways of strengthening and preserving these institutions in a North American context.

The flaw that statesmen identified was that the prerevolutionary American governments had been too democratic, too subject to popular pressures. The first concern of the new colonial government must therefore be to reinforce the royal or executive power. The governor's council was therefore made appointive and responsible to the sovereign's local representative, who could make or unmake its members. The Executive Council was a form of cabinet, if by cabinet we can conceive of a group of politically oriented civil servants appointed to do the bidding of an official appointed from London. The Executive Council did not have the power to ratify legislation; in theory at least it did not make laws but enforced them. The making of laws was the job of the Legislative Council and the Legislative Assembly, acting, it was hoped, in concert. Naturally the laws they made had effect only in Upper Canada. Only the legislature could levy taxes on the King's Upper Canadian subjects — taxes such as tariffs on goods coming across the American frontier. The British Parliament had given up, in 1778, any claim to tax the American colonies, and that British surrender still applied. There were, however, means of raising revenues through licences, land sales, and administrative fees that did not have to pass through the legislature, and whose effect was to confer a certain independence on the Upper Canadian executive.

The ultimate executive, at least on the western side of the Atlantic, continued to reside in Quebec City. The governor of Quebec now became the governor-in-chief of Canada. When the governor-in-chief came to visit his Upper Canadian province, he became its *de facto* executive. But the journey up the St Lawrence was long and tedious, and the governor-in-chief seldom came. In practice it was the lieutenant governor of Upper Canada who ruled the Great Lakes.

John Graves Simcoe was the man chosen to give flesh to Grenville's dream. A career officer with a taste for verse, Simcoe had commanded a Loyalist unit, the Queen's Rangers, in the American Revolution. Through his service in America Colonel Simcoe had come to admire loyal Americans, but he even managed to admire certain things about the disloyal kind. They were enterprising and energetic; they knew how to settle a country and bring it to prosperity. Perhaps they would get over their republican spasms and bring themselves to perceive the inherent absurdity of their new government. It followed that Upper Canada must succeed, both politically and economically, and that it must be seen to succeed. Simcoe saw no harm, and much positive good, in attracting Americans to his province, and he proceeded to shape his policies to bring about that happy result.

His instrument was land. Land was owed to the king's loyal subjects, first, and since 1784 it had been dispensed to the Loyalists, according to grade and rank in the late war, free of charge. Loyalists and their children — specially designated "UE" or United Empire as a mark of distinction — were entitled to grants, and also to trade their entitlements, which as late as the 1830s were opening up new lands for settlers who might never have set eyes on a living Loyalist. Land could be used to induce loyalty and to attract entrepreneurs and projectors to open up and then to people the townships of Upper Canada. Finally, land was a fitting reward to the servants of government, and there were few public servants who left Upper Canada without a few thousand acres to their credit. Simcoe himself was no exception to the rule; on his departure from the province in 1796 he left behind thousands of acres which his family only gradually sold off.

There was a contradiction in the land grants. They could accelerate development through concentration of effort and application of (American) expertise in settlement, but they could also retard development. By leaving land uncleared and unpeopled, the developer could wait until the surrounding townships were opened, and then sell off his properties at a good speculative profit. Nor were the grants conducive to perfect harmony among the inhabitants of Upper Canada. It was obvious that friends of government, and more particularly of the governor, had a greater chance to acquire land and wealth than the average subject. It is quite possible that the smoke of rumour was greater than the fire of patronage, but it is not surprising that tales of land grants became political currency in the years that followed, and that public officials had their names blackened for their supposed greed for land as well as office.

In addition to land grants, there were the clergy reserves, established in the Constitutional Act. The reserves were meant to support a ''Protestant clergy'' in Upper Canada, and were immune to virtually any enactment of the local legislature. Their abolition would require the consent of the British Parliament, whether tacit or explicit. The clergy reserves posed the same problem as the undeveloped grants. Lying in the midst of settled farms, and constituting one-seventh of the surface of any given township, the reserves placed a burden on their neighbours in developing roads.

The reserves were meant to support a Protestant clergy. But which Protestant clergy? The meaning was most unclear. To the various Protestant sects it meant, or should have meant, all. To Lieutenant Governor Simcoe it meant the Church of England as by law established in England. The fact that Great Britain had two established churches, the Church of England and the Church of Scotland, cut no ice with Simcoe, who stubbornly reserved the lands for Anglicans alone. This might not have been an insurmountable difficulty had God favoured Upper Canada with a deluge of Anglicans sufficient to drown the sectarians — Baptists, Presbyterians, Methodists, and the like. Sadly, His will was expressed in other ways, with the result that the favoured church was supported by only a minority of the population. The Anglicans attempted to solve the conundrum by appropriating to their faith all those who professed no religion, but their reasoning did not impress.

The fruits of these policies were not immediately apparent before the end of Simcoe's term, in 1796. That would take time, and even now historians are not beyond disputing the precise relationship between land tenure and political dissatisfaction. But no one could doubt that land, in its earthly as well as its transcendental application, was at the centre of politics.

Simcoe's other policies did have results before he left Upper Canada, but they were not the results intended. When the lieutenant governor arrived in 1792, British troops still occupied the forts of Oswego, Niagara, Detroit, and Michilimackinac on the American side of the 1783 frontier. The Americans naturally wished to possess them, according to treaty, but the British were mindful that the Americans themselves had not fulfilled all the terms of the treaty of peace. Both sides had good reason to bury their differences and seek agreement: the Americans because of problems internal and external, the British because of the outbreak of war in Europe between themselves and revolutionary France in 1793, a war that would last with intermissions until 1815. The British government was not anxious to tangle with the Americans when it had more serious enemies closer to home, and the result was Jay's Treaty of 1794, which provided for the evacuation of the western posts on June 1, 1796. On that day the British troops moved back across the various rivers and lakes, and American soldiers took their place.

Jay's Treaty did little more than ratify a change in the balance of power between the Indian tribes, the British, and the Americans. In 1794 at the battle of Fallen Timbers the Americans eliminated the Indians of Ohio as serious rivals for the possession of the Ohio valley. The prospective Indian confederation of which the more ambitious native leaders had dreamed was indefinitely postponed. At the same time the Iroquois of the Grand River made another discovery — that their cousins on the American side of the border had, through land sales, achieved a tidy income at the expense of their former territories. Joseph Brant was soon agitating for the right to sell off some of the Grand River land to white settlers or speculators, and reluctantly the government gave in. It could not afford to offend Brant, and if the price of happiness was the disappearance of some of the Iroquois patrimony, so be it.

The last years of the eighteenth century, then, saw the confirmation of the international boundary in the form in which it exists today. Soon there would follow customs agents and tariffs and frontier posts. There would also be international trade, for the merchants and farmers of Upper Canada were delighted to supply the United States army at Forts Niagara and Detroit for an appropriate price. But behind the border the situation remained unstable. The Indian tribes of the northwest were not yet resigned to the American appropriation of their land, and the possibility of trouble remained. Nor were relations between the United States and Great Britain free of acrimony. The first decade of the nineteenth century was punctuated with quarrels between the British and American governments, over the rights of neutral American ships at sea and the ability to the Royal Navy to stop, search, and conscript ("impress") seamen it claimed as British deserters. Politicians were not lacking in the new American federal capital of Washington to demand that the British be chased out of North America altogether and the Great Lakes region reunited under the flag of liberty, the Stars and Stripes.

There were those in Canada who welcomed such talk. The land-granting policy of Simcoe and his successors had indeed been successful in attracting thousands of American immigrants to Upper Canada. Many of the Americans who came thought that settling in Upper Canada was the most natural thing in the world, barring only a few anachronisms like the Union Jack and a British administration. Travellers in Upper Canada found American sentiments rife among the population. At Queenston on the Niagara

River a visitor found "a determined partiality towards the United States and a decided and almost avowed hostility to the British government."

The government of Upper Canada was not ignorant that such views were current. The government had been located at York (later Toronto), across Lake Ontario from the exposed first capital of Newark (now Niagara-on-the-Lake). There the lieutenant governor, his councils, and the assembly met and legislated the future of the province, and quarrelled over land, place, and patronage. The details of the politics of the 1800s need not detain us, except for two points: they showed that the various parts — east, centre, and west — of the sprawling province had decidedly different complexions in terms of population, interests, and politics; and that these differences were to have descendants in the political factions and issues of future decades. The fact of political strife was important in itself, as were the numbers and personalities ranged on the opposing sides of issues. But the issues themselves were transitory and soon overshadowed by the far greater issue of war.

War was declared by the United States on Great Britain on June 18, 1812. It was a war that the American politicians who brought it about confidently expected to win. The United States had a vastly larger population than the British colonies in North America. The British were still involved in fighting France in the mountains and plains of far-away Spain. Between Upper Canada, population 136,000, and the adjacent American states of Ohio, Pennsylvania, and New York, the disparity was even greater. To defend Upper and Lower Canada the British had only a few battalions of regular troops, to which could be added the citizen soldiers, the militia, of the two provinces. The militia were almost completely untrained. Those in Upper Canada were estimated at about 11,000 in number, "of which it might not be prudent to arm more than 4000" as the governor-in-chief, Sir George Prevost, put it.

Prevost, who had the rank of general in the British army, held overall command in North America. The local defence of Upper Canada devolved on Major General Isaac Brock, the administrator of the province during the absence of the lieutenant governor who had left the previous year and would not return until 1816. Brock faced several options. His troops, fewer than 1600 in number, were scattered from Fort Malden on the Detroit River to Kingston on Lake Ontario. They depended on a long, thin line of communications, which the Americans could cut by seizing Montreal, crossing the St Lawrence River, or dominating Lake Ontario. Brock nevertheless urged that Upper Canada could and should be defended. Prevost reluctantly consented.

The Upper Canadian population did not share Brock's enthusiasm. Writing in July 1812, the general complained that his situation was ''critical, not from any thing the enemy can do, but from the disposition of the people — The population, believe me, is essentially bad — A full belief possesses them that this Province must inevitably succumb.'' The drooping morale of the civilian population inhibited defence, but despite that, Brock added, ''I however speak loud and look big.''

To firm up the loyalty of the population, Brock knew that he must move rapidly. A small force seized Michilimackinac, with the happy result that the Indian tribes of the northwest joined in the conflict on the British side. The next target was Detroit, where the American commander, General William Hull, had attempted a brief and timid invasion of Upper Canada. Fearing British and Indian retaliation, Hull took refuge behind the walls of his fort, only to find, at the beginning of August, that he was surrounded by the British and their Indian allies. He surrendered on August 16, along with 2100 of his troops.

Brock quickly moved back east, to the Niagara frontier where, he correctly judged, the next American attack would occur. It came on the morning of October 13, at the village of Queenston. The Niagara River there was narrow and swift, and though the terrain on the British side was difficult — a steep cliff rising abruptly just inland from the river — its capture would allow the Americans to command the whole Niagara peninsula. The Americans actually seized the heights; Brock led a counter-attack only to die in the attempt. It took regular troops led by Major General Roger Sheaffe (a regular, though born in Boston) to clear the Americans off. Handicapped by the refusal of the New York State militia to cross the river, the Americans on the Canadian bank finally surrendered. American losses were about 1300, killed, wounded, and captured; the British lost about 100.

Brock was credited with the victory, but, as a historian of the war has pointed out, Sheaffe had also shown himself a brave and competent commander. Brock's primary aim was secured: the Americans had been turned back and, with their twin defeats at Detroit and Queenston, disloyal sentiment in Upper Canada subsided. An American minister in Upper Canada later observed that "After this event, the people of Canada became fearful of disobeying the government — some that had fled to the wilderness returned home — and the friends of the United States were discouraged, and those of the King encouraged . . . The people now saw that it was as much as their property and lives were worth to disobey orders, and now what they had been compelled to do, after a while they did from choice." Not all chose to obey, but those who did not were compelled to decamp and seek their fortunes in the United States.

1812 was capped by an inconsequential American demonstration near the St Lawrence, following which the two armies went into winter quarters along most of the frontier. In the extreme southwest, beyond Detroit, the winter was a lively one. A premature American attempt to recapture Detroit in January 1813 was defeated with heavy loss to the Americans at Frenchtown on the River Raisin; 400 Americans were killed and 500 captured. Nevertheless the Americans, under a new and considerably more competent commander, General William Henry Harrison, were soon able to replace their losses and when, in September 1813, the British were defeated in a sea battle on Lake Erie, Detroit could no longer be held. The British commander, General Procter, ordered a retreat into Upper Canada. At Moraviantown on the Thames River the Americans caught up with the fleeing British and Indians and decimated them. Few survivors reached the safety of the British garrisons further east; among the slain was the Shawnee chief Tecumseh, the principal Indian leader in the American northwest. The western part of Upper Canada now passed under American occupation and remained so for the duration of the war.

The eastern part of Upper Canada was also invaded. In April 1813 an American force raided York, where they drove off the British garrison and occupied the town. An easy triumph was converted into a disaster for the Americans when the British exploded a powder magazine and with it about 40 American troops; another 222 were wounded. There was some minor looting, the destruction of military buildings and stores, and the burning of the provincial legislative building. The Americans sailed away but returned for another foray at the end of July. More government property was burned before they departed; otherwise the damage was slight and temporary.

The American depredations did not go unopposed. The fleet that raided York was based in Sackets Harbor at the east end of the lake. Their British counterparts were located at Kingston, in the northeast corner. The two fleets manoeuvred up and down the lake, while their shipyards on shore laboured to build bigger and better ships to outgun and outclass the rivals. No major engagement resulted between the two fleets, neither of which was ever able to achieve a decisive superiority over its enemy. Nevertheless, as long as the British fleet remained, Upper Canada's communications along the lake were secure.

The Niagara River was not secure. The Americans crossed the river in force in May 1813 and took Fort George, opposite Fort Niagara. The British army retired towards ''the Beaver Dam beyond Queenston Mountain,'' on top of the Niagara Escarpment. Then the British moved back to the head of Lake Ontario at Burlington Bay. The Americans followed, but were checked at Stoney Creek just outside modern Hamilton. Two American generals were captured and the American army retired in some haste and discomfort towards the river. Then, on June 24, a detachment of Americans tried to take a British outpost at Beaver Dam by surprise. The British commander, Lieutenant Fitzgibbon, was warned by Laura Secord of Queenston of the American plan; when the Americans arrived as predicted, they were surrounded by a force composed almost entirely of Caughnawaga and Mohawk, and surrendered. Fitzgibbon and Secord got most of the credit, but the unsung commander on the British side was Captain Dominique Ducharme of the British Indian Department, who actually commanded the Caughnawaga. As a result of these actions, the British army remained in control of most of the Niagara frontier.

The Americans did not finally abandon Fort George until December, and when they did they burned the surrounding village of Newark and part of Queenston. It was a rash and unjustified move, and it provoked resentment and retaliation. The advancing British crossed the river and took Fort Niagara on December 19; then, at the south end of the river, another force crossed and burned the villages of Buffalo and Black Rock on December 29. Like the inhabitants of Newark, their citizens were turned out in the snow to fend for themselves.

The conflict was not entirely between regular armies, or even between the respective militias. The Americans had begun the war believing that a large part of the population was simply awaiting a convenient opportunity to exchange one flag for another. There is no doubt that many Upper Canadians, including some of Loyalist descent as well as the American-born, wanted just such a change. Three members of the Assembly — two Americans and one British-born — passed over to the enemy. The latter, Joseph Willcocks, organized a force which he called the Canadian Volunteers to fight on the American side, and it is believed that Willcocks had a hand in the burning of Newark in December 1813.

The government responded by requiring Americans refusing to fight for the crown to leave the province. In 1814 the assembly authorized the suspension of *habeas corpus* and expelled its disloyal members. Residents of Upper Canada continued to fight on the American side, and frequently participated in raids designed to harass their former neighbours and destroy their property. The ravages were particularly severe in southwestern Upper Canada, where raiders could descend by boat across Lake Erie or from the American garrisons at Detroit or Amherstburg on the Canadian side. As late as 1816, almost two years after the war ended, a traveller crossing Upper Canada from Niagara to Detroit commented that he was "most sensibly struck with the devastation which had been made by the late war, formerly in high cultivation, now laid waste; houses entirely evacuated and forsaken; provisions of all kinds very scarce; and, where once peace and plenty abounded, poverty and destruction now stalked over the land."

Rebels unlucky enough to be captured in arms against the king could be severely dealt with. In June 1814 nineteen such men were tried at Ancaster; one pleaded guilty, four were acquitted, and fourteen convicted. Eight were subsequently hanged at Burlington Heights in July, giving the incident its usual name: "the Bloody Assizes" of Ancaster. The rest either died in prison or, after the war, were exiled to the United States.

The third year of the war was no more conclusive than the first two. Bloody battles were fought along the Niagara frontier, the opposing fleets continued cruising up and down Lake Ontario, and the British army, reinforced from Europe, made an unsuccessful attempt on Plattsburg in upper New York State. The Royal Navy was by this time virtually unopposed off the American east coast, and raided and blockaded at will. In August 1814 a British army seized Washington, driving out President Madison and his wife Dolly and burning the White House, ostensibly in retaliation for the burning of the Upper Canadian legislature at York.

By this point both countries were heartily sick of the war. The British could not win it without a disproportionate effort, which they did not care to make. The Americans could not win it, period. Many Americans, particularly in the northeastern states, were opposed to the war. Some, indeed, made a good living selling provisions to the British army in Canada, while others even threatened to take New England out of the United States unless peace was made.

Peace was made, on Christmas Day 1814, in the little Belgian city of Ghent. Both sides agreed to return what they had captured: the Americans gave back the western part of Upper Canada, and the British returned Fort Niagara and part of Maine, which had been seized earlier in 1814. Outstanding boundary questions were left for special commissions to regulate. Both sides promised to stop fighting the Indians, but the Indians did not otherwise receive any benefit from the treaty. They had to resign themselves to living under the national flag which fate, and the treaty of 1783, had given them.

The postwar boundary commissions duly occurred. With them was made an agreement to limit armaments on the Great Lakes, the Rush-Bagot agreement of 1817, named after the American secretary of state and the British ambassador of the period. Rush-Bagot only affected armaments sailing on the lakes, and not fortifications around them. But it was a step, even if a small one, towards a different way of regulating disputes between Canada and the United States.

General Brock became a hero. A column was erected at Queenston to commemorate his name. Blown up by disgruntled citizens, it was rebuilt and stands today, a monument to Upper Canadian pride in the repulse of the enemy in the face of overwhelming odds. John Strachan, the Anglican archdeacon of York at the time, gave his own interpretation as early as November 1812: "It will be told by the future Historian, that the Province of Upper Canada, without the assistance of men or arms, except a handful of regular troops, repelled its invaders, slew or took them all prisoners ...." To this effusion Professor C. P. Stacey, a twentieth-century expert on the war, replied that the defence and survival of Upper Canada owed more to General Brock and the small number of regular troops under his command than it did to the miraculous exploits of Upper Canadian civilians, however loyal. There is no doubt that the war was important, in that it helped to give Canadians the pride and confidence that Brock found so sadly lacking in June 1812. It encouraged a fair amount of myth-making, both about the heroism of the brave Upper Canadians and about the despicable nature of their American invaders. There was, to be sure, a large portion of justifiable resentment on the part of Upper Canadians who had suffered from American guerrilla-style raids, and observers at the time detected a coolness in the view that even American-born Upper Canadians took of their republican neighbours.

The War of 1812 thus marks a dividing line. To its contemporaries, the American Revolution had not settled matters finally. Men like Simcoe on the British side, or the American politicians of 1812, had not accepted the boundary or the settlement as final. The war made it so.

Was Upper Canada worth fighting about? Obviously to its inhabitants it was, but how rich, how prosperous was it? What did its inhabitants do, and what was the result of their efforts?

Much of our evidence is impressionistic and scattered. The first settlers necessarily lived in tents or in shanties, lean-tos made of wood that kept out the worst of the cold in winter and the mosquitoes in summer. Agriculture was necessary for survival and, in the early years of the province, if crops failed, hunger was not far behind. Fortunately there were government stores and rations, but these supplies were not always sufficient.

The easiest access was along the lakes, to the settlers lucky enough to live on "the front" of settlement. Behind the lakes Simcoe built military roads, Dundas Street from York to the Thames River, where he hoped to locate the future provincial capital (the eventual London), and Yonge Street from York to just south of Lake Simcoe. Neither street would be immediately recognizable as a road in today's terms: they were, rather, stretches of stumps over which wagons could proceed at their own risk. But they were good enough to bring settlers in, and, after a certain time, crops out.

The production of crops followed the American model, naturally enough, considering the origins of the Loyalists and later colonists. It involved hard work, long hours, and, at first, small rewards. Clearing the land for a shack came first, and then clearing the land for crops, which meant chopping down trees and uprooting stumps. Even before all the stumps were gone crops might be sown, and between sowing and harvest the farmer might work elsewhere to earn money. The better-off immigrant was, by the 1830s, hiring gangs of workmen to accomplish these tasks. Immigrants of all kinds discovered that farming was a mixed business, since profit could be derived from burning the wood to make potash, while there might be a market elsewhere for the timber.

With communication difficult, except near water, it became necessary for immigrant farmers to lay in large quantities of supplies if they could afford them. From these stocks it was possible to sell to the neighbours, so that many settlers, without originally intending it, became storekeepers on a minor scale. Those placed on or near rapids or waterfalls were in a position to develop mills; the difference between farming and commerce, and between commerce and industry, was rather less rigid than is frequently believed, and it was possible for one activity to lead quite naturally and almost imperceptibly into another.

Methods of agriculture varied from place to place, as did the crops sown. Writing in September 1826 an English farmer named Joseph Pickering commented: "Saw six acres of new cleared ground, with its first crop on; *viz.*, corn, oats, peas, kidney beans, turnips, cabbages, cucumbers, melons and tobacco, and all very fine. The owner said this first crop would pay for clearing the land, and all other expenses attending the crop." Pickering drew attention to the tobacco, which he judged highly profitable: "while it continues to be used so generally, and I fear excessively, it will pay the cultivator much better than any grain crop." Tobacco had attracted an unusual variety of immigrant labour — "black slaves" who had run away from servitude in Kentucky, the nearest slave state in the United States, and had found freedom in Upper Canada where slavery had long since been prohibited.

Grist-milling was an important industry in the province, and Upper Canada early on began to export wheat and flour across the Atlantic to the British Isles. British policy between 1800 and 1846 generally encouraged the importation of colonial grain by fixing a lower tariff duty on such imports than was available to foreign countries, but the policy fluctuated as the government, during periods of low grain prices, tried to protect British agriculture. This complicated policy was embodied in the so-called Corn Laws (corn being a British word for what North Americans call grain). Thus the terms and conditions that the British government laid down for the protection and development of its own farm industry had a direct effect on the distant frontier of Upper Canada. Certainly the prosperity of many Upper Canadian farmers was linked to the grain trade, and it became a matter of great concern to them just how the terms of trade between Britain and its North American colonies were managed. Since this was a political as well as an economic question, the Corn Laws became a matter of political importance.

Policy decisions arrived at in London also demanded the presence of large British garrisons in the colonies. The garrisons protected the local territory, but for the colonists the fact of defence was outweighed in importance by its cost. Forts had to be built, soldiers paid, and supplies bought, and the money thereby engendered went into the pockets of the local inhabitants. The stone fortifications at Fort Henry, near Kingston, have held troops, prisoners of war, and tourists over the 150 years since they were first piled up. The credit for the great limestone edifice belongs to the local contractors and workers as well as to the soldiers who designed and used the fort.

The most spectacular example of imperial expenditure in Upper Canada is today another notable tourist attraction. The Rideau

Canal runs north from Lake Ontario beside Kingston, through the Rideau lakes, and along the Rideau River system until it reaches the Ottawa River in the heart of present-day Ottawa. From Ottawa navigation proceeds via the Grenville Canal near Hawkesbury down to Montreal. The Rideau Canal therefore bypasses the St Lawrence and provides an alternative means of water transport between the head of navigation at Montreal and Lake Ontario. Its purpose was to create a second supply route between the lower and upper provinces in case the Americans cut the St Lawrence in a new war. Under Lieutenant Colonel John By of the Royal Engineers, work began in 1826 through a swampy and unsalubrious countryside rife with mosquitoes and swamp fevers. On May 24, 1832, the canal was open for business, 130 miles of it, cut to a depth of 5 feet, with 47 locks. The cost was £1 million, all of it contributed by the British taxpayer, a stupendous sum in terms of the time (annual expenditure on the army and navy in the late 1820s was in the area of £7 million, worldwide).

Upper Canada had another useful function as far as the military were concerned. The end of the Napoleonic wars released a large number of soldiers from service. Those desiring to settle in British North America would receive free grants of land (100 acres for enlisted men, 200 for officers), tools, and government support. Soon the back townships between the St Lawrence and the Rideau rivers began to receive new-model British immigrants, equipped, as the Loyalists had been, with government-issue tools and supported by government-funded services including medicine and education. These services would be discontinued as and when the new settlers achieved an income sufficient to support them. There were, as well, government-assisted civilians, who received an assisted passage across the Atlantic and a refund of their fare payable in three years' time.

The effect was a considerable rise in British immigration to Upper Canada. Poor Scots and Irish, encouraged to move by a government desperate to rid itself of surplus population, settled Lanark county in eastern Ontario and Peterborough to the northeast of York. Army and navy officers who wished to make the move were allowed to trade their commissions for land grants, a move that the historian of Upper Canada, Gerald Craig, considers to have been largely successful, by reason of the vigorous and well-educated men it brought into the province.

At the same time that British subjects were being encouraged and assisted to emigrate to Canada, emigrants of another kind were being discouraged. Americans were not in favour in official quarters in York, where it was keenly remembered that they had been less than a bulwark during the recent war. The lieutenant governor, now Sir Peregrine Maitland, a retired general, and his advisers were convinced that something must be done to limit the political rights of American immigrants. Their attempt to do so, however, led them directly into a conflict with the Legislative Assembly. A complicated and apparently endless quarrel followed, centring on the issue of the naturalization of "aliens," even though the aliens in question might have resided in the province for thirty years and damned themselves in the eyes of their former country-men by serving in the Upper Canadian militia during the War of 1812. Elections were fought on the matter, an anti-government majority was formed in the Assembly, and deadlock ensued be-tween the Legislative Council and the Legislative Assembly. The "alien question" was referred several times across the sea to Britain, and was finally resolved in 1827 on terms that repre-sented an almost complete victory for the "alien" side.

The alien issue went beyond politics or political rights to in-clude property and land, for it was assumed by many that what affected, or removed, political rights also touched an immigrant's right to hold property. Although this was never intended, it gave cause for alarm and contributed to the bitterness the alien issue aroused. Nor was this the only land issue of the 1820s. The old problem of land grants resurfaced, as it became apparent that far more land had been granted than was actually being farmed. To resolve the problem, Maitland and his advisers tried to dispossess the idle of their grants, but their efforts were better in intention than in effect. It did not help that by this point the governor and his advisers were acquiring a name and reputation that did neither much good: the Family Compact.

The Family Compact was supposed to encompass a small and privileged group of government followers clustered around the lieutenant governor of the day. Its opponents would have described a typical member of the Family Compact as rich, privileged in the matter of government grants and income, and Anglican. John Beverley Robinson, the attorney general, a man of Virginian ancestry; John Strachan, the archdeacon of Toronto and later the city's first Anglican bishop; William Allan, a wealthy business-man and land speculator; and D'Arcy Boulton, the solicitor general, were all likely candidates for the title. They were not incapable men, by any means, but origin, education, social connection, and experience, especially during the War of 1812, had hardened their attitudes and made them rigidly and unbendingly "loyal." Their opponents, it went without saying, were at least suspect and at worst disloyal, as the traitors during the war had been. To the Family Compact, loyalty to the British crown, the preservation of the government set up by the Constitutional Act of 1791, and the cultivation of an established, government-sponsored church, the Church of England, were matters of principle and more: they were the bulwarks against the tide of republicanism that had almost overflowed into Upper Canada in 1812.

Opposition to the Compact and its actions was episodic. There had been division even among the appointed officials in the years after 1800, a controversy that left a legacy in inherited politics and political loyalties. There was a brief flurry in 1817–18 over the activities of a disgruntled immigrant Scot, Robert Gourlay, who surveyed the province with a questionnaire and, having discovered abuses to be remedied, summoned conventions to discover the appropriate ways and means. His action was interpreted as a challenge to constituted authority, in that he was trying to substitute himself and his followers for the legislature. The conventions came to naught, but their failure did not prevent the provincial authorities from prosecuting Gourlay under Upper Canada's Sedition Act. After spending eight months in jail awaiting trial, Gourlay was exiled from the province in August 1819.

There were further quarrels, including conflicts among the appointed officials and judges, that tended to confirm lines of division and, by that token, to furnish potential leaders to the opposition or reform cause, as it was coming to be called. Events in the 1820s, for example, awakened the dormant "reform" sentiments of a prominent York family, the Baldwins. The Baldwins, Irish Protestant immigrants, carried over from their Irish background a conviction both of free parliaments within the British empire and of parliamentary supremacy over the executive as the foundation of the British constitutional system. During the 1820s first William Warren Baldwin and then his son Robert secured election to the Upper Canadian legislature. There they joined a motley crew of oppositionists, whose main point in common was that they did not like the way in which Upper Canada was governed.

The most prominent, and certainly the most vociferous, of the opposition leaders was another recently arrived Briton, William Lyon Mackenzie, a native of Dundee in Scotland who had come to the new world in 1820, at the age of twenty-five, to seek his fortune. After a spell as a shopkeeper, Mackenzie felt the call to own a newspaper, and it was as proprietor and editor of the *Colonial Advocate* that he made his name. At first he used his paper to sustain the orthodox causes of the British connection and the clergy reserves, but soon he veered into opposition, and not merely opposition. Mackenzie had an unrivalled capacity for spying out conspiracies against the public good and for vilifying the supposed conspirators. Employing a talent for denunciation and abuse almost unequalled in Canadian history, he questioned the motives, character, and ancestry of those he perceived as enemies. These included most of the prominent members of the Family Compact.

Some of the Compact children — young men in their twenties — took offence, and rashly punished the scandal-monger Mackenzie by dumping his press into Lake Ontario. Mackenzie, who had fled to the United States to escape his creditors, now returned triumphant to collect damages in the courts. The damages, which were far in excess of the actual loss he suffered, re-established his credit and gave him a new lease on financial life. Soon Mackenzie was in the legislature representing York County, which at that time included most of south-central Upper Canada. There followed a series of petitions to the British government — in which Mackenzie still believed — for the redress of grievances. Mackenzie himself became a political issue early in the 1830s when a legislature dominated by the friends of the government, or Tories, repeatedly expelled him from the Assembly and removed his right to speak.

The political turmoil in Upper Canada landed on the doorstep of the Colonial Office, the British department of government charged with colonial administration, in London. All too often Upper Canadian politicians landed there too, and were joined by their counterparts from Lower Canada and even occasionally from the Maritime provinces. In an effort to see whether something better could not be accomplished, the British government in 1836 sent out a new lieutenant governor, Sir Francis Bond Head, an English engineer and magistrate with a talent for prose and, as it later appeared, melodrama. Bond Head had considerable ability in politics, though not in planning events over the long term. He was instructed to reform some of the abuses in the administration and, at the same time, to try to reconcile the reform opposition to British administration.

The new lieutenant governor started off by inviting two reformers, Robert Baldwin and John Rolph, into his Executive Council. They remained there for some months, until they realized that Bond Head, though not a Tory in the usual sense of the word, was nevertheless determined to have his own way and to run the government as he thought best. The reformers thereupon resigned, and Bond Head called an election. Personally leading the government forces, appealing to British loyalties and mobilizing the large numbers of recent British immigrants to the province, Bond Head swept the field. Even Mackenzie lost his seat, an unpleasant jolt for the veteran agitator.

From outside the legislature, Mackenzie continued to denounce the government, and gradually, in 1837, his disgruntlement sought a shorter and more certain solution. He set up "committees of vigilance" and harangued his large crowds of supporters. In turn, his people were attacked by groups of government supporters, particularly by Orangemen, members of the Orange Lodge. The Orange Lodge had been imported into Upper Canada from Ireland, where it was an ultra-Protestant and ultra-loyal secret society. In Upper Canada it became almost an arm of the government, and an important factor in the politics of the province. It would remain so for over a hundred years.

Mackenzie was not the leader of a united reform movement. The most conservative reformers had moved off some time earlier, following the Methodist leader Egerton Ryerson into an attitude of loyal support to the British constitution and the British connection. Ties with the Baldwins also frayed. William and Robert Baldwin identified themselves with the cause of "responsible government," which meant the supremacy of the legislature over the executive but which declined to take matters one step further in the direction of severing the British connection. The Baldwins believed that they were merely upholding British institutions, however imperfectly Bond Head and the Family Compact understood these matters.

And so, when Mackenzie passed over the line into rebellion in the fall of 1837, he could count on only a fraction of supporters in the central and western parts of the province. The rebellion was concerted between Mackenzie and his rural followers north of Toronto, as York had become in 1834 (Mackenzie was its first mayor). The two sides got their signals crossed, with the result that the rebels from the north marched prematurely on the city, accompanied by Mackenzie, but not by Mackenzie's chosen general, who would only arrive, on time, a few days later. They marched to a few miles north of the city, and then lurked around Montgomery's Tavern, a radical watering-hole in Hog's Hollow near where Toronto's York Mills subway station now sits. An attack on the city was repulsed on December 5, and two days later loyal volunteers from Toronto and the surrounding area drove off the rebels from their tavern. The "baboon Mackenzie," as one loyalist called him, was sent fleeing for the American border, which he reached on December 11.

The drama was not over yet. Mackenzie's fight for freedom attracted American support, many Americans seeing in the rebellion a distant echo of their own revolution sixty years before. With American support, Mackenzie seized an island in the Niagara River and supplied it from the American side using an American boat, the *Caroline*. Loyalists rowed across the river and set the *Caroline* adrift and afire; one American was killed and another injured. This operation resulted in a famous case in international law a few years later, when a Canadian, Alexander Macleod, indulged a taste for heavy drink and loose talk on the United States side of the border and claimed to be one of those who had burned the ship. Arrested for murder, it took the combined efforts of the American and British governments to get him back safely to the Canadian side of the frontier.

For the next few years there were alarms and excursions up and down the border, from Prescott, where rebels and their American friends seized a windmill and had to be blasted out of it by British cannon, to Windsor. The American government, fortunately for Canada, wished to keep out of the quarrel, and without official support and with a great deal of official discouragement, the transborder raids petered out.

The rebellion was restricted in terms of actual fighting: the inglorious excursion to York and a few scattered gatherings in southwestern Upper Canada were the sum total of overt disloyalty. They were easily put down by the militia and volunteers, all the regular British troops in the province having been sent to Lower Canada to deal with a more serious rebellion there. The two rebellions, Upper and Lower, were not co-ordinated, and even the Upper Canadian version was notable for its lack of coherence and cohesion. Mackenzie was not a master organizer, to say the least.

Why were some people loyal and others rebels? A recent study by the historian Colin Read of the southwestern part of the rebellion suggests that economic discontent was not the difference. The rebels by and large came from prosperous and comparatively long-settled townships, and as individuals they seem to have been reasonably well-off. It is true that they tended to be either native-born Upper Canadians or American immigrants, but obviously they were still a minority within both categories. Nor is there any conclusive link between membership in the American-derived Protestant sects and participation in the rebellion; still, it is true that members of the official church, the Church of England, were loyal. The true causes of the rebellion therefore seem to lie in political postures, alliances, and influences. Individuals took up arms, or scythes, for many reasons, some personal, some general. Many were reformers who took their politics one step beyond the norm. Others were misled by false reports.

The aftermath of the rebellion saw rebels or suspected rebels suppressed. Active partisans of Mackenzie were arrested if they could be found. Two rebels, Samuel Lount and Peter Matthews, were hanged; others were transported to Van Diemen's Land (Australia). Many others, whether active rebels or not, chose to leave the province for Michigan and other points west. Some would later return, but the majority would not, and they and their descendants became prominent in the public life of American states from Michigan to Texas to California.

The immediate effect of the rebellion was to strengthen the dominance of the Tories in the life of the province. Eastern Upper Canada was already strongly Tory in sentiment, and for a while the Tories became dominant in the west too. British garrisons went to London and St Thomas and reformers found it advisable to speak softly and refrain from too active politics. The imperial government in London was also concerned in the aftermath. Sir Francis Bond Head was removed from office and replaced by Sir George Arthur. A new Governor General came out, Lord Durham, who briefly toured Upper Canada and retired to write a report on the grievances of and remedies for the Upper and Lower Canadians. Durham, who held office for less than a year in 1838, was succeeded in 1839 by a British politician, Charles Poulett Thomson, who shortly became Lord Sydenham.

Sydenham's task was to implement the British government's new scheme for the two provinces of Canada, the first large-scale overhaul of their government since 1791. Upper and Lower Canada were to be united as a first step, as Durham had recommended, and Thomson came himself to Upper Canada to secure its co-operation in November 1839. "The country was split into factions animated with the most deadly hatred to each other," he reported. The finances of the province were "deranged," the state of the government was low and sinking, and people were leaving the province in droves. With the assistance of a rising young Tory politician, W. H. Draper, Thomson got what he wanted from the Upper Canadian Assembly. Against its own inclination and decidedly against its better judgement, the Assembly voted for union on British terms.

In 1840 the British Parliament voted an Act of Union for the two Canadas, and in February 1841 it took effect. Upper Canada as a separate political entity vanished from the map. Its future would depend on what Upper Canadians could make of their unsought union with the largely French and Catholic population of the lower province. But while Upper Canada's distinct political identity was submerged, it was not extinguished. The traditions and attitudes established during the province's first fifty years were too deeply rooted to be lost now, whatever else the future might hold.

The Province United — and Divided

An aerial view of Upper Canada early in the 1840s would have disclosed some differences from the 1780s. The forest cover of the province was diminishing. Settlement was well north of the Great Lakes, was surrounding Lake Simcoe, and was spreading along the Ottawa and Rideau rivers in the east. Linking the farms and towns were slashes through the bush — roads — some built by Simcoe's troops as far back as the 1790s, others of more recent vintage. The roads were usually considered "indescribably bad," a consideration which did not prevent travellers from describing them, usually at length. In spring, summer, and fall the rivers and lakes opened up for navigation. There were small boats (*bateaux*) on the St Lawrence, and larger ones on the lakes. These could be either sailing ships of varying sizes or steamships, the first one, the *Frontenac*, having been launched in 1816.

Navigation was assisted by canals. The first canals were built around rapids west of Montreal between 1779 and 1783; they were always inadequate and in time became more of a bottleneck than a pass-through for traffic. Far better was the Lachine Canal, dating from the 1820s, which offered passage to boats to a depth of five feet as far as the mouth of the Ottawa, from which boats could proceed via the Grenville and Rideau canals up the Ottawa and Rideau rivers to reach Kingston by way of Colonel By's masterpiece, the Rideau Canal. This cumbersome journey might have been necessary in wartime, but it did not commend itself to travellers who wanted a quick and direct route to Lake Ontario. The Upper Canadian legislature studied the question, surveyed the St Lawrence, passed resolutions, and eventually, in 1834, construction started. The Cornwall Canal, beside the town of the same name, was completed in 1843. It was eleven miles long, and cost $1.8 million. It was, in a word, expensive, especially in terms of the time, and it points up one of the features of canals and canal-building: the necessity for bountiful finance.

The canal enthusiasts of the late eighteenth and early nineteenth centuries were not daunted by the comparatively minor problem of money. That could be furnished by the credit of the province, occasionally assisted, as with the Rideau Canal, by the generous donations of the imperial government itself. The building of canals proceeded. The most exciting project was a canal around Niagara Falls from Port Dalhousie on Lake Ontario via the Welland River into the Niagara River above the falls, and thence on into Lake Erie. This canal, the brainchild of W. H. Merritt, was completed in 1829. In combination with the St Lawrence canals, it became possible to sail from Montreal as far as Sault Ste Marie, as early as 1843.

At the same time, the Americans built the Erie Canal from the Hudson River along the Mohawk valley to Buffalo on Lake Erie. Finished in 1825, the Erie Canal offered an alternative exit for Upper Canadian products destined for overseas, and throughout this period it gave the more northerly lake-and-river system a run for its money.

The money needed to finance canals came increasingly from the public pocket. Although the Welland Canal was originally a private project, it swiftly acquired public ownership and swallowed ever larger amounts of public money. William Lyon Mackenzie, whose newspaper diatribes are a good barometer of the state of public excitement and indignation for the period, naturally saw the canal as an iniquitous fraud: ''The Welland Canal,'' he wrote in 1834, ''has been a hoax from first to last.'' It was, at least, a hoax along which steamships could sail and exports could flow.

The western part of the province — "western Canada" as it was then called — lay athwart the great migration route from New York State through to Michigan. To western Canada had come the American settlers whose presence caused so much unease during the War of 1812 and after. Much of the settling was done along the shores of Lake Erie, in what are today Essex and Elgin counties, but which in the 1830s and 1840s were the domain of Colonel Thomas Talbot, the despotic projector of southwestern Ontario. Talbot had made his career in the British army, which had sent him to Upper Canada as aide-de-camp to John Graves Simcoe. On the outbreak of an interlude of peace in 1803 Talbot left the army and returned to Upper Canada, there to found a settlement in his own image and to increase his landed wealth to a point undreamt-of in his native Ireland. By the time of his death Talbot had a well-deserved reputation for extravagant behaviour and eccentric politics, which were directed at preserving intact the status quo. Talbot had done well by the status quo, and he stood by it through the War of 1812 and the Rebellion of 1837, keeping "the Scoundrels" in order with what he called "twigs." Talbot, at the time of the rebellions, possessed 48,000 acres; childless, he left his estate to his servants when he died.

Talbot's methods were not popular, but no land speculator, however well he managed his land grant, was ever well-regarded for very long. The Canada Company, a British land development firm whose Canadian agent was the novelist John Galt, purchased almost 3 million acres from the Upper Canadian government and sold them off to immigrants through the 1830s and 1840s. The consensus among historians seems to be that the Canada Company gave good value both to Upper Canada and to its clients, but no one could ever be satisfied with its efforts. The Canada Company's Huron Tract brought settlement to the shores of Lake Huron — what is now Huron County — around Goderich.

At the other end of the province there was another, much less significant, experiment in speculative tyranny, of a kind closer to the Talbot Settlement than to the Canada Company. The thirteenth laird of clan McNab in Scotland decided to recreate the vanishing days of Scottish feudalism in the Canadian wilderness. His experiment, unhappily for himself, ran into the egalitarian and democratic ways of the new world, and ended messily in a series of lawsuits. The laird returned to the old world, leaving his colonists behind in what is today Renfrew County, at the northernmost end of the province's farming country. Like the settlers who had preceded them on the shores of Lake Erie and Lake Huron, the clansmen of Renfrew turned to the forest for their livelihood.

In Upper Canada around 1840 lumbering was everywhere. In its most elementary form it was called timbering: after cutting down a tree it was "squared" with an axe, hauled to the nearest large river or lake, and gathered into a "boom" or "raft" to drift downstream towards Montreal or Quebec City and the British timber ships waiting to carry it to its destined market in Great Britain. The ships that hauled timber in one direction brought immigrants in the other; and the immigrants in turn furnished the labour force that would cut more timber. As the trade developed, the square timber was sawn into planks, called "deals," and was similarly exported to a British market that favoured colonial imports under a series of timber duties designed to discourage imports from the closer forests of Scandinavia and the Baltic. The timber duties persisted as late as 1860, although they were substantially reduced in the 1840s, and as long as they lasted, so did large Canadian exports of wood.

Britain was not the only export market. Square timber started to head south in the 1830s, to the United States. It became what is called a "staple," defined by economic historians as an export consisting largely of a primary resource; it was also a staple in a different sense: an important, basic, natural product. Since timber accounted for 50 percent of Canada's exports in the 1820s, it was a true staple as well as a means of growth and development in the future farmland of Upper Canada. White pine was the foundation of the timber trade, as it was to be, a few years later, for lumbering.

Lumbering was the first large-scale manufacturing industry in

Upper Canada. It depended on machinery and water power, and of course on the abundance of trees. The lumber barons of the Ottawa valley — the Egans, the Edwardses, the Bronsons — were the most prominent in the trade, but virtually no Upper Canadian locality was without its saw mill powered by the rushing waters of some nearby stream. "The machinery is on a gigantic scale," one traveller wrote of a visit to a mill near Peterborough in the 1850s. "One hundred and thirty-six saws were working with tremendous velocity, reducing huge logs to planks at the rate of nearly fifty an hour." The mill in question worked day and night, and absorbed 70,000 logs in a nine-month season, but whatever it produced, it could sell. And this was far from the largest. The Egan Company in the Ottawa valley employed 3800 men in the woods in the winter of 1854–55, as well as 1700 horses and 200 bullocks.

Lumber destined for the American market went by water too, down to Kingston and then by schooner across Lake Ontario to Oswego, and thence to market via the Erie Canal. Timber could even be exported to Britain through the port of New York, and some Ottawa valley timber travelled south to go east, instead of going more directly through Quebec. Lumbering depended to a large extent on the infusion of American technology, capital, and entrepreneurs. E. B. Eddy, a New Englander, built up a vast lumber company at the Chaudière Falls between Bytown, the modern Ottawa, and Hull, Quebec.

Water power drove not only lumber mills but grist mills too. Wheat exports occurred early in Upper Canadian history, and wheat and flour exports were encouraged by the British Corn Laws, as we have seen. Preferential treatment in the British market encouraged investment in flour mills in Upper Canada, but the sudden repeal of the Corn Laws was an equally tangible set-back. Writing in 1848, a Methodist preacher described a mill "which must have cost many thousand pounds in its erection ... standing still."

The set-back was temporary. During the 1850s wheat prices and markets recovered, and the acreage devoted to wheat in Upper Canada increased steadily. Land prices rose as well, as farm-land became more desirable, and it became an attractive speculation to invest in land on the very edge of the Canadian Shield, in Haliburton north of Peterborough and in Bruce and Grey counties. But while wheat became an Upper Canadian staple, it was a transitory one. By the 1860s informed observers were predicting that wheat had reached its peak and would diminish in importance thereafter, a prediction that later proved quite correct.

Other forms of economic activity were appearing. Manufacturing, on a small scale, occurred as soon as the first settlers required crude farm implements and local blacksmiths were able to make them. For many years much of Upper Canada's and later Ontario's manufacturing activity was on a scale so humble that today's observers might be forgiven for mistaking it for something else. Even to contemporaries, it seemed natural that manufacturing would be concentrated where population and experience demanded it: in Lower Canada, and particularly in Montreal, Canada's largest city and the metropolis of the St Lawrence and Ottawa valleys.

It is not surprising that Upper Canada's population grew rapidly as mid-century approached. In 1831 Upper Canada counted 237,000 inhabitants and Lower Canada, 553,000. By 1842, despite the rebellion and subsequent emigration, Upper Canada had 487,000 residents; two years later Lower Canada had 697,000. Immigration was still on the rise, and the occurrence of famine in Ireland stimulated a new flow in the late 1840s that would push Upper Canada's population higher than the lower province's. At the same time, the effect of immigration was to place British immigrants in a numerical majority in Upper Canada for the crucial years in the middle of the nineteenth century. Upper Canada in 1840 or 1850 was very different from Upper Canada in 1800 or 1810.

The question of population, strange as it might seem, was a political matter. The Act of Union of 1840 that brought Upper and Lower Canada into an uncomfortable symbiosis also equalized representation between the western and the eastern provinces.

Even if Lower Canada's population was much larger, proportionately, than Upper Canada's, it was mostly French-speaking and therefore potentially disloyal. By adding Upper Canadians, who were at least English-speaking even if not entirely trustworthy, to the balance, French Canadians were bound to be outnumbered by a combination of western representatives and Lower Canadian English-speakers. The French resented this development, but then, when the Upper Canadian population surpassed that of French Canada in 1851 (952,000 to 890,000), the tables were turned. The politics of the 1850s acquired a new slogan, "rep by pop" (representation by population), just as old issues concerning the alien question and the clergy reserves were dwindling into insignificance.

Economic developments were not foreign to the politics of the period. The Canadians of the 1840s were keenly interested in economic development, and even more concerned with the question of who was going to pay for it. Popular interest in canals had a price, and the price was paid in taxation. But banks, currency, industrial growth, and railways were also interesting, and local politicians rose and fell according to the measure of satisfaction they could bestow on the communities that elected them. In the economic measures that were adopted in the 1850s and 1860s we can begin to discern the shape of many Canadian institutions that are still familiar; and the familiarity grows even greater when we consider such institutions as schools, universities, and hospitals, and counties, towns, and cities. All, in one way or another, took their basic shape in this period. It was a busy time for the legislators.

First the legislators had to clear the decks of the burden of the past. The burning issues of the 1830s were not solved by the rebellions, and certainly not by the reaction the rebellions induced. The rebellions did, however, jolt the British government into thinking about the administration of the Canadian provinces in a more creative way. The Governor General sent to supervise the establishment of the united province of Canada, Charles Poulett Thomson, was himself a politician, and a highly skilled one. He carried with him a British promise to guarantee a £1 million loan to re-establish the finances of the colonies, and to develop the province by pushing ahead vigorously with canals. Thomson, who became Lord Sydenham, formed a broadly based administration by appointing a combination of Tories and Reformers (the terms Conservatives and Liberals would shortly come into common use) to advise him. He intended to be both the political and the administrative head of the Canadian government and, had he survived, a different politics might have resulted. But Sydenham, having launched the new Canadian legislature in his new capital of Kingston, died. He was succeeded by Sir Charles Bagot, the former British ambassador to the court of St Petersburg.

The political personalities of the day were more constructive, and possibly more talented, than their predecessors had been. W. H. Draper, who had guided union through the Upper Canadian Assembly, remained prominent as a "moderate" Conservative, certainly preferable in the Governor General's eyes to the Upper Canadian mossbacks, such as Sir Allan MacNab, who had opposed the union root and branch. On the Reform or Liberal side there was Robert Baldwin, whom we have met agitating for "responsible government" back in the 1830s. Baldwin was allied to a Protestant Irishman, Francis Hincks, who has frequently been described as a man of measures rather than of principles. Supple where Baldwin was rigid, prone to compromise where Baldwin was stubborn, Hincks also beheld the world through a different perspective. Baldwin, pre-eminently a lawyer and a constitutionalist, as well as a man of considerable private wealth, was isolated from some aspects of political reality. Hincks, who had made his own way, was a man for progress and the modern era. He was that rarity among Canadian politicians, a man who understood economics and finance, and who was prepared to make them work for the development of the country as well as for his own advancement.

It was Hincks, too, who took the first steps towards the historic compromise of Canadian politics. Making contact with Lower Canadian Reformers, under Louis-Hippolyte LaFontaine, Hincks established the basis of a political alliance between the two groups, an act which virtually guaranteed the Reformers a natural majority in the first legislature of united Canada. A natural majority, that is, but for the exertions of Lord Sydenham, who outmanoeuvred both men only to have his successor captured by them.

The 1840s saw governments rise and fall, and politicians made and eclipsed, by whether they stood for a continuation of rule by the Governor General with a government-made majority in the Assembly — the traditional or Tory position, as Sydenham had made it — or whether they plumped for rule by a government sustained by the legislative majority, irrespective of the Governor. As every student of Canadian history knows, the battle was eventually won by the reformers, and lost by the Tories. Baldwin and LaFontaine formed a ministry in 1848, after an election gave the majority to the reformers.

Thereafter, all Canadian governments would ultimately depend on their ability to get themselves elected, and at its base the government of 1848 was the same kind of government Canada has today. It had its differences, of course. Many of the offices bore different titles. The inspector general, for example, was the minister of finance. There were two attorneys general, one for each section of the "united" province. There were only two jurisdictions whose needs had to be considered, Upper and Lower Canada, but within that limitation, jobs and politics proceeded with all due regard to local sentiments.

Party loyalties, not to mention the parties themselves, were drawing together into a form that is almost, but not quite, recognizable. Members of the Canadian legislature could belong to a dozen different groupings or factions. There were moderate as well as extreme Tories from Upper Canada. The extremists took their stand with Sir Allan MacNab, the squire of Dundurn Castle in Hamilton; but what they stood for was becoming increasingly archaic and irrelevant. Moderate Tories showed an increasing tendency to favour John A. Macdonald, the young lawyer-member for Kingston, whose supple ways and administrative ability

commended him to other politicians. Baldwin had his own following, and Hincks had his; but neither man completely trusted the
other, and both were united in mistrusting the vocal editor of the
recently founded *Globe* newspaper, George Brown of Toronto.
Brown, in turn, found that there was entirely too much compromising going on among the provincial politicians, and struck out
increasingly on his own, away from the moderate reformers of
the Baldwin stripe towards the grass-roots Clear Grit movement.
(The term Clear Grit appears to be uniquely and authentically
Canadian: it is confined to Upper Canadian Liberals from the
western part of the province in its original sense.)

Baldwin was the first casualty of the emerging factional politics, in which it was no longer enough to be labelled a reformer.
He made his mark before he departed, however. He reformed
local government in Upper Canada, dividing the province into
counties with local autonomy and revenues, and abolishing the
older "district" system by which the province had been governed
since before the days of Simcoe. Baldwin passed a University Act
establishing a secular provincial university (University College)
on the ruins of an Anglican college that had been envisaged by his
Tory predecessors. A provincial university was long overdue, by
North American standards: south of the border the American
states were establishing and endowing state universities and colleges by the dozen. Important as these enactments were, their
significance was dimmed by the appearance of Clear Grit agitation in Upper Canada. In its original form, Clear Grit doctrine
demanded that Baldwin go one step further, in the direction that
his Municipal Corporations Act established, by making everything elective. Baldwin viewed this step as a threat to parliamentary
forms of government, and resisted, but the criticism did not die
down. Disgusted, disheartened, and ill, he resigned in 1851; he
would die in retirement at the early age of fifty-four, in 1858.

Francis Hincks was Baldwin's logical successor. Hincks' abilities were self-evident, but the same talents that made him an
original and dynamic administrator also raised hackles and cre-

ated distrust. He was the first Upper Canadian leader of the railway age, the prophet of a new technology. It is no exaggeration to compare enthusiasm for railways to certain forms of religious mania, especially those forms that promise earthly benefits and infinite satisfaction. Railways were the true sign of the modern age, the harbingers of prosperity as well as of enlightenment, breaking down the isolation of rural areas and bringing everyone within the range of metropolitan centres.

The metropolitan centres were not necessarily located in Upper Canada. To transport lumber to Boston and New England, for example, a railway snaked across the border at Prescott on the St Lawrence to connect up with Bytown and the lumber country on the Ottawa. To join Montreal with the Great Lakes basin another railway, the Grand Trunk, was projected. But the first railway actually started was the Great Western, running from Buffalo to Detroit and designed to connect two sections of the American railroad system across the shortest distance between them. Colonel Talbot, virtually the last relic of the eighteenth century and of Governor Simcoe's time, turned the sod at London in 1849.

The Great Western was a notable, though belated, advance. Upper Canada's politicians, however, were looking for bigger projects, and they found one in the conception of a "main line" railway to traverse the whole province. Translated into the Grand Trunk, promoted by no less than Francis Hincks, financed from England and built by Great Britain's foremost railway contractor, the Grand Trunk was chartered in 1853. Its most important section, from Toronto to Montreal, was completed in 1856. By 1859 it reached Sarnia, on the St Clair River, and linked with Detroit via a line on the American side. To the east, the Grand Trunk absorbed another railway to take itself to Quebec City, and then to Rivière-du-Loup on the lower St Lawrence.

From the start, the Grand Trunk received a mixed reception. There was no doubt that it greatly increased the convenience of getting around, no doubt too that it gave people access to a wider world. It was, however, by no means certain that people wanted everything that a wider world had to offer. Railways were, by the standards of their time, giant corporations, the prototypes of modern industrial organization. They required elaborate financing, and when the receipts of the railway failed to satisfy the hopes of its promoters, the financing could well fall on the public purse. Such was the case with the Grand Trunk.

The Grank Trunk disappointed everyone. It disappointed its British shareholders, and continued to do so. It disappointed the Province of Canada, which had to find revenue to pay for its thousand-mile trackage from Detroit to Rivière-du-Loup. It disappointed its passengers, especially those who had travelled on other trains, because its roadbed could sustain speeds no greater than twenty-five or thirty miles per hour; on poorly built sections, trains crept along at ten. The Grand Trunk had strong political support in the Canadian cabinet. Its president sat in the cabinet, its bankers were also those of the province, and it could apparently rely on a majority of the legislature when its cash ran out. But this strength was also a weakness. Standards of public conduct were considerably more relaxed in the nineteenth century. There was no bar to a minister doing business on the side, as long as there was no evident bribery. Nevertheless, the feeling grew that the cabinet was in the railway's, or the railway's bankers', pocket. Especially in agrarian Upper Canada, resentful and mistrustful of the distant metropolis, the Grand Trunk was an alien and hostile intrusion.

It was not the only one. The farmers of Upper Canada, and particularly those of the western peninsula between Lakes Ontario, Erie, and Huron, had benefited from an economic boom in the 1850s. Farmers seized the opportunity to improve their holdings. New houses, barns, and roads were built. Money was easily obtained from the bank. The Bank of Upper Canada, the province's banker, was glad to advance money on the strength of land; land, after all, was rising in value every day. The province kept its cash in the bank, a sure sign of stability. In 1857 the boom went bust. Land lost value, and mortgages went down with the price of land. The Bank of Upper Canada found itself perched precariously on the edge of a precipice. The government's deposits, it is true, stayed with the bank, because to withdraw them might finally push the bank over the edge into bankruptcy. Thus the bank's weakness became its last source of strength. The slump saw a contraction in farm credit, and, as the stronger banks pulled their money out of land and placed it in more profitable or at any rate safer investment, western Canadian farmers grew irritable and resentful. The money power was at work, squeezing them, in conjunction with the Grand Trunk.

Much of the blame was directed at Montreal and its banking and political community, and at the French Canadian members of the legislature who sustained the government. It was a new government by the time the Grand Trunk started up: the Reform party had split apart and a Liberal-Conservative coalition had been formed on its ruins. The French Canadian supporters of the Baldwin-LaFontaine government now coalesced with Upper Canadian Tories and a few ministerial Liberals. Sir Allan MacNab became premier in the new government, but the real Upper Canadian Tory leader was increasingly John A. Macdonald of Kingston. Confronting Macdonald across the floor of the legislature was the tail end of Upper Canadian reform, now little more than the Clear Grits of western Canada and some scattered Liberals from the St Lawrence area.

The outstanding personality on the reform side was, and remained, George Brown. Brown had an unenviable reputation among many of his contemporaries. Dour, self-righteous, demagogic, he was ideally equipped for factional strife. A convinced Protestant, he supported public schools and opposed government funding of religious institutions; in other areas of politics he sustained the democratic and popular interest and promoted the advancement of his own section of the province. Brown, however, was more than a parochial or regional politician. It is true that he sometimes confused the interests of a particular group of Torontonians with those of Upper Canada as a whole, and true that he could, on occasion, assume political blinkers of the most remarkable opacity. It is also true that Brown was a genuine political representative of nineteenth-century British liberalism, with its faith in equality and opportunity, in the absence of privilege or preference, whether in matters of religion or in secular affairs. Brown's interest in public affairs was anything but abstract: politics was associated with the progress of Toronto and Upper Canada, with the railway lines snaking in and out of the Lake Ontario city, and with Toronto's emerging rivalry with Montreal.

Toronto was indeed acquiring an identity and institutions of its own. The Bank of Upper Canada was there, as were a number of railway offices and mercantile establishments. There were grain elevators to handle the grain trade, barracks for the British garrison, a large jail of pleasingly classical design, and the provincial lunatic asylum on Queen Street. To service the railways there were railway shops, one of which, the Toronto Locomotive Works, produced its first engine in 1853. A stock exchange of sorts was set in motion in the 1850s, although it took a number of years before it achieved a stable existence.

The city did not, however, achieve one of its larger ambitions. It did not become the permanent political centre of united Canada, although the provincial capital moved there temporarily in a rotation arrangement with Quebec City. The permanent capital, it was decided in 1857, would be Ottawa, formerly Bytown, an unlovely little lumber city on the Ottawa River. Bytown had the advantage of a magnificent natural location, on cliffs overlooking the Ottawa and the Rideau Falls, and it was midway between French-language Lower Canada and English-language Upper Canada. The decision would stick when the Dominion of Canada was established in 1867; and government became a permanent part of Ontario's business — even if government was located on the province's furthest frontier.

The 1850s left other, equally lasting, consequences behind. The financial strains of the decade resulted in the establishment of Canada's tariff policy. Not everyone in Upper Canada favoured this development. Farmers exporting wheat from the province wished to buy their supplies as cheaply as possible, and looked askance at the imposition of a revenue tariff. But manufacturers took a different point of view. Publicists like Isaac Buchanan argued that a protective, not just a revenue, tariff was a foundation of greatness and prosperity. If foreign goods were taxed off the market, then Canadians would have no choice but to turn to the home-grown product. The British government, which at first resisted the province's attempts to establish an autonomous high tariff policy, eventually conceded the issue. At least, thanks to the union of 1841, Upper and Lower Canada were no longer imposing tariffs on each other.

The union also saw the establishment of a publicly supported common school system in Upper Canada. The chief architect of the common schools was a Methodist divine, Egerton Ryerson; such were Ryerson's personality and abilities that he dominated the school system, making it over in his own image. Education was envisaged as a means of inculcating morality as well as learning, and of assimilating a heterogeneous population to a standard of behaviour. The religious sects, Ryerson hoped, would put their quarrels to one side. No one sect could be favoured over any other; better that doctrinal differences be left to the churches to deal with on their own, with their own money and in their own time. This "voluntarist" view, as it was called, commended itself to most of the politicians in largely Protestant Upper Canada, but it did not appeal to the Catholic clergy.

And so, just as the issue of the clergy reserves was being dealt with (they were done away with in an act sponsored by John A. Macdonald in 1854), the separate school issue appeared on the horizon. The Catholic clergy did not believe that faith and morals could properly be inculcated in common schools. They had an advantage, for the great majority of Lower Canadian representatives in the legislature were Catholic. The Lower Canadians were sensitive to the fact that the English Protestants of Lower Canada had been granted their own schools, and when the Catholic bishops of Upper Canada appealed to them for help in granting the same privilege to Upper Canadian Catholics, they could hardly resist the call. In 1853 the bishops got some of what they wanted, a concession that Upper Canadian Catholics could be exempted from school taxes if they wished to pay their levies to their own school system. But the Supplementary School Act that made the concession was hedged with qualifications and limitations, and no one believed the measure to be anything more than a stop-gap.

A second, broader measure was passed in 1855. The original act had conceded separate schools to anyone who wanted them, but it was now amended to grant such schools only to Catholics. There were, however, still limitations and complications. These problems were finally resolved in 1863 by the Scott Act, named after Richard Scott, the Catholic member for Ottawa who first introduced a bill on the subject in 1860. This act simplified the administration of the 1855 act and made possible the establishment of separate schools in rural areas. Subsequently, the Scott Act was embodied in the great constitutional settlement of Confederation in 1867, and it remained the basis of Ontario separate schools for over one hundred years.

One final development in education is worthy of note. The provincial university was established on a firm basis, after being secularized and placed in Toronto. A faculty was hired and a university building begun. Dr. John McCaul became principal of the new establishment, which was situated just to the west of a lunatic asylum. It did not help that Dr McCaul was cordially hated by his professor of history, Dr Daniel Wilson, "a hatred most religiously returned," as an amused bystander commented. The building proved to be an interesting combination of Gothic, Byzantine, and Italian Renaissance styles, and it withstood the attentions of the Governor General, Sir Edmund Head, who had little else upon which to expend his energies. Despite a host of natural enemies, for the religious sects each wanted a piece of the endowment and other localities proved to be jealous of Toronto's good fortune, the university survived.

In its growth and development Upper Canada was not very different from other mid-nineteenth-century jurisdictions. It was, however, unusual in the complexity and difficulty of its political system, and that difficulty was about to be augmented. In 1861 the Province of United Canada held a census, which showed that Upper Canada had 1.4 million inhabitants, 280,000 ahead of Lower Canada. The effect was to augment the agitation of George Brown and his allies for representation by population — "rep by pop" — to extinguish the iniquitous French Canadian domination of the Assembly, something that would, among other things, make impossible the imposition of a separate school system by the representatives of the lower province.

But 1861 was more notable for the outbreak of civil war in the United States. There the country had divided into two parts: the northern states had largely abolished slavery; the southern states had not. Slavery had become a great moral issue in the decades after 1815 and by the 1850s the American political system could hardly bear the strain. Escaped black slaves from the south were assisted on their way north by an "Underground Railway" to Canada, where slavery had long since disappeared and where slave-catchers operating under American law could not pursue them. When, in 1860, an anti-slavery party, the Republicans, captured the American presidency and eleven southern states separated ("seceded") from the American union, President Abraham Lincoln determined to oppose them by force.

The war posed ticklish problems for Canada. Canadians were divided in their sympathies, not so much on the issue of slavery as on the question of the preservation of the American union. The division of the United States into two parts would make each separate part less strong and less of a threat to Canada. The south claimed to be fighting for its culture and its local autonomy, and some Canadians thought that on both counts the southern variety was preferable to the northern equivalent. Newspapers and politicians took sides, although the newspapers were necessarily more vocal than political leaders ever could be. The United States was just across the lakes and northern politicians were inclined to be resentful of criticism.

Great Britain was officially a non-belligerent in the war between north and south. The British position masked the divergent hopes and fears of the British government as it looked westward across the Atlantic. Non-belligerence almost slid into war when, in the fall of 1861, an American warship stopped a British steamer, the *Trent*, and removed two southern pseudo-diplomats en route to Europe to agitate for their new country's cause. The British sternly protested and demanded the return of the southerners. The north was inclined to refuse, and for a while it seemed that there must be war.

If there were war, Upper Canada was bound to be a battleground. Through the winter of 1861–62 British troops arrived in the province. The Canadian legislature dithered over how much money to spend on defence; failing to agree, it traded one government under John A. Macdonald for another under Sandfield Macdonald, a moderate Liberal from Cornwall. Although the danger of war subsided, it did not entirely pass. Southern sympathizers and agents made a nuisance of themselves along the border and there was always the danger that southern activities on Canadian soil directed against the north would finally provoke the United States government into retaliation.

Border tensions were costly for the Canadian government. A volunteer army was raised and equipped. Every second Canadian became an officer, or so it must have seemed from the regular reports of drills, reviews, and military balls that filled the daily press. When the American Civil War ended in a northern victory in April 1865, the danger for Canada did not abate. It is true that the American army was very speedily demobilized. The soldiers who were left were sent to the western frontier or as an army of occupation to the conquered south. Among the disbanded soldiers there were many who had another cause in mind, now that the south was no more and the slaves were free. Their cause was the liberation of Ireland from England, and the means to that end, they believed, were ready to hand. The British American provinces were rich, sprawling, and vulnerable. The road to Dublin lay through Toronto. Let the British be defeated in North America, and their colonies used as bargaining counters in obtaining the freedom of Ireland.

The Canadian government understandably viewed the situation with alarm. The Irish patriots — Fenians, as they were called — were numerous. They had support in the American Congress and among many ordinary American citizens. As veterans of a long and arduous war they were certainly more experienced than anything the Canadian government could throw against them. When the Fenians actually crossed the border, in June 1866, they speedily defeated a Canadian militia force sent against them, at Ridgeway near the Niagara River. Fortunately the Fenians' steam ran out at that point, and they retired before reinforcements could stage another battle.

The Fenian incursion was a sign that the Canadian provinces were exposed and disunited. There were three possible courses of action. The first was to turn British North America into a permanent British encampment, with a large proportion of the British army permanently stationed between Montreal and Windsor. This alternative was considered, but not for long. It cost too much money. It used up too many soldiers, who could be more usefully employed elsewhere in the vast world-wide British empire. In any case, all the Americans needed to do was to cross the St Lawrence and capture Montreal, and the rest of the Province of Canada would fall into their laps, and with it the British garrison. On mature reflection, the future of Upper Canada would not be a military one.

The two remaining courses could be followed in tandem. The first was to negotiate with the Americans on the assumption that the United States had no fundamental quarrel with Great Britain. This proved to be correct, and although it would be a considerable exaggeration to say that relations between the two countries, or between Canada and the United States, were cordial, they were good enough to make war only a very remote possibility for the rest of the century, and, indeed, thereafter. The third course implied a change of status for the British North American provinces. It travelled under the name Confederation, and between 1864 and 1867 it too came to pass. For the British government, the union of its American colonies promised a welcome relief from expense and bother. At best, the British Americans might be persuaded that in union there was sufficient strength to encourage them to defend themselves. At worst, their union might permit the British government to disengage itself from expensive trouble of the kind that had already occurred between 1861 and 1866.

To understand the process whereby the provinces of Canada, Nova Scotia, and New Brunswick (and eventually Prince Edward Island and British Columbia too) became part of Canada, and to explain Upper Canada's role in the process, we must go back a few years. The 1850s were a period of prosperity, down to 1857. Prosperity picked up again in 1861, and the years down to 1867 were good ones for British Americans in general and Upper Canadians in particular. Canada's economic situation had been considerably simplified in 1854 when a Reciprocity Treaty had been negotiated with the United States. Reciprocity simply means an exchange of favours, in this case tariff concessions on natural products such as grain, fish, and lumber. Upper Canada's primary exports were therefore favoured, but American manufactured products had somehow been left out of the equation. When the Province of Canada raised its tariffs in 1858–59, in part to pay for the Grand Trunk, the Americans complained that the Canadians were violating the spirit, although not the letter, of the Reciprocity Treaty. In 1865, in the aftermath of some southern-inspired border incidents, they cancelled the treaty, effective on April Fool's Day, 1866.

By then an alternative was in prospect. If British America were to be thrown back on its own resources, then the resources should be concentrated. For a number of other reasons, too, the idea of union advanced to the head of the political agenda. The political

balance between Upper and Lower Canada, based on equal representation in the legislature, produced deadlock. Upper Canada
voted mostly Liberal or Reform, and Lower Canada voted mostly
Conservative or *bleu*. The minorities in each province, Conservative in the upper province, and Liberal in the lower, were just
large enough to bring the two political groupings (party is too
strong a word) into a nearly perfect equality. Governments rose
and fell on the switch of a few votes.

It was obvious that political stability required more than simple
immobility. To break the deadlock, some kind of constitutional
reform was essential, and despite the bitter personal rivalries
which were so prominent a feature of nineteenth-century Canadian politics, some of the partisan leaders were convinced by the
summer of 1864 that they had no alternative but to compose their
differences and seek a broader solution. George Brown for the
Liberals, and John A. Macdonald for the Conservatives, with
their respective followers, formed a grand coalition in June 1864,
with the object of purging Canada's political constipation by a
broader union.

The coalition lasted long enough to secure agreement among
the provinces, first in a conference at Charlottetown attended by
the Maritime provinces and Canada, and then at another in Quebec City in October 1864. The bases of a union were agreed.
There would be a federation of the British American colonies,
those that cared to join, and in the federation Upper and Lower
Canada would be separated. The two provinces were to assume
their original boundaries, but not their original constitutions. Lower
Canada would be reborn with both an Assembly and a Legislative
Council, but Upper Canada would have just an Assembly.

John A. Macdonald, who became the principal Upper Canadian
representative in the government when George Brown dropped
out in 1865, had no intention of permitting the several Canadian
provinces to wander off in directions of their own choosing. Local
government under the union would be severely restricted to what
he considered to be local, even municipal, matters. But compro-

mises were necessary, and while the resulting British North America Act was strongly weighted in favour of the central power, it did leave the future provinces some leeway.

There was, first of all, taxation. The central government got the tariff, the main source of revenue in the mid-nineteenth century. Indeed, it got the power to tax both directly (the modern income tax is an example) and indirectly (as with the tariff). The provinces could only tax directly. The central government undertook to pay out subsidies to the provinces for the support of their local governments, at a fixed per capita rate. The central government received "residual" powers — matters not specified in the constitution — but it had, in addition, a formidable array of specific powers. The provinces also had such a list, without the residuals. Broadly speaking, the provinces were to have jurisdiction over education, roads, social policy, and "property and civil rights." These things were considered to be primarily a matter for local initiative, and it was proper that a provincial government keep them adequately regulated.

Macdonald fervently supported the project, as did Brown even after he had left the government. Most Upper Canadians would have agreed with them—that their province's opportunities would be greatly enhanced in a broader sphere and that in the new union they could not fail. What was the choice, after all? John A. Macdonald argued that Upper Canada on its own would be nothing more than "a miserable little back state." As the historian J. K. Johnson has pointed out, Macdonald expected Upper Canada to go on much as before, a thriving agricultural community, as befitted "the more favored section of the Province," while Lower Canada, with its "industrious and frugal population" and abundant water power, would become "a great manufacturing country." In balance and in true reciprocity the two great halves of central Canada would strengthen each other under the new system, and not dissipate their energies in pointless sectional quarrels. Some Upper Canadians went further than Macdonald: they believed that Upper Canada had an industrial destiny too; or they foresaw the province and its people spreading across the great unpopulated plains of the northwest, soon to be freed from the archaic grip of the Hudson's Bay Company and placed under the tutelage of the new federal state.

These matters still had to assume final form, and final form was bestowed at a conference in London in 1866. There the new country got a name, "the Dominion of Canada," or, as Canadians for the next eighty years would usually call it, "the dominion." Its capital would be Ottawa. It would have four provinces — Nova Scotia, New Brunswick, Quebec, and Ontario. How Ontario got its name is most unclear; W. L. Morton, one of the historians of the period, has concluded that it originated in the British Colonial Office and that it scotched a proposal to name the new western province "Toronto," something that the non-metropolitan parts of the place would surely never have forgiven.

Ontario would have the largest number of seats in the new dominion's House of Commons—eighty-two. It would have twenty-four seats in the appointive second chamber, the Senate, balancing off Quebec and the Maritimes. But it would have its own local government too, and that government would return to Toronto, the province's largest city as well as its commercial and banking centre. The new Dominion of Canada and the new Province of Ontario would come into existence on July 1, 1867.

Across the dominion it was a fine day. This was taken as a good omen, and prominently recorded for posterity:

> The Temperature.
>
> July 1st. Monday.
>
> Taken at noon in the shade at Atkinson's Drug Store. King Street, Oshawa. 78 degrees. Fine.

In Toronto, the volunteer soldiers paraded and were reviewed by the local British general commanding the garrison. (The general, Major General Stisted, also became Ontario's first, though temporary, lieutenant governor.) There were parades everywhere in the province. Band concerts followed and, in the evening, fire-works. There was, of course, dancing. George Brown sat through the small hours in the office of his *Globe* newspaper, composing 9000 well-chosen words to hail the birth of "a new nationality." In the excitement, very few people paused to notice that it was also the birthday of the province of Ontario.

Prosperity and Provincial Rights

The extent of the province of Ontario in 1867 was a matter for dispute. Maps generally showed Ontario as occupying the western part of the old province of Quebec, with its northern boundary following the height of land that separates the drainage basin of the Great Lakes from that of Hudson Bay. Settlement still hugged the southern fringe of the Canadian Shield, running along a line from midway up Georgian Bay through the Kawartha Lakes over to Lanark County, near Perth, and then northwards to the northern fringe of Renfrew County, north of Pembroke. During the 1860s Manitoulin Island was bought, in part, from the Ojibwa and Ottawa, but north of Manitoulin there was little more than an occasional outpost: Sault Ste Marie, Fort William, Fort Frances, and Rat Portage, the modern Kenora.

By the time the traveller got to Rat Portage, which consisted of three log houses roofed with bark and surrounded by a palisade, he was well out of Ontario and closer to the further end of the Canadian Shield. Beyond lay Red River, a small agricultural and hunting settlement, and beyond that nothing but Indian territory, all the way to the Rocky Mountains and British Columbia. Distant though they were, Red River and the prairies were to play an important part in Ontario's history, and soon. For despite the fact that at least half of the new province was unpopulated, there was no inclination to look for new land in Ontario. The prospective migrant looked west, to Red River, or the United States.

The lack of available agricultural land was widely known and even more widely commented upon. The *Globe* had noticed the "disappearance" of "wild land" as early as 1855. Its editor and proprietor, the reform politician George Brown, was concerned. Brown's political base lay among the farmers of Upper Canada, but as the historian Doug Owram has pointed out, he was equally concerned with the interest and destiny of the city of which he was a prominent ornament. If Upper Canadian farmers needed more land, so did Toronto. What they wanted to settle, Toronto would use as a market. It was the best hope of the little metropolis to rival its American counterparts south and west of the lakes, by reaching out across the Shield and tapping the fertile prairie.

There was, of course, an alternative. Ontario had excellent connections with the American west, where settlement was moving into the great plains in the 1860s. It was easy to move to the United States; by 1871 almost 500,000 Canadians had migrated, up from 250,000 ten years earlier. Ontarians in particular moved to Michigan, where the climate and land were similar to what they were leaving behind, but there was no prairie state without its Canadian contingent; and most of these prairie settlers from north of the border came from Ontario.

Left behind in Ontario in 1871 were 1,621,000 people, scattered over a considerable range of country. In the east, French Canadians had been drifting in, settling the counties of Prescott and Russell and moving the frontier between the English and French languages right into the federal capital of Ottawa. The English-speakers "up the valley" from Ottawa were different from the descendants of the Loyalists and soldier-settlers to the south and west of the capital: up the valley prosperity depended on the lumbermen and the forest hinterland, while further south the apple orchards and stone houses of the early settlers imparted a real stability to the landscape, a stability that was reflected in regional politics — more conservative than the provincial norm.

The surface prosperity of eastern Ontario was not uniform. There were pockets of bad land, rocky and swampy, in Glengarry, in Russell, and more and more as the farms verged on the Canadian Shield. As the traveller approached Kingston the scenery improved — resort hotels were making their appearance around the Rideau lakes — and the quality of farmland declined. It would take many years to persuade the farmers of the Kingston hinterland that their ancestors had made a terrible mistake, but even in the nineteenth century those who could leave, did. Good land picked up on the other side of the Shield — only fifty miles wide at this point — along the Bay of Quinte. From Belleville to Lake Huron real farming, the money-making variety, was once again the norm. Where farming had been difficult before, thanks to swamps and marshes, advances in the technology of drainage, through small canals and drainage tiles, made agriculture possible for the first time. A Drainage Act passed by the provincial legislature in 1879 enabled farmers to borrow on easy terms. Nowhere was the improvement more noticeable than in Dufferin County, "the roof of Ontario" at 1300 feet above sea level, but afflicted with a swampy and unpromising terrain.

Wheat was the predominant crop in southern Ontario in the 1860s, but wheat was highly dependent on the American market. When the Reciprocity Treaty was cancelled in 1866, farmers found it desirable to switch to barley and other coarse grains and thereby contribute to the American brewing industry which, during this period, preferred Ontario barley to all others. As an American investigator explained to a congressional committee in 1886, Canadian barley "produces a better color and more extract than the barley raised in the United States, as well as makes a beer with a delicate flavor, which will keep better in hot climates and stand export without deterioration." All the first-class breweries, he observed, depended on Ontario barley.

Other commodities exported included peas, apples from the St Lawrence valley, and peaches from the Niagara peninsula. There, farmers had discovered and cultivated the grape, and in 1866 had organized the Vine Growers' Association to promote their product. The Vine Growers shipped grapes to Toronto and other Ontario towns, but they had also started to use whatever was left over to make wine. Distilleries were a much older phenomenon: our records show that distilling was first tried in the 1790s. But rye, on which distillers depended for rye whisky, was an unpopular crop among farmers, who held that even growing the stuff was a reflection on the quality of their farms. Nevertheless, Ontario distilleries were increasing in size and importance, and the names of the houses of Seagram, Walker, and Gooderham were becoming well known.

The greatest change in agriculture occurred in dairying and cattle-raising. Dairying was extremely uncommon before the 1850s. During that decade cheese and butter production got started in a small way, but it took the American Civil War to stimulate the large-scale industry. Paradoxically, while the Civil War brought on high prices, the end of reciprocity, which cut off the supply of cheap American cheese, stimulated what was called ''cheese-on-the-brain,'' what R. L. Jones, Ontario's agricultural historian, has called a ''mania'' for cheese-making. The advent of refrigeration, at first using ice, made it possible to transport cheese and butter over long distances and helped create an export market. Starting in 1877 there was even a weekly cheese and butter train speeding from Stratford, Ontario, to the port of Montreal for export to Britain.

In appearance, Ontario's farmhouses moved in the direction of greater solidity and more obvious prosperity, even while keeping abreast of international styles of architecture. Early farmhouses were generally of wood, and of a simple uniform design: boxlike, with a summer kitchen extending out the back. In style, there was little difference between Ontario and Ohio, although architectural historians have detected more gravity and less imagination in the Ontario standard. By the 1860s Victorian forms were predominating: the sharp angles and curlicues of the Gothic Revival, accentuated by brickwork in two colours, usually red and yellow. Both in the countryside and in the older urban areas, much of this period's architecture has been preserved. In the cities, however, multicoloured brickwork was a sign that the builder's pretensions did not reach as high as the upper class, which by the 1870s was inclined to regard a yellow and red brick house as distinctly lower or lower-middle class.

In the cities and even in small towns there was already a distinct difference between lower-class and middle- and upper-class housing. Row housing was the housing of the poor, and it proliferated around Ontario during the 1860s and 1870s. In Toronto, Hamilton, Ottawa, or Port Hope, there were mill hands or factory workers to be accommodated. Most factories were not large, and most cities were by later standards very modest. Toronto, although it was by the 1860s a large grain-trading centre as well as Ontario's regional banking metropolis, was still under 50,000 in population — less than half the size of Montreal. And Toronto dwarfed its rivals: Hamilton, Ottawa, Kingston, and London.

Politicians were conscious of the cities and their problems. The dominant political class was overwhelmingly a town or city-dwelling species, drawn from law, medicine, or, sometimes, business. Occasionally, as with William Warren Baldwin, father of Robert Baldwin, it was from all three. Provincial politicians had to balance carefully among regions, farms, business, as well as inherited political prejudices. They also had to take into account religion.

Most Ontarians still lived on farms and were, by the 1870s, native-born. They were predominantly English-speaking and Protestant. Language excited almost no comment, except in the border towns along the Ottawa River; but religion was a matter of concern and excitement. From the 1830s onwards sectarianism played a part in politics. The Conservative party, and its predecessors, found a ready support in the Protestant Orange Order. The Orangemen were an import from Protestant northern Ireland where, by word, deed, and song, they commemorated the victory of Protestant William of Orange over the Catholic James II in the battle of the Boyne in 1690. Protestant Irish immigrants brought the order to Canada, where its traditions were reinforced by decades of struggle against American republicanism and the ever-present machinations of the pope.

The strength of Orangeism had not prevented compromise between Protestant and Catholic, or between English and French Canadians. Orange leaders found it possible and even desirable to join coalitions with Catholic partners, and Canadian streets were not filled with riot and murder on a daily basis as Protestant mobs did battle with the hated Catholic. But these things occasionally did happen, and it was always possible for animosity to be triggered by elections or other political phenomena. Even where a sense of common interest customarily prevailed, it was likely to be set aside for a ritual parade or sectarian squabble.

It is ironic that the first premier of this Protestant and Orange-tinged province should be a Catholic Highland Scot. John Sandfield Macdonald was based in Cornwall, in eastern Ontario, and his political reputation placed him more or less on the Liberal or reform side of politics. As a member of the first Parliament of the Dominion of Canada, he took his seat with the Liberal opposition. But as a member of the first legislature of the province of Ontario, he was the leader of a Liberal-Conservative coalition and the local ally of Sir John A. Macdonald, the Liberal-Conservative prime minister in Ottawa.

Macdonald became premier of Ontario as something of an afterthought, on July 15, 1867. His cabinet was an unlikely coalition of Liberals and Conservatives, which Macdonald himself dubbed the "patent combination." The patent combination duly swept the first provincial elections, held in August and September in conjunction with the first dominion elections. The number of constituencies in the provincial legislature equalled that in the first dominion Parliament — eighty-two — and the result of the election was also similar: a (Liberal)-Conservative majority both in Toronto and Ottawa. Many of the members were the same too, for until 1872 it was legal and even desirable for one man to sit in both the dominion and provincial assemblies. Supporters of "dual representation" claimed that this system insured that first-rate men would be found for the local legislatures; opponents denounced it as a scheme to subordinate the provincial power to that of the dominion.

Sandfield, as he was called to distinguish him from his ally in Ottawa, was accounted a man of the most rigid personal honesty. He was no better, and no worse, than the majority of his political friends and foes in subscribing wholeheartedly to influence and patronage as the necessary fuel for his political and administrative machine. Once, when the citizens of Strathroy petitioned their premier to locate the lucrative government prison in their municipality, Macdonald repulsed them with the question: "What the hell has Strathroy done for me?" Hamilton, which already had the provincial Deaf and Dumb Institute, made the mistake of defeating one of the premier's friends. The Deaf and Dumb Institute was promptly moved to Belleville, which had the good taste to return a government supporter; the Institute remained in Belleville for many years.

The premier's political style was scarcely different from that of his predecessors under the union, which is not surprising since politicians raised under the union dominated Ontario politics from the organization of the province down to 1896. The first legislature of Ontario maintained many familiar characteristics. It met, for example, in the old Upper Canadian legislative building in downtown Toronto. Its members' allegiances were not especially rigid, and it was possible for a government to dissipate its support among the members. Most important, the government's agenda was little different from those under the union. Education, railways, agricultural colonization, and natural resources continued to rank as important considerations for any government. The old colonial constitutional issues diminished and then vanished altogether with Confederation, as far as Ontario was concerned. The British government became something remote and, as its remoteness increased, altogether admirable to the distant gaze of the British subjects resident north of the Great Lakes. Instead of fighting with London, the government of Ontario would try to reach conclusions with Ottawa. Provincial rights and dominion-provincial relations now appear for the first time as important issues in Ontario politics.

The prerequisite for the issue of provincial rights was the establishment of parties. Party politics was already engraved on the Ontario political system. Parties existed before the union, and despite appeals to non-partisanship, they would exist after it. Sandfield Macdonald's attempt to describe his government as Liberal-Conservative was ultimately a failure, for the old reform leaders, men like George Brown or Alexander Mackenzie of Sarnia, refused to accept his leadership. A Reform party, small but well organized, sat in the first Ontario legislature, and gradually it took back the title of Liberal that Sandfield had appropriated.

It was less Sandfield than John A. Macdonald who was the opposition's favourite target. When the senior Macdonald refused to help local banks or favoured the Bank of Montreal, when he preferred Montreal interests to those of Toronto, or when he gave Nova Scotia extra money to induce its politicians to accept Confederation, the Liberals of Ontario professed great indignation. When the northwest was finally acquired, in 1869, and had to be brought into the dominion by force as well as persuasion, and when an Ontario Orangeman, Thomas Scott, was executed by the Red River rebels under Louis Riel, the opposition in Ontario exclaimed, and pointed the finger of blame, at both the dominion government and its local representative, Sandfield Macdonald and his patent combination.

The Liberal leader was now Edward Blake, who had succeeded to the position in 1869 at the age of thirty-four. Blake was a more modern specimen than Sandfield. Self-consciously brilliant, hard-driving, and ambitious, Blake had swept all before him. He was a leader of the bar, earning $20,000 a year in his practice, a princely sum and far beyond the salary that any premier could hope to command. Blake's logical capacity made him a natural leader for the Liberals, as the opposition attack centred on the rights and wrongs done to Ontario by John A. and Sandfield, and on the unsupervised spending habits of the government. When an election was held, Blake appealed to the "intelligent judgment" of the electors. In case that line failed, he also appealed, in the same sentence, "to Him without whom not a sparrow falleth to the ground — to appeal to Him in this crisis of our national existence and to call upon Him, as I ask you to join with me in doing, in the prayer that God may defend the right."

God, in the election of 1871, did just that, but not very decisively, especially given the complicated manner in which nineteenth-century electoral contests were carried out. Customarily the electors rendered their decision and then, if it proved unsatisfactory, it would be taken to the courts or to a legislative committee to have the wrong results thrown out and new elections called. Sandfield Macdonald preferred to go to court, and so when the legislature assembled in December 1871 it was lacking a certain proportion of its membership. That made no particular difference. The opposition first defeated the government on a motion condemning its conduct from 1867 to 1871. When Sandfield held on, the opposition passed another motion of censure, by one vote. The government next tried to adjourn the house, but that failed, and by a much larger margin. Sandfield finally took the hint, and resigned on December 19.

Edward Blake became Ontario's second premier. He was a most reluctant first minister and accepted the job only under protest. By-elections had to be held because of a requirement that newly appointed ministers submit themselves to the voters a second time for approval. The by-elections were fought over the corpse of Thomas Scott, by then two years dead, and over the fugitive Louis Riel, in flight from the newly organized province of Manitoba. With this crucial issue wrapped up, Blake and his party were ready to govern.

Blake's program, revealed in his provincial budget, was more of the same. There would be assistance to colonization through road-building and the encouragement of immigration. The government of Ontario would continue to offer assistance to railway building, and in the same way that Sandfield had done. The government wanted to improve the financial lot of teachers and schools, but it left Ryerson's edifice undisturbed. Finally, the Blake government abolished dual representation, effective at the dissolution of the first dominion Parliament. When that came, in the fall of 1872, so did Blake's resignation.

He was succeeded, not by any serving politician, but by a judge, the vice-chancellor of Ontario, Oliver Mowat. Mowat was a political warhorse whose career stretched back to articling in John A. Macdonald's law office in Kingston. He had been a Conservative in those days. Changing allegiance, he once provoked Macdonald to rush upon him in the old Canadian legislature, screaming, "You damned pup, I'll slap your chops." Mowat was no pup by 1872. Aged fifty-two, he was only five years younger than Macdonald himself; and like Macdonald he had great tenacity and endurance. He would be premier of Ontario for twenty-four years, longer than any other single individual. His sheer political longevity guaranteed that he would have a considerable impact in shaping Ontario's policies and traditions; possibly more than any other nineteenth-century Canadian except John A. Macdonald, Mowat shaped the Canadian constitution and the direction in which relations between the dominion and the provinces were to travel. Mowat's most recent biographer, Margaret Evans, claims for Ontario's third premier two titles bestowed during his lifetime: "Christian statesman" and "practical politician." The former characteristic was to be found in the premier's anxiety to compose religious differences and to seek social harmony and labour peace; the latter reflected the fact that these goals were very useful to the premier's political success, based as it was on combining the Catholic vote with the Protestant.

Mowat's government outlasted all its contemporaries. It survived John A. Macdonald and his four Conservative successors during the 1890s. Surviving, it even brought the dominion government around to its way of thinking, and since that way of thinking represented a reversal of the balance of the Canadian constitution, the British North America Act of 1867, it is worth pausing to examine it.

Macdonald, George Brown, and most of the rest of the Fathers of Confederation believed that in establishing the Dominion of Canada they had placed responsibility for national policy firmly in the hands of the dominion government. There were to be no quarrels between central government and local government of the kind that had paralyzed the United States during the 1850s and that had brought on that country's civil war. The government in Ottawa was to be a truly national government; the provincial governments would be little more than housekeeping concerns, accepting direction on important matters from the national centre. To signify the true balance of forces, the dominion government was given the power to disallow — negate, or veto — provincial statutes. The lieutenant governor, a dominion appointee, paid by Ottawa, could be instructed to reserve a provincial bill for the pleasure of the dominion government, or even to veto a bill outright. These were colonial powers, familiar to any mature Canadian politician: they were, in fact, precisely the powers the British government was no longer willing to wield over its Canadian colony, but which the Dominion of Canada was nevertheless authorized to brandish at the provinces.

Against this situation Edward Blake and then Oliver Mowat used two arguments. Local autonomy was good and even politically essential. Distant parliaments, whether in London or in Ottawa, could not hope to legislate on local matters to the satisfaction of the citizens. Too great an infringement on local autonomy by a central authority would only serve to alienate the citizenry from the national government and bring on the disunity that centralization was intended to avoid. The second argument went further. It contended that the whole Canadian confederation was the result of an agreement, a "compact" among the various British North American colonies. The provinces existed before the national government. They had created it, and they had endowed it with certain specific powers. But let no one forget that the provinces came first, and that the federal power must carefully respect their rights and responsibilities. Historically this view is nonsense. There can be no doubt what the Fathers of Confederation in the 1860s intended to do — to create a centralized rather than a decentralized state. They never intended to limit the powers of their creation by giving all the powers not specified in the British North America Act to the provinces. Indeed, they had done, or thought they had done, the exact opposite. But the Fathers had reckoned without the ingenuity of Edward Blake or the legal talents and persistence of Oliver Mowat. They had reckoned without the courts as well.

Disputes between a province and the central government can be resolved politically, by a trading-off of interests between a provincial government and its federal counterpart, or they can be handled judicially, with each level of government arguing against its adversary in a court of law. There is little doubt that the first method is the least expensive and most convenient, and it is also the most used. Unfortunately, it is seldom documented and history notoriously concentrates on the great exceptions rather than on the daily grind of routine. Compromise, in other words, is seldom dramatic enough even for contemporaries to notice and, as a consequence, the history of Canada's federal system takes on an adversarial and rhetorical quality that may make the reader forget that on most issues, most of the time, the federal government and even the most cantankerous and obstreperous province get along because they must.

Canada did not, of course, become independent in 1867. There was still a British-appointed Governor General in Ottawa, there were still British troops and ships at Halifax, Nova Scotia, and Esquimalt, British Columbia. The British Parliament could still make laws for Canada, and whenever the British North America Act required modification, it did, and continued to do so down to 1982. Canada's laws were still part of the British empire system, which meant that the final court of appeal for Canada and any other colony was an institution called the Judicial Committee of the Privy Council — despite its name, a court. The Judicial Committee sat in London, and over the years Oliver Mowat was a frequent visitor to its chambers. He seldom lost a case.

Mowat's first case, if it may be called that, was the question of Ontario's boundaries. The eastern and southern ones had been fixed for years, but the northern boundary was lost in the mists of bad geography and worse maps, back in the eighteenth century. The question became acute when Canada acquired the Hudson's Bay Company lands, and more acute still when small settlements began to spring up.

We have already met some of these settlements: Fort William, Fort Frances, and Rat Portage, all old trading posts. In the 1870s they suddenly became staging points for road traffic between Lake Superior and Red River and then construction camps for the new transcontinental railway, the Canadian Pacific. Attempts to negotiate the boundary between Ottawa and Toronto proved fruitless. Both sides believed, as Prime Minister Macdonald wrote, that "The mineral wealth of the country is likely to attract a large immigration into these parts" and both sides therefore attached importance to a speedy solution. Unfortunately, Ottawa and Toronto were so far apart on the issue that no negotiated settlement was possible.

Even when a Liberal government under Alexander Mackenzie held power in Ottawa between 1873 and 1878, and Edward Blake was dominion minister of justice, negotiations moved slowly. Finally, with the defeat of the federal Liberal party a virtual certainty in elections in the fall of 1878, the two Liberal governments hurried through an arbitration in August of that year. This agreement gave Ontario everything it could have hoped for: a territory 300 miles further west than the original federal offer, and a frontier that reached as far north as James Bay, along the Albany River. Oliver Mowat was pleased.

Sir John A. Macdonald, who returned as dominion prime minister in October 1878, was not pleased. Oliver Mowat was just another political opponent as far as Macdonald was concerned, and a peculiarly low member of the species. Macdonald would not co-operate in implementing the arbitration award. Instead, he gave the disputed territory to Manitoba. The stage was set for the memorable Battle of Rat Portage.

In 1882 Ontario and Manitoba appointed competing magistrates at Rat Portage, supported by rival jails and opposing police. The police spent their time arresting one another. There was a jail-break, and, in the summer of 1883, there were even competing provincial elections. The citizens of Rat Portage, it seemed, preferred to belong to Ontario, while the government of Manitoba steadfastly refused to get excited about the affair. After years of dispute a compromise was in order, and it was finally achieved through a reference to the Judicial Committee of the Privy Council. Mowat set sail for London in 1884, and returned, award in hand. Macdonald, however, refused to pass the legislation necessary to complete the transfer to Ontario, and it took another law case and another reference to the Judicial Committee before Macdonald gave in. The legislation was duly passed in 1889, and the great Ontario boundary dispute was over.

As a result Ontario gained 90,000 square miles of territory, increasing its size to 200,000 square miles. There was a great deal of timber in what was called "New Ontario" and, it was hoped, a great deal of minerals. How much, nobody knew, but in this case optimism proved to be right. Other things were hoped for too. With so much land, there must be farmland, a new frontier. The fact that climate and soil were, except in a few scattered areas, most unfavourable failed to impress the promoters of a northern farming frontier, and for many years the Ontario plough, paid for by the province, furrowed intractable clay and hacked away at rocks in the hope that something could be grown in the ninety-day frost-free growing season north of Lake Superior. As it was, only a few regions proved profitable for farming: the Rainy River area, New Liskeard, and some truck farms near logging or mining communities where proximity compensated for climate and soil. Good, bad, and indifferent, Mowat had won it all.

Mowat was greeted with throngs and fireworks. A triumphal ode was composed for the occasion (beginning, ''The traitor's hand is at thy throat, Ontario, Ontario,'' it does not bear repetition). But securing the boundaries was only part of the battle. Constitutionally, it may well have been less important than Mowat's next struggle. He likewise prevailed in a battle to establish the sovereign status of his province, and with it, all other provinces too. The province and the dominion quarrelled over which government had the power to license the use of rivers and streams. The power had considerable implications for patronage, for clearly the Conservative government at Ottawa had no desire to concede the patronage of rivers to its Liberal rival in Toronto. Macdonald used the federal power of disallowance to beat back Mowat's attempts to encroach on federal jurisdiction; but after Mowat's right to act was sustained by the Judicial Committee, Macdonald abandoned the fight.

The two men fought over liquor licences, another patronage plum with obvious party implications. Every community had its tavern-keeper, and with him a possible spokesman for the party in power from whom he got his licence and therefore his livelihood. It can be said that Macdonald prevailed over Mowat as long as he was prepared to use the power of disallowance. Disallowance, however, proved a blunt instrument, and it could not give Macdonald the power to supersede Mowat. Instead, it created a vacuum, through which neither party could proceed. Maintaining the vacuum consumed valuable political and parliamentary time and effort, and Macdonald tired of the effort sooner than Mowat did.

Mowat's final achievement on the dominion-provincial front is more dubious. He was the moving spirit behind an interprovincial conference in Quebec City in 1887 at which the Liberal premiers of Quebec, Ontario, Nova Scotia, and New Brunswick, and the Conservative premier of Manitoba, agreed on a common front of demands to be made upon the dominion government. The principle involved was the lowest common denominator or, as we could call it, ''something for everyone.'' Mowat wanted sympathy for his fight against disallowance, and he got it. Disallowance should be abolished, the provinces resolved. There was insufficient provincial influence at Ottawa: let half the Senate be appointed by provincial governments. The dominion government was intruding on provincial jurisdiction through the use of its legal powers: let it cease and desist. In return, Mowat agreed to a proposal that would have increased the subsidy the dominion paid the provinces under the provisions of the British North America Act. The premiers got no joy from Macdonald, who steadfastly regarded the conference as a dismal political confidence game. But the premiers had discovered a political instrument, and one that would have a long future.

Despite the excitement that Mowat's court battles engendered, there is no evidence that his struggles with Macdonald had any immediate electoral consequences. Elections, Mowat knew, turned on smaller issues, matters of domestic policy and practical politics. What counted was the creation and location of a provincial institution — an institute of technology, for example, or the latest modern jail. What counted too (and still does) were tradition, economic interest, and religion.

The most significant political development to affect Ontario during Oliver Mowat's golden age was federal in origin and jurisdiction, so that not even Ontario's militant premier could raise his voice in protest. Tariffs and external trade were indisputably the business of the dominion government. Ottawa raised most of its revenue from the tariff, and the tariff served as a crude barometer of the strength of the national economy. During the late 1860s and early 1870s receipts from the customs houses were high and plentiful: it was a good time for business; factories expanded; merchants imported; farmers sent their goods abroad in increasing quantities; and cities grew as the workforce increased.

Suddenly, in 1874, receipts dropped. Businesses failed, and workmen were thrown out of work. Political consequences followed. The Liberal government of Alexander Mackenzie in Ottawa was obliged to raise the Canadian tariff to maintain its revenues, but it was reluctant to commit itself to a high tariff as a path to prosperity and incidental job creation. That role was left to the Conservatives under Sir John A. Macdonald, who adopted the part with gusto. Macdonald and his Conservatives won the dominion election of 1878, and with it the majority of Ontario's seats. They proceeded, in 1879, to enact a "National Policy" of high, protective tariffs, behind which, it was argued, Ontario industry would survive and then, possibly, flourish after it had recovered from the harsh blast of foreign competition.

High tariffs were nothing out of the ordinary in the late nineteenth century. The Americans had them, and had used them to keep Canadian goods out of their markets. Continental European countries had them too, and promoted them as a means to economic growth. High tariffs had popularity, and they contributed to the Conservatives' popularity among the manufacturing interest in Ontario's urban areas. That included, naturally enough, the manufacturers, but it also included their workmen, who were attracted to a program that promised to secure their jobs. Macdonald even leached away at Liberal support in the Clear Grit bedrock of southwestern Ontario, but there his touch was less certain and less consistently successful. It was a truism that what appealed to the city — secure jobs and high prices for the consumer under the national tariff policy — did not necessarily appeal to the farmer, who had to buy city-made goods at those same prices and whose own markets were not particularly advantaged by high tariffs.

The Liberals attempted to capitalize on farm dissatisfaction, and from time to time they succeeded, as in 1891 when, running on a platform of "unrestricted reciprocity," the Liberal leader Wilfrid Laurier swept the heartland of Protestant, agrarian Ontario. Laurier did not win; instead, Macdonald, buoyed by appeals to protectionism and patriotism, prevailed for the last time. Farm discontent was obviously not alleviated by this result. For the next few years, in the provincial election of 1893 and the dominion election of 1896, independent farmer candidates were run under the banner of the "Patrons of Industry." In 1893 they actually won seventeen seats in the legislature, not enough to overcome the Liberal government's fifty seats in a house of ninety-four. The Patrons appealed to an explicit occupational interest and banned everyone but farmers and labourers from membership in their association. They lacked staying power, however. By 1896 they were down to three federal members elected, and by the next provincial election, in 1898, they were gone. The old parties prevailed once again.

The old parties also prevailed in the cities, although there political allegiance was amalgamated with religion and occupation. This was predictable enough in a society where religious traditions, unless carefully controlled, spelled animosity. The ability of the Protestant sects, including the Anglicans, who were divided on whether they were Protestant or not, to submerge their differences in a variety of voluntary and non-denominational labours was well established by the 1870s. It was the foundation of Egerton Ryerson's school system, which was universal, compulsory between the ages of eight and fourteen, founded on a commonly agreed basic curriculum which was the same all round the province, and which started off with the Lord's Prayer each morning and ended with a Bible reading every afternoon. The great exception to the Christian non-denominational rule of "the Reverend Doctor," as his critics sarcastically called him, was the Roman Catholic church.

The Catholics were different. They proclaimed their difference. They would not accept Ryerson's system, even though they admitted that it had its points. It did not take much for Protestants to become suspicious of a church whose head, the pope, was their historic enemy, the symbol of a system against which Protestants had been revolting since the days of Martin Luther. The pope was suspected of designs on the state, of attempting to control what was said and thought, and how citizens voted.

Let us take a minor example. Ontario students were subjected to a standard diet of prose and poetry, including, in 1882, Sir Walter

Scott's poem "Marmion," which was prescribed for the entrance examinations for the provincial university in Toronto. Archbishop Lynch, the Catholic prelate of Toronto, objected, understandably enough, since "Marmion" presented a vision of medieval catholicism that was anything but flattering. The minister of education, Adam Crooks, agreed with the archbishop, and removed the poem from the curriculum. The news leaked out, as it was bound to do, and the incident placed the archbishop and the minister in a most unflattering light. It was a classic case of censorship, classic in the sense that both sides to the controversy had some right to complain and from which neither would emerge the winner. The suppression of "Marmion" was presented as proof that the Ontario Liberals were knuckling under to the pope and his minions. Good Protestants, brought up on tales of sixteenth-century martyrs and the cruelties of the Inquisition, instinctively knew what was afoot: "priestly tyranny," as the Conservative press delicately put it.

As it happened, the only party to suffer for "Marmion" was the Conservative opposition, which derived no benefit and fewer votes in the by-elections and elections that followed the airing of the controversy. But the subject was never far from the surface. The Liberals, and the archbishop, were accused of tampering with Bible readings in the schools, by suppressing certain Protestant texts. As a Protestant school trustee put it, when offered the government's collection of inoffensive scripture: "No!" pounding his fist on the table. "We want the whole damned Bible, and nothing but the Bible!" Nor would the matter rest there. Amendments to the status of separate schools in 1886 provoked another round of denunciation, and this time the complaints were linked to the existence, in the Catholic schools of eastern Ontario, of education in French. The Liberals were taken by surprise. Eastern Ontario generally voted Conservative, and was considered by the Liberals to be a region of darkness for reasons other than language.

Controversy over education was the upper level of religious disputation. Lower down were the annual riots between Orange and Green in towns large enough to have a substantial representation from the Emerald Isle. The occasion might be St Patrick's Day or it might be the Glorious Twelfth of July. If the rioting was especially bad there might occur the paradoxical spectacle of the Orange militia being called out to confront an Orange mob and to prevent them from doing too much damage to Green institutions and property. Religion could, and did, make a difference to everything from school to housing to politics, and it was beyond the power of most nineteenth-century politicians to do very much about it. Few politicians in Ontario attempted to capitalize on ethnic and religious hatreds; after each riot tempers subsided, as if a certain ritual had been successfully performed, as recent historians have observed.

We have made no mention of how the government organized its finances. Taxation is a subject that governments prefer to avoid, but it is one of the staples of politics. How did the Ontario government pay for itself between 1867 and 1896? For an answer we must revert to the British North America Act, which laid down an annual subsidy from the dominion to the provinces, based on a calculation of population derived from the 1861 census, the closest prior to Confederation. The money that Ontario made from the subsidy, in addition to revenues from fees, licences, and natural resources, was, apparently, enough to convince the provincial government that it was doing very well. There was nothing new in this. Ontario governments had always raised their money from land and licences, and if the tariff had been taken away, so had some heavy expenditures. Ontario managed very frugally with what it had. The provincial civil service was tiny, and modestly paid: at the turn of the century it was estimated that there were no more than seven civil servants for each member of the legislature (the figure is now six hundred per member, and for a larger legislature).

Revenue from land and natural resources was the most flexible source of funds, but, as had been the case in the past, the province's concern was twofold: it wanted money, but it wanted development too, whether settlement or the opening up of new lands for lumbering or mining. That being so, the provincial government, of whatever political stripe, adopted a generous attitude towards developers of virgin territory. Mines, for example, were open to any prospector who could locate a mineral, stake his claim, and register it. Of course, the prospector had to pay first for a licence to prospect, and he had to pay a dollar an acre for whatever land he wanted to stake. But after that, what lay beneath the ground was entirely his, or his company's.

The mines discovered in the 1860s, 1870s, and 1880s attracted investment, generally American. More minerals were uncovered as railways were thrust into and across the Canadian Shield. There were gold and silver deposits, rich but transitory. In 1883, however, nickel was discovered near Sudbury on the Canadian Pacific's main line. Mining promptly started, and as it proceeded it became obvious that the nickel field of Sudbury was of truly incomparable extent and wealth. The exploitation of minerals on this scale encouraged the Mowat government to think twice about its preference for development over revenue. It would be just to explore the possibility of turning over some of the wealth to the public purse, from a royalty on production, as was customary in other jurisdictions. A royal commission was appointed to assist the government in its deliberations. Some of the commission's recommendations were useful, such as the creation of a professional provincial Bureau of Mines, and others were truisms. But the government was anxious to go further, and quickly. In 1891 a provincial minister informed the legislature that nickel offered a strong potential for revenue, enough, he said, "to ward off the bugbear of direct taxation for many years to come." This was important because the government was spending more than it was taking in, and the deficiency had to be made up somehow. The solution was to charge more for registering claims, and to charge a royalty on minerals taken out of the ground. Mining interests protested, but their protests counted for less than the call of revenue.

Ontarians were not accustomed to thinking of themselves as

mineral-rich. They were even less accustomed to thinking about energy. The province's original energy sources grew in the ground, and were cut down into timber or firewood as settlement moved north from the lakes. Trees gave way to coal as the nineteenth century advanced, and gave Ontario's Victorian cities a hazy and sooty aspect as thousands of furnaces and fireplaces offered their particles to the sky. Steam engines used in factories added to the pollution, and so, momentarily, did another invention of the Victorian age. Electric light was demonstrated in the United States in 1877 by the son of an Upper Canadian refugee of 1837, Thomas Alva Edison. (At almost the same time, in Brantford, Ontario, a Scottish immigrant, Alexander Graham Bell, was conducting experiments in telephonic communication.) Electricity could be produced by steam generators, and, at first, it usually was.

Electricity could also be produced by hydraulics — by the natural movement of water down a rapid or over a fall, driving turbines and generating electric power. It was a thrilling prospect. Bright light would no longer depend on gas jets (usually artificial and produced from coal) or on candles or coal oil lamps. At first electricity was tried out rather tentatively, as an adjunct to manufacturing. A small hydro-electric plant was opened in Ottawa in 1885, and others were established around Peterborough. The first transmission of electricity over any distance was at Georgetown, Ontario, in 1888: a two-mile line was strung to power the Barber Paper Mill.

The single largest source of hydro power in Ontario was at Niagara Falls. Interestingly enough, the provincial government was more concerned with the aesthetics than the economics of the situation. Seeking to preserve the falls for posterity, the Mowat government shopped around for someone to maintain it as it deserved, as an unspoiled wonder of the world. An attempt to give the falls to the dominion government for a national park failed. Next, a provincial body was appointed to supervise the development of the falls, but its main concern was to prevent crass commercialization and to obtain a steady source of income to keep its park afloat. It got the money from a syndicate of American capitalists, who won the right to exploit the hydro-electric power on the Canadian side of the falls, an option they wished to reserve rather than take up, since they were already fully occupied with the American side.

Electricity would soon have an impact on the potential of the Ontario economy. It revolutionized mining, making the exploitation of northern mining properties cheaper and much easier. It attracted industry to sources of hydro power; on the American side of the Niagara River it made Buffalo into an electricity-consuming boom town. Ontario as yet had no policy for the infant industry. Although it involved the sale or lease of a public resource — water rights — there was no sense that the development of hydro-electricity required public intervention. That would occur soon, but only after public opinion had seized the opportunities that government intervention and regulation presented. That, in turn, would take time and a change in long-established mental attitudes.

The politicians of the later nineteenth century were moving slowly in the direction of change. As long as the ultimate power was held by a generation that had entered politics in the 1840s, and which interpreted the world in terms it had learned a half century before, profound change was unlikely. Mowat was a man for economical, even minimal government. He reformed, but slowly. He added to the responsibilities of the provincial government, but without upsetting the balanced budget he had established in the 1870s. Mowat was also, as his enemies knew to their cost, an extremely durable political general. In the legislature or on the hustings the premier was virtually untouchable, even when his local lieutenants dipped into their pockets (or someone else's) to buy votes or to abscond with influential opponents as voting day approached. As long as Mowat lasted, so did the Liberal party's dominance in southwestern Ontario.

Admittedly, the persistence of the Catholic and French issues into the 1890s did Mowat no harm. Sir John A. Macdonald, reflecting on his ability to evoke a Conservative majority in Ontario in the dominion elections of 1883 and 1887, as contrasted with the unsuccessful performance of the provincial Conservatives, concluded that it was the Catholic vote that made the difference. At the federal level it was split; at the provincial level, a few stalwarts apart, it went to Mowat, and it would continue to do so as long as Conservative firebrands denounced the pope and the French Canadians. Macdonald was doubtless right. Unfortunately, he failed to persuade even some of his own followers in the dominion Parliament, and the stage was set for a period of "nativist" agitation under the banner of an organization calling itself the Protestant Protective Association.

The resurgence of militant Protestantism in the 1890s coincided with great events elsewhere in Canada. In Quebec, a nationalist government under Premier Honoré Mercier regulated a thorny political question by compensating the Jesuit order for the loss of their property in a complicated series of events almost a hundred years before. Here, in the eyes of militant Protestants, was proof of the collusion between the French Catholics and the pope. An outcry resulted, at the same time as the Liberal majority in the Manitoba legislature abolished the official use of the French language in that province and restricted the rights of Catholics (and other sects too, as if they cared) to the teaching of religion in publicly supported schools. The Manitoba School Question was launched.

It was a question of some interest to Ontario, not least because of the linkages that had developed between the two provinces in the 1870s and 1880s. When Manitoba entered Confederation in 1870 the French element in its population was influential if not predominant. There was little French immigration in the decades that followed. There was, however, a steady inflow from Ontario. Forty thousand settlers arrived in Manitoba between 1876 and 1881, and the great majority of them came from Ontario. They brought with them ideas about the proper organization of government — on the Ontario pattern; they imitated Ontario names for their towns; they believed that church and state should be separate. Ontario had implanted its identity on a province whose original institutions were, in fact, quite different from those Ontarians were leaving behind. In moving to alter Manitoba's constitutional balance, the provincial Liberals believed that they were being true to the best aspects of their British, Reform, democratic Ontario past. They had gone one better on Ontario. The elder province had been saddled with a separate school system. That was in the Confederation agreement, and there was nothing that could legally be done about it. Manitoba, however, would have only one publicly supported school system, and there was nothing, the immigrants believed, that the Catholics could do about it.

In fact, there was a great deal that they could do about it legally, but nothing in a practical sense. The federal government, still Conservative, intervened on behalf of the French and Catholic minority. The provincial government resisted the intervention. A complicated quarrel ensued, the details of which need not concern us here. What is of interest is that the quarrel aroused public opinion in Ontario as well as Manitoba, both on behalf of endangered provincial rights and local autonomy and of embattled Protestantism. It was embarrassing that the leader of the Canadian Liberal party was both French and Catholic, but the leader had the sense to entrench himself behind a smokescreen of provincial rights verbiage and refused to allow his position to be clarified.

The Liberal leader, Wilfrid Laurier, defeated the Conservative prime minister, Sir Charles Tupper, in the dominion general election of June 1896. Laurier had not done it unaided. In Ontario he had the support of Oliver Mowat, who at seventy-six bestirred himself to run for the dominion Parliament, pointedly throwing his considerable prestige behind a Liberal leader whose own support among the Ontario electorate was infirm. Laurier did well in Ontario during the election, though not as well as he had hoped. He did well enough elsewhere, particularly in Quebec, and his government reflected both ability and strength.

Mowat's departure made way for younger men and newer measures. It was the end of an era for the province, and for the provincial Liberal party. He left the party strong, and in the hands of experienced successors. But none of Mowat's many successors as Liberal leader had the same sure touch, the same ability to compromise or to appeal to widely scattered sections of the province's population. With Mowat's departure the comfortable era of Victorian liberalism, with its stress on equality, fair play, and economy as the three pillars of government, took its departure. The new era would be considerably different.

La Salle on the Toronto carrying-place, August 1681, on his way to the Mississippi. Drawing by C.W. Jefferys.

Lieutenant-Governor Simcoe opening the first Legislative Assembly of Upper Canada, 1792.
Watercolour by C. W. Jefferys.

Public Archives of Canada C-6060

The first lumber raft down the Ottawa River, 1806. Watercolour by C.W. Jefferys.

Naval action on Lake Ontario, 1813. Drawing by C.W. Jefferys.

Battle of Stoney Creek, 1813. Drawing by C.W. Jefferys.

Pioneer Peterborough, 1837. Sketch by Anne Langton.

Reformers and Supporters of Law and Order
IN THE COUNTY OF LEEDS

FRIENDS AND FELLOW SUBJECTS!

Often we hear it asserted by those who fatten on the spoils of office, those who enjoy the smiles of the Executive, and those who are looking forward with sycophantic adoration and servile obsequiousness for the gilded honors of the *powers that be,* that we possess "the very image and transcript of the Constitution of the Mother Country." I shall not now stop to point out how unfounded such an assertion is,—all who can or dare reflect for themselves, know its falsity, its absurdity, its delusiveness; but granting, for argument that it is what the adulators of, and aspirants to power pretend, I ask where is the proof in its practical operation? Where is the boasted liberty and protection which Englishmen are said to enjoy while exercising their rights?—When we assemble at the polls, we are met by a band of lawless ruffians armed with clubs and sharp instruments; our old men and peaceable inhabitants are knocked down and beaten, their clothes torn, and pointed weapons thrust into their flesh, and while their blood—yes, the blood of faithful subjects of the King; the blood of descendants from those who, during the American Revolution, fought for British rule and afterwards settled this country, converting it from a howling wilderness into fertile fields and cultivated plains,and rendering it a desirable and tempting home for the surplus population of the British realm; the blood of peaceable English, Irish, Scotch and Canadian Reformers has been spilt upon the ground; electors have been obliged to abandon their right of voting for Representatives and fly for their lives! Reformers, can you endure this!— Scotchmen, from the land of a Wallace and a Bruce, will you see your McPhersons, your Camerons, your friends and neighbours beaten and abused, and flying for self preservation from the polls! Englishmen, on whose name glory attends, will you be tame and inactive spectators of such scenes! Irish Reformers, respecting the rights of your fellow subjects, and with bosoms fired with the flame of liberty and justice, will you permit the re-enactment of the disgraceful riots and violence which at the last election gave to Gowan and Jameson a temporary but ignoble triumph! Canadians, whose loyal and valorous conduct during the last war with the United States, taught the foreign enemies of your country,that its soil could not be invaded with impunity, and that you were not to be frightened or seduced from your allegiance, will you again allow violators of the law to rob you of your elective rights! To one and all I say, WILL YOU ? *Will you, I repeat?* Nay, if I could, *I would thunder,* WILL YOU !

FELLOW SUBJECTS!—My heart bleeds when I behold the prostration of civil power in this country; when I see the Magistracy, the sworn conservators of the peace, shrink from the performance of their duty, and encouraging violence by their timidity and inaction; when I see a Sheriff who is bound to suppress riot and disorder and cause the laws to be respected, while acting as Returning Officer, permitting scenes of lawless violence about the hustings, by men armed with bludgeons and pointed weapons; when I see an Attorney General, the sworn asserter of the laws and whose especial duty it is to have them maintained, encouraging outrage by approving looks, and pretending that he is there as a Candidate, not as Attorney General, as if he could at pleasure lay aside the law and his sworn duty; when I see the King's Representative, Sir John Colborne, (who is bound to protect the subjects of the country,) by again appointing that Sheriff to be Returning Officer and ordering the coming election to be held at Beverly, after that same Sheriff admitted under oath that he considered the place improper, giving apparent proof that he (Sir John) approves of the recent violation of the laws, the abuse of our peaceful inhabitants, their forcible hindrance from exercising the elective franchise and the destruction of the freedom of election ; when I see all this, and reflect that these things occur in a country boasting of British laws and British protection, can I fail with sorrow to exclaim "Oh my country, thou art fallen indeed!" But who that has a bosom fired with the generous glow of liberty, justice and love of country, can witness such conduct and not burn with deep,honest,heartfelt indignation! Or who that has one spark of real British patriotism or British spirit, but will resolve to assure for himself that protection from insult, injustice and violence which the civil authorities withhold from him!—Inhabitants of the County of Leeds! you who are well disposed, arouse from your slumbers and pour forth in multitudes to the approaching election—shew the wicked and evil inclined by your numbers, your union, your spirit and persevering determination that you are resolved to seek for yourselves that protection which the Magistracy and those in power have denied you. Has it come to this, that you must either set for defence of your rights, or to see them wrested from you and be content hereafter to submit to abuse and insult from lawless ruffians,urged on by more lawless and black hearted leaders! Ask yourselves if you are willing to come under the domination of men, who, pretending to Britishfeeling, showed at the last election by their conduct and outrage, that they were actuated alone by feelings which were a disgrace to the name—feelings which every high-souled Briton and Canadian must detest and abhor !

But hold!—Indignant as I feel, and as you must all feel at the outrage of the last election, (proved to the satisfaction of the Committee of the Assembly which tried and annulled the return) I would not urge you to acts of aggressive violence or revenge. Far be it from me to desire to violate the laws, trampled upon and insulted though you have been. No, I would not do this, but I would arouse you to a lively sense of your wrongs, a keen perception of your rights and a firm determination to maintain them. I would stir you to one and all, to appear at the hustings, and present the noble spectacle of a body of united,peaceably disposed, but resolute freemen, in such numerical force as will strike terror and dismay into the hearts of the lawless and abandoned desperadoes, who at the last election fouly robbed you by force of the exercise of your most valuable right, and who may hereafter again attempt to repeat the same wicked and iniquitous scenes.

FELLOW SUBJECTS! Mark what an official has assigned as a reason why Sir John Colborne again ordered the election for the County to a place so improper as Beverley. "It must be," said he, "because Sir John thinks the laws ought to be sustained as much in one part of the District as another, and that if he had ordered it in a different place, it would be admitting that the rioters could with impunity triumph over the law at Beverly !" Do you believe 'it ? Has Sir John's conduct hitherto proved any strong desire on his part to suppress violence and outrage when proceeding from the party ever ready to laud the acts of his administration ? But suppose him to be the enemy of rioters and violators of the law, and anxiously desirous to maintain peace and good order in society and to secure to the subject the free exercise of his rights, and see how far his Sheriff, his Returning Officer, his Magistrates and his Majesty's Attorney General went at the late Election to sustain the laws! See them either shrinking from or neglecting their duty or conniving at violence and outrage! Behold peaceable subjects and respectable inhabitants when attempting to go forward to vote, beaten, stabbed, their clothes torn and compelled to seek safety by flight, in sight of Sir John's Officials! If they desired peace why did they not strive to maintain it ? Why did they not put the law in force against the first man who presumed to transgress it? Why did they not cause every man who appeared on the ground carrying a club or unlawful weapon in a time of great excitement to be disarmed ? Why did they not show a proper indignation and abhorrence of the outrages committed by the partizans of Gowan and Jameson ? Why did not the whole Magistracy of the District,when they heard of the violence and iniquity perpetrating at the Election, go forward nobly in a body to support the laws and afford protection to His Majesty's subjects, instead of shrinking from their duty and remaining at their homes ? If they had thought that Sir John wished them to be prompt in upholding the law and protecting the freedom of Election on the occasion, do you believe they would not have turned out readily and acted energetically ? But if it be true that Sir John wishes the laws upheld and the rights and persons of His Majesty's subjects protected in every part of the District, another Election is at hand ; another opportunity is about to be afforded to the Magistracy and Officials to exhibit their respect for his Excellency's motives and desires and their zeal to keep the peace and sustain the laws of their country. We shall see if they will appear at the Hustings and be prompt and upright in exercising their authority and duty. We shall see, if they attempt to act, whether they will not manifest insincerity and reluctance and swear in as special Constables the actors and men who caused the riots and disturbance and trampled on the rights of the subject at the last Election. We shall see how they will act. If, however, they show a becoming zeal and go forward manfully to put down outrage, let us aid them with that alacrity and that anxious desire to preserve peace and good order in society which has always characterised us. Such conduct on their part will entitle them to public approbation and go far to remove the unfavorable impression that they are unwilling or negligent in the discharge of their duty. But if they hang back and leave us without the shield of official power to direct and protect us, although we will not violate the law by attacking others, yet if we are attacked it cannot be expected, after the long forbearance we have shown, that we will not defend ourselves and repel force by force.

But,my friends,let me entreat you,while smarting under the sense of your wrongs, not to give way to enraged feelings. Fired with indignation as you must be, yet curb your passions and appear at the hustings in the cool, moderate, rational dignity of human nature. Firm in your purpose to exercise your Elective Franchise let reason and moderation govern your conduct. Exhibit union and spirit but avoid imprudence. Enter into no useless discussions with any individual who may seek to rouse your anger and embroil you in a quarrel to afford a pretext for violence and outrage. Waive all disputes with your opponents. Assault no one, but conform to the laws and preserve peace as far as lies in your power. Remember that a legal election must be carried by legal means, not through riot and disorder,excited and inclined by the triumph of a party. Sustain the honorable character which has ever been your's, for obedience to law ; and if the civil authorities shall fail or fail to put down any disturbance that may arise, nobly and promptly second their efforts. If attacked, however, while peaceably seeking to exercise your elective rights, remember that the laws of nature and the laws of the land equally permit necessary self defence. Defend yourselves then under such circumstances promptly and energetically, and show the enemies of public liberty and public order that you will not carry another Election by violence and outrage upon peaceable members of the community.

Finally, and in an especial manner, let me entreat—let me urge —let me enjoin on you one and all, young and old, who respect the laws, by all that you hold most dear,—your liberties, the honor of your King and Country, your future peace and welfare and the peace and welfare of your children, your regard for good institutions and good government, and your desire to ensure them, to rally and press forward to the polls. Let there be such a collection on Monday next, at the hustings in Beverly, of the friends of the law, as was never before assembled in the County ; when there, keep together, and appear day after day, till the election is over. If you do this, the cause of Reform, the cause of your country, the cause of peace and order must and shall triumph.
ONE OF YOURSELVES.

County of Leeds, 24th February, 1835.

Election poster, Leeds County, 1835.   Archives of Ontario, P-1815

Settling the bush, Opeongo Road, Renfrew County.

Sir Oliver Mowat, Ontario's third premier, 1872–96.

Lumber as big business: aerial view of the Edwards Lumber Company, Ottawa, 1919.

Empire Ontario

5 The province of Ontario at the turn of the century was a comfortable place. Visitors noted the wide, leafy streets of its towns, the busy factories, the railways that criss-crossed the southern part of the province. Further north, there were mineshafts being sunk, new towns being carved out of the bush, and two new transcontinental lines across the rock and bush of the province's northland, "New Ontario." New Ontario was growing. In 1912 Ontario's limits were extended northward, angling northeastward until they reached Hudson Bay at latitude 56°50' north. The province now totalled 412,000 square miles (roughly 1 million square kilometres).

The inhabitants of the province seemed to be generally content. They turned out on Dominion Day, July 1st, to celebrate their pride in the Dominion of Canada. They got fireworks on May 24th, Queen Victoria's birthday, when children sang, "And if you don't give us a holiday we'll all run away." The old Queen expired with the old century, in January 1901, but the holiday remained. Almost no one could remember when a king had sat on Britain's and Canada's throne. Sir Oliver Mowat could, comfortably ensconced in the lieutenant governor's mansion, Chorley Park, on a grassy hillside overlooking the Don River. But Sir Oliver was not long for this world; he would die in office in 1903, virtually the last link between Ontario and the daring nation-builders of 1867.

Mowat had grown up in an era when to be a Liberal, a reformer, was to be concerned about real abuses in a colonial constitution that, in the reformers' view, must be changed. It had been changed, and many things with it. Before that could happen, there was a rebellion, the first significant event of Queen Victoria's reign. By the time she died, the rebellion would have been assimilated into Ontario political legend. The rebel, William Lyon Mackenzie, had even returned to Toronto to sit as a member of the Canadian legislature, on the Liberal side, of course. The Liberals were now the government of Ontario, as they had been for thirty years. Their leader was a proclaimed prohibitionist, the veteran politician.George W. Ross. Sitting across the floor from Ross was the leader of the opposition Conservatives, James P. Whitney, the son of an American immigrant and a man of reform stock, as he liked to say. No one could be prouder than Whitney of his British heritage, or more scornful of the doubtful blessings of the American constitution.

Whitney and Ross, men in their fifties, had been brought up in a rural province, where farmers were the dominant class and elections were won and lost in village halls and along concession roads. But the farming element was ceasing to grow. In 1891, of Ontario's 2.1 million people, 60 percent lived on farms. In 1901, the first year of the new century, Ontario had hardly grown at all — to 2.2 million. All the growth had been in the cities and towns of the province; rural areas had actually lost 50,000 people over the last decade, in absolute terms. Counting the natural increase — subtracting deaths from births — of the 1890s, the loss of population was very severe. That worried pundits, who filled newspaper columns and magazine articles with their concerns. The trend would continue, so that by the census of 1911 Ontario's rural blood had thinned still further, down by another 50,000 people. But by 1911 the province's population had gone up, to 2.5 million. All of the increase was in cities, and for the first time Ontario's urban population was greater than its rural counterpart, 1.33 million to 1.2 million.

Toronto was incomparably the largest city. That city had bulged from 181,215 people in 1891 to 376,538 in 1911. Ottawa, the nearest rival, was increasingly far behind, although the national capital did reach 87,000 by 1911. Then came Hamilton, 82,000, London, 46,000, Brantford, 23,000, and Kingston, 18,000. For the first time the provincial capital was approaching Montreal, its great rival, which until 1891 had been the only city in Canada to count more than 100,000 inhabitants. The cities were remarkably homogeneous, especially considering the great and simultaneous influx of European immigration to the American eastern seaboard and to the Canadian west.

The largest ethnic group, if it can be called that, was "English" — 701,413 out of the 1901 total of 2.2 million. There followed "Irish," north and south, and Scots, 400,000 of them. The next largest ethnic group was the Germans, with the French, at 158,671, far in the rear. Methodists were the largest religious sect (666,000), followed by Presbyterians (477,000) and Catholics (390,000). The racial and religious complexion of the province, together with traditions and memories inherited from struggling forefathers, shaped its politics.

It was political wisdom that the "peninsula" (which some liked to call "Old Ontario"), "Yankees and Covenanters, the most yeasty and unsafe of populations" according to Sir John A. Macdonald, voted Liberal, and that the eastern counties tended to vote Conservative. This is a serviceable generality, although every election brought new exceptions. If the rule were reduced to a township-to-township basis it becomes clearer and truer: some towns and townships never voted anything but Grit, and some never anything but Tory. The rule was further modified by the Catholic issue, which the Conservatives so fatally embraced in the 1880s and 1890s, and by Protestant and Anglo-Saxon agitation over the French Canadian "invasion" of the eastern counties.

Between 1896 and 1905 Ontario, after being politically stable for a generation, suddenly turned over its politics. The Conservatives moved from a minority to a majority, and even to a heavy majority, breaking the Liberal hold over southwestern Ontario while consolidating their own areas of strength. The reasons for the turnover will never be precisely clear, but they fall into two broad categories. First, the change in the character of the province, from rural to urban, from agricultural to industrial, took its toll on "old" issues. Where before agriculture and related issues were the sinew of politics, politics now concentrated on matters like sanitation, factory legislation, and workmen's compensation. Growing towns like Brantford or London (up in population by 30 percent between 1901 and 1911) searched for ways and means to consolidate their growth as well as for further means to expand. There was a much greater willingness to invoke legislation to accomplish social and economic goals, and to rely on coercion where nineteenth-century politics had favoured laissez-faire. Second, there were particular political reasons that led to the long-term decline of the Liberal party.

The best example of our first category is the question of hydro-electric power. This question was left in an unfinished state by the Mowat government, and Mowat's successors, A. S. Hardy and G. W. Ross, did little to resolve it. Basically, the towns and cities of southwestern Ontario wanted a reliable, cheap supply of electricity. Electricity, like railways before it, was the key to growth and prosperity. There were considerable local sources of water-power in southern Ontario, but the greatest single resource was the great falls at Niagara. Niagara Falls, however, had fallen under the domination of large investors, foreign and domestic. They wanted electricity for their own purposes, and not those of the province or the people.

A confrontation was inevitable. Agitation for public power transmission lines beat against the Ross government, but its response was half-hearted and feeble. It became apparent that decisive action would not quickly emerge from the existing government, and that a drastic change was indicated. A powerful, volatile issue was emerging in just the region where the Liberals had previously had their greatest strength.

There are other examples too. Through the late nineteenth century pressure grew for "temperance," and eventually prohibition of alcoholic beverages. Temperance counted as a progressive response to the genuine evil of excessive drink. The government responded by licensing the liquor trade, but early on it became apparent the liquor inspectors or commissioners were a fruitful avenue for patronage. The Ross government took refuge in plebiscites and in the desperate hope that prohibition was constitutionally a matter for the dominion and not the province. When the courts decided otherwise and the anti-drink forces called Ross to account, the premier's response to their insistent questions was at best disappointing. At worst it placed a time-bomb inside the Liberals' electoral prospects, because temperance reformers were encouraged to seek their goals by active intervention in provincial politics.

Faithful Liberals were increasingly disgusted by the inertia and paralysis of the Hardy and Ross administrations. Nothing of any importance was transpiring in successive sessions of the legislature. The government's majority was narrow and could be endangered by any leakage of support. Elections were won and lost by extremely narrow margins, so narrow that it often became possible for a creative politician to intervene in the electoral process with two-dollar bills, bottles of whiskey, and other occasional favours in the hope of buying just enough electors to put the appropriate candidate into the legislature. Both major parties played the electoral game, but as the 1890s wore on the Liberals seemed to get caught at it more often. A member of the lesiglature confessed in open court that he had been a party to corrupt practices. A steamer, the *Minnie M.*, ferried Americans over from Sault Ste Marie, Michigan, to Sault Ste Marie, Ontario, to cast their votes for the local Liberal. After a particularly close election in 1902 a Conservative member, R. R. Gamey, announced that he would give his support to Ross and the Liberals instead. But when the legislature met, he explained that it was all a hoax, and that the Liberal provincial secretary had in fact attempted to buy his support.

The scene, according to eye-witnesses, was unforgettable. Hector

Charlesworth, a reporter sitting in the gallery of the Assembly, recalled that the provincial secretary, Stratton, "paled and was like a man of stone. The Prime Minister [Ross] sat with bowed head, his beard on his chest, almost a stricken man. Their followers were dumbfounded .... The bulletins were up on the downtown newspaper offices almost as soon as they could get the messages through, and going back a few minutes later into the press gallery, whose broad windows looked southward through Queen's Park down University Avenue, I presently saw a most remarkable sight. Hundreds and hundreds of people were running towards the Parliament Buildings. The news had spread magically and everyone wished to be on the scene."*

The Gamey revelations occurred at the beginning of 1903. A commission of judges exonerated the Ross government, and the Liberal majority in the legislature censured Gamey, but it was apparent that the Liberals had suffered one scandal too many. Bribery, manipulation, and a cynical policy of inaction had taken their toll. The government had, in effect, defeated itself, and when an election was called for January 1905 the result was entirely predictable. The Conservative party, under James P. Whitney, swept the province, and took office with a sizeable and stable majority.

The Whitney government lasted from 1905 until the premier's death in September 1914. Whitney won four general elections, in 1905, 1908, 1911, and 1914, and each time was returned with a decisive majority over the Liberals. The government saw itself as a reform administration, with a mandate to clean up Queen's Park and to cut the red tape of the previous administration. Whitney was, nevertheless, a practical politician, and despite his reforming noises he did not hesitate to imitate Ross by appointing solid Conservatives to lucrative posts. It is, however, probable that he did it less, and less obviously, than his hapless predecessor.

---

*Hector Charlesworth, *More Candid Chronicles* (Toronto, 1928), 138

The most solid monuments of the Whitney administration were the creation of the Ontario Hydro-Electric Commission and the reform of the provincial university, the University of Toronto. The premier placed the university on a firm financial footing, reformed its administration, and appointed a new president. The roots of the movement for public power were humble. As cities grew they required services: water, sewage, and gas. Franchises were doled out to private entrepreneurs, who thereupon did their best to wring a profit out of what would prove to be first an unco-operative, and then unwilling and eventually ungrateful public. Municipal services generally ended up back where they started, in public hands through the purchase of established rights and facilities. As a historian of Ontario Hydro, Ken Dewar, has persuasively argued, electricity fitted a long-established pattern.

In Ottawa, for example, electricity came early, in 1885, courtesy of the Ottawa Electric Company founded by Thomas Ahearn. Ahearn was enterprising and inventive, boasting in August 1892 that he had created the world's first "electric dinner": "the first instance in the history of the world of an entire meal being cooked by Electricity," from Consommé Royal through Saginaw Trout with potato croquettes through Beef Tongue and Sugar Cured Ham through Larded Sweetbreads with Mushrooms, finally arriving at Black Currant Tart and Cocoanut Drops. More practically, the year before Ahearn had formed the Ottawa Electric Street Railway Company, with ten streetcars made in St Catharines, fitted out with a polished oak interior and red plush seats and heated in winter by Ahearn's own heating system in the floor.

With Ahearn controlling electric light and electric transport, the city fathers of Ottawa began to have second thoughts about their benefactor. They tried encouraging competition, but Ahearn bought up the competition. When it seemed, in 1905, that the last competitor was about to be swallowed up by Ottawa Electric, the city in desperation bought up the competition, only to find that it could purchase no power from the only available source. Under the circumstances, the advent of the Ontario Hydro Electric Commission, under its dynamic and ruthless presiding genius, Sir Adam Beck, was more than fortuitous; it verged on the miraculous. Through the commission, Ottawa got the necessary power and resold it to its customers; but until 1950 the city continued to carry on competition with the Ahearn interests, before the Ottawa Electric Company was finally folded into the municipal Ottawa Hydro.

Ottawa's story, with variations, was repeated across the province. Corporations and monopolies, charging high rates to helpless consumers, encouraged those consumers, in their own self-image, to band together and take action. In Adam Beck, a minister without portfolio in the Whitney government and previously mayor of London, they found a leader who managed to be a symbol of the public power movement. Whitney, together with Beck, who became the first chairman of Ontario Hydro, overcame all resistance in a classic political battle between "the people" and "the interests" — the corporations that squeezed the consumer. Hydro, as the Hydro-Electric Power Commission was called, was created in 1906, constructed and operated transmission lines and thereby linked municipally owned power systems with the great sources of power. Private companies were not put out of business immediately, as we have seen in Ottawa's case, but over the long term Ontario Hydro came to manufacture as well as distribute electricity, and in the process to become a major factor in the development of the province. Not unexpectedly, electricity remained a political issue.

The creation of Hydro was not without incident. Existing interests at Niagara Falls appealed to the federal government to intervene and disallow Whitney's legislation. The premier knew that the Ottawa Liberals were most unlikely to do so, and he was right. There were protests from investors, domestic and foreign. The province was seizing private property without due compensation, it was argued. Whitney was acting arbitrarily and changing the rules of the game. But arbitrary or not, the government's actions stuck, founded as they were in a grassroots political reform movement that appealed to the mood of the moment. Seen in this perspective, public power was a blow for the ordinary citizen against privilege, a scenario remarkably like the themes of reform agitation in old Upper Canada seventy-five years before.

The Whitney government's reforming efforts did not end there. The premier knew that the school system was distinctly uneven in quality. Rural teachers were underpaid, school texts were expensive, and protests to Toronto had gone unheeded. Whitney established a minimum salary for teachers ($300 a year), and, when rural boards of education protested that this was too much, he subsidized them. School books were reduced in price, breaking, as Whitney thought, a schoolbook combine in Toronto, friends of the former government.

One of the more underprivileged areas, in terms of education, was eastern Ontario. Investigation showed that children in the eastern, French-speaking townships were receiving an inferior education: objective inspection, Whitney was told, showed that this was the case. In a narrow sense the school inspectors were probably right. In a larger, political sense they were disastrously wrong. There were both English- and French-language schools in eastern Ontario. The latter, which were both separate and public according to choice or accident, were styled ''bilingual.'' It was understood that ''bilingual'' was a sham, and that pupils in bilingual schools were in fact being taught in French, and were learning very little English. Indeed, as French Canadian leaders themselves recognized, their schools were not doing a particularly good job of teaching French.

With the existing situation clearly unsatisfactory, the government had the options of extending more money and assistance to the bilingual schools in order to improve their curriculum and the quality of their teaching or of bringing the bilingual schools more into line with schools elsewhere in the province: English-language schools, whether public or separate. Whitney's own attitude on this issue, which gathered force between 1906, when the problem was first raised, and 1912, when the government finally took a position, was complex. The premier was no bigot and prided himself on healing the rift between the Conservative party and the Catholic church. He quietly sent his daughter to a French-language convent school in Ottawa, appointed French Canadians to his cabinet, and attempted to understand French Canadian points of view. But however laudable the attempt, it is clear that Whitney, when faced with a choice between efficiency and "Britishness" on the one side and the desires of the French Canadian community on the other, lacked the imagination to respond sympathetically and creatively to the problem.

There was one further factor that helped to complicate matters. French-language immigration into eastern Ontario in the late nineteenth century helped overturn the balance inside the local Catholic church. Dioceses that had once been Irish were now French. Irish separate-school taxpayers were being taxed to pay for French schools. English-language Catholic school officials protested. So did English-language bishops, most notably Bishop Macdonnel of Alexandria and Bishop Fallon of London. The bishops had influence, and their arguments were based, in Fallon's words, on the fact that Ontario was "an English-speaking Province on an English-speaking continent where the boys and girls going out to fight the battle of life must be equipped, first with English, [and] that at all hazards ... "

The government found the bishops' logic persuasive. After considerable thought, the provincial Department of Education issued Regulation XVII to ban the use of French in Ontario schools beyond a junior elementary level. From the moment that the regulation was issued, in June 1912, the eastern counties of the province, and particularly Ottawa, were convulsed by a dispute over language rights whose ramifications spread far beyond the borders of Ontario.

Whitney resisted the pressures brought upon him, but he did not live long enough to observe the full consequences of his educational policy. Failing in health, the premier spent most of the year 1914 in bed, emerging for one election rally during that year's provincial contest. Dying in September, he passed his mantle on to William Hearst.

Whitney's legacy was, on the surface, wholly sound. The province's growth was accelerating. Toronto, and to a lesser extent the other major cities of Ontario, were attracting migrants from the countryside and from other countries. The migrants went to work in Ontario's factories, 8000 of them, mostly small but some by 1914 very large indeed. The immigrants tended to concentrate downtown: in Toronto they clustered in the shadow of the city's handsome Gothic city hall. They did not, by existing standards, live well. Observers were affronted by the uncleanliness, the noise, the disorder of the slums where the immigrants dwelled. As one generation of immigrants acclimatized itself to Canada and moved off to improved housing, another group came to take its place. Better-off Ontarians, proud of their British heritage and their solid (or stolid, according to preference) way of life, worried about ''alien'' influences and sought reassurance from social commentators or social workers, whose profession was just getting its start.

It was becoming the era of the expert. There were inspectors, enforcing building, sanitation, and health codes. There were public hospitals, and sanitoria for tuberculosis victims. It was too much to expect that the government could prevail on farmers to adopt the new-fangled French method of pasteurization of milk to kill bovine tuberculosis germs, but there were stricter regulations for the production and cleanliness of milk, and of other products too. Meat packers found it in their interest to co-operate with meat inspectors, so as to reassure their customers, domestic and foreign, that they would not die from eating their product. The Ontario Agricultural College in Guelph, founded in 1874, was enrolling over a thousand students by the 1910s, to encourage them in scientific farming. At home these students had new machines to operate: steam generators powered threshing and other harvesting machines. Provincial ministers boasted of the prosperity of Ontario farmers, and guessed that the province's thrifty farmers had put away over $100 million in savings, while in 1901 it was estimated that the total value of all farm property exceeded $1 billion for the first time.

Science and regulation also affected other natural products. In 1878 the government first took steps to prevent forest fires, by banning fires in "Fire Districts"; in 1885 forest rangers were hired to enforce the regulation. In the 1890s, after considerable study, a large provincial park was established between the Ottawa River and Georgian Bay: Algonquin Park where, it was hoped, the province could control the cutting of increasingly scarce timber.

The most significant action taken by the government had to do with the products of the forests. Angered by American legislation banning the importation of sawn lumber from Canada, the government of Ontario after much hesitation imposed a "manufacturing condition" on timber cut on crown lands — in other words, on most forested land. Ontario wood could leave the province in the form of lumber, cut and processed in Ontario mills, or it could simply not leave at all. The manufacturing condition enjoyed some success, although, as H. V. Nelles has pointed out, the success may have owed as much to improving business conditions at the turn of the century as it did to government intervention. Attempts to control the export of pulp logs, for conversion into pulp and paper in mills south of the border, had much less success until Quebec was persuaded to impose a manufacturing condition of its own in 1910. No longer able to play one Canadian province off against another, the American newspaper interests gave in. In 1913 the United States dropped all tariffs against Canadian pulp and paper. Simultaneously, large pulp and paper mills started up in both Ontario and Quebec: as far south as Thorold on the Welland Canal as well as across the north, from Fort Frances to the Quebec border, and down the Ottawa River.

Mining was also booming, stimulated by the extension of railway lines into the Canadian Shield. The government hoped for an agricultural colony in the Clay Belts of northern Ontario. It got its colony, though at high cost and low population. Two timber cruisers (in effect, scouts for lumber) found the great silver-cobalt-nickel-copper deposits of the Little Clay Belt, near Haileybury. W. G. Miller, later the Ontario Provincial geologist, christened the site Cobalt, and to Cobalt flocked a small horde of miners, prospectors, and, of course, speculators.

The speculators, if they did not come from Toronto, passed through the metropolis on their way up the railway to the north. It was a provincial railway, the Temiskaming and Northern Ontario, that took them there after 1904. In 1907 a "Cobalt Special" was started up, leaving Toronto at nine every evening and arriving at Cobalt just after breakfast the next morning. Stephen Leacock described the impression it made as it chugged through Orillia en route to the north:

> On a winter evening ... you will see the long row of Pullmans and diners of the night express going north to the mining country, the windows flashing with brilliant light, and within them a vista of cut glass and snow-white table linen, smiling negroes and millionaires with napkins at their chins whirling past in the driving snowstorm.

The millionaires brought investment, Canadian and American, in the mining properties. Toronto became known as a centre for mining finance, and also for mining fraud, for there were far more properties promoted than ever saw production or even the breaking of ground. After the Cobalt silver boom there was gold, further north at Kirkland Lake and Timmins, in the Abitibi country, and across the border at Rouyn-Noranda in Quebec. Gold from Kirkland Lake went into the first gold coins ever minted in Canada, an achievement more important for its symbolism than for its actual contribution to the country's financial history.

Toronto was more than ever a financial, transportation, and distribution centre. The city enjoyed most kinds of industry, from iron foundries and the garment trade to paper-making and publishing, but it was not primarily as a manufacturing centre that Toronto made its mark. There had always been banks in the city:

the Canadian Bank of Commerce, Bank of Toronto, Dominion Bank, Imperial Bank. There were insurance companies. There was a stock exchange, which moved to new and more spacious quarters on Bay Street in 1912. There were new suburbs to house the new rich, and even the old rich who found their downtown dwellings too close to traffic and business. The old houses were beginning, by the time of the First World War in 1914, to descend in the social scale, towards their eventual service as rooming houses, restaurants, and parking lots. The face of the city was changing as prosperity altered its shape and increased the numbers of the middle and upper classes.

Toronto was also well known across the province and across the country as a centre for the retail trade. The great department stores of Eaton's and Simpson's confronted one another at the corner of Queen and Yonge streets, in downtown Toronto. They also ran mail order businesses, competing for favour across Canada with profusely illustrated catalogues promising most of the miracles of the modern age. Especially tempting were the new electric goods, which promised a future of relative ease and comfort. The electric age was by 1914 well established in the cities and towns. The countryside was another matter. The Hydro Electric Commission did its bit to promote rural consumption by sending around a caravan of electric miracles: electric milking machines, domestic gadgets of all kinds, and of course electric light. It would take a while for transmission lines to catch up to the commission's propaganda, and it would take well into the 1940s for rural electrification to be proclaimed complete.

Electricity also contributed to the province's transportation network. Most cities had electric streetcars, but it has been forgotten that between the cities there were also electric railways that trundled passengers and freight from Toronto to Lake Simcoe, Waterloo to Port Dover, or Windsor to Leamington. The intercity radials, as they were called, reached their peak soon after 1914. They took a long time to decline, and the Lake Erie and Northern carried its last passenger in 1955 and its last freight in 1963.

Such services were useful in the absence of a proper network of provincial highways. It can reasonably be stated that Ontario's roads, down to 1914, were a major incentive to travel by rail. Roads were, until the twentieth century, a municipal responsibility. During the first decades of the century the provincial government gradually intruded itself into the road system, until in 1918 a provincial highway system was finally inaugurated. The first provincial highway, of the paved variety, ran between Toronto and Hamilton. It would later be extended, as Highway 2, from Windsor to the Quebec border; but that would be a development of the 1920s.

Another form of transportation was developing. The settlement of the prairies during the first decade and a half of the twentieth century meant a rise in Canadian grain production. By 1914 Canada stood third among grain-exporting countries, and most of Canada's exports travelled by rail to the Great Lakes and by freighter — ''laker'' — along the lakes towards the Atlantic and markets. The twin cities of Port Arthur and Fort William at the head of the lakes, on Lake Superior, became grain ports. A revolution in the design and construction of concrete buildings at the turn of the century permitted the building of long rows of repeating silos, great cylinders for the storage of grain, along the lakeshore. The elevators were not only at the lakehead, but also along Georgian Bay, at Collingwood and Midland, at Toronto, and eventually on the St Lawrence River, at Prescott.

The eventual destination of Ontario's exports or of the exports that passed through Ontario was a matter of academic concern to most of the province's citizens. The world was a stable place for Ontarians, who knew that their security and prosperity was symbolized as well as guaranteed by the great British empire, of which they were all subjects — highly contented subjects at that. The two prewar premiers, Ross and Whitney, proudly wore their imperial honours (''Sir George'' and ''Sir James'') and preached the vigorous patriotism of the empire. Whitney had no hesitation in pressuring the dominion government in Ottawa to contribute to the British Royal Navy; he could be confident that most Ontarians would agree with him. The history taught in Ontario schools was British history, in its original and its colonial form. Ontario children memorized the Anglo-Saxon kings of England, and learned that their own British parliamentary system of government was especially favoured and far preferable to the confused republican institutions of the neighbouring American republic. Fortunately, the Americans who came to the province en route to resorts along the lakes or in the interior did not mind; but then, they probably did not notice.

The summer of 1914 saw Canadians flock to vacation resorts too. Those who could not afford to leave the cities and towns played or observed sports: baseball, rowing, tennis, lacrosse. Sir Robert Borden, Canada's Conservative prime minister since the defeat of Sir Wilfrid Laurier in 1911, spent a week in the fashionable Muskoka resorts, playing bridge. Towards the end of July Sir Robert's vacation was interrupted. The international situation in Europe was grave, the prime minister was told. He should return to Ottawa as soon as possible.

By Saturday, August 1, those who cared to read the newspapers or to saunter past the bulletin boards outside newspaper offices knew that the world was on the brink of war. Germany and Austria were confronting Russia and France. In London the British government was considering what it must do. In Ottawa the government was standing by to learn what Britain proposed. Since Canada was still a British colony, even though a very large and senior colony, it was obvious that if Britain went to war, Canada would go too. Crowds gathered outside government and newspaper buildings, anxious for the latest word.

The word came in the evening of August 4. Britain was at war with Germany. Canadians, and especially Ontarians, needed no convincing that the British cause was just. Members of the militia reported to their local armouries (the period before 1914 was especially prolific in the construction of these large brick and concrete buildings across the province). There they learned that the dominion had scrapped its existing mobilization plan in favour of a fervent call to arms. Canadians would fight in an entirely new way, in numbered units called battalions (a battalion, in 1914, contained about 1000 men). They would volunteer, then proceed by train to the military camp at Valcartier outside Quebec City for preliminary organization and training prior to embarkation for England.

The first volunteers probably underestimated what they were getting into. The war, it was held, might be over by Christmas. A First Contingent was raised, then a Second, then a Third. The Third went overseas in 1915, and by then there was little doubt that the war would last longer than at first expected. It lasted four years and three months. Canadian — Ontario — soldiers fought mostly on the Western Front, in northern France and Belgium. The conditions under which they fought were at best grim: water-logged trenches, unimaginative tactics, a well-prepared and determined German enemy. Casualties were high, and continuous drafts of reinforcements became necessary. Efforts to raise recruits therefore became more and more intensive as time passed; eventually the dominion government was obliged to resort to compulsory service — conscription — in 1917, a move with serious political consequences both on the national level and in Ontario. By June 1918 Ontario, out of a population of 2.5 million, 31 percent of the Canadian total, had recruited 231,191 young men, or 43 percent of Canada's enlistments — and the war had still five months to run.

The Ontario government announced that it would support the war effort as soon as the war started. It contributed flour and dehydrated apples to Britain and raised $500,000 for an imperial fund. Sir James Whitney, dying, roused himself for one last patriotic pronouncement. It would be left to his successor, W. H. (later Sir William) Hearst, to lead the province through the war. Hearst, amiable and anxious to please, struggled manfully with the task. It would not be the fault of his intentions that he did not succeed very well.

The most serious immediate consequence of the outbreak of war for any Canadian province was that it transferred the centre of political interest and power to Ottawa. The British North America Act permitted the dominion government, in times of emergency, to pre-empt provincial powers and responsibilities. Because Hearst and Borden were of the same political stripe, Conservative, it was natural that the dominion and the province should try to submerge any differences for the sake of the great cause of the war effort. The corollary, however, was that Hearst would take political responsibility for many political decisions that were not his to make.

It helped that the provincial opposition, the Liberal party under its leader, Newton Wesley Rowell, was if possible as patriotic and determined as the government party. Rowell would eventually abandon provincial politics altogether and join Borden's government in October 1917 as a pro-conscription Liberal, in opposition to his erstwhile national leader, Laurier, who opposed conscription. Rowell's stand was consistent with the widespread sentiment among Ontarians that personal liberty was a necessary sacrifice to the organization of victory.

It would not be the only sacrifice. Hyperpatriotic citizens took a severe view of words or actions intended to encourage the enemy. The dominion government's war powers were exercised broadly and, when challenged by individuals or groups, were sustained by the courts. Censorship began immediately. The press was under orders not to report military information, but newspapers were inclined to take a positive as well as a negative interpretation of their war duty. They were assisted in their attempts to encourage patriotism by the vigorous, not to say lurid, propaganda efforts of the allied governments, and by the increasingly extreme pronouncements of political leaders. The teaching of German, the language of the enemy, went by the boards. German professors at the university were barred from their classes, although their conduct was considered to be above reproach. In the schools, the provincial Department of Education provided booklets entitled *The Children's Story of the War*. Music was most affected, and songbooks were purged of German or Austrian selections written after 1850. The German language continued to be taught, however, and no attempt seems to have been made to remove it from the curriculum.

The war's effects went far beyond what was contemplated or intended. The first effect was, of course, the drawing off of large numbers of young men to the army, where $1.10 a day was a private's wage. That was better than unemployment, which had been particularly severe in 1913-14 because of a business downturn. The downturn continued for some months after war's outbreak, owing to the disruption in normal markets that the war entailed. By 1915 business was picking up, and by 1916 it was positively booming.

Companies large and small adapted to war work. Because so much of Ontario industry was small or local, subcontracting was common. But even by spreading work around there was soon a labour shortage. In the single year 1915 the number of workers in iron and steel across Ontario rose from 4300 to 9400; workers in foundries and machine shops increased from 9000 to 13,000. Welfare offices closed and employment offices opened. The government assisted by recruiting schoolchildren for work on farms and women for munitions factories.

Employers were initially dubious, but the labour shortage allowed for no hesitation. During 1916 the number of women workers rose, and it rose more and more sharply during 1917 and 1918. Women were used for work of all kinds: bank tellers, although bankers doubted that they could cope with the noon rush; conductors on streetcars; ordinary munitions work; and eventually work with explosives.

The war also opened attitudes and lowered barriers that had seemed insurmountable. There had been no disposition on the part of the Ontario government to grant the vote to women before

the war. Suddenly, in 1917, Premier Hearst announced the introduction of appropriate legislation, and it was done. The dominion
followed suit later in the year, although on the federal level the
vote was at first given only to women with husbands, sons, or
brothers serving overseas.*

Up to this point the interests of the dominion government and
those of its Ontario counterpart had been compatible. The war,
however, cost money — a great deal of money. Prices rose sharply
as governments outbid one another for limited supplies of essential commodities. Inflation followed, but in the inflation after
1915 wages did not generally keep pace with the cost of living.
There was, moreover, pressure on the workforce for increased
production. Labour trouble was the result, with strikes commonplace across Ontario in 1916, 1917, and 1918. The labour difficulties were not as serious in Ontario as they would prove elsewhere
in Canada. This was partly because labouring men seem to have
shared the general outlook of their government towards the winning of the war, and partly because union leaders in eastern Canada were strongly inclined to co-operate with the government.

Farmers were also increasingly discontented, and basically for
the same reason. They were called on to produce more, and to
invest more in their farms in order to do so. But their returns were
not proportionate to their investment. Crops fluctuated, costs rose.
Prices were controlled, at least for farm products. The same
patriotic impulse that kept Ontario cities firmly behind the war
effort right up to 1918 was less in evidence on the farms, while the
greatest single issue of the war, conscription, provoked very different responses from farmer and city dweller.

Conscription, by focusing attention on manpower and population, touched on a very sore issue in rural Ontario. That much of
the province had been losing population for some time had been

*Much of the material in this section has been derived from the excellent book by Barbara
Wilson, *Ontario and the First World War* (Toronto, 1977).

obvious, although its effects were concealed by the use of aggregate statistics. Certain areas suffered much more heavily than others. At one extreme, a township in Grey County lost almost 50 percent of its homes in the single decade 1900-10. Losses of between 5 and 10 percent were much more common, with the result that abandoned farmhouses became a feature of the rural landscape, at least in the more distant and less fertile parts of southern Ontario. Regardless of prosperity in one year or another, there was a growing sense that things were not going as they should; the uneasiness could easily be transferred to politics and, in particular, to the politics brought about by the war.

Farmer spokesmen were profoundly unimpressed by pleas for recruits from the farms. There were few enough people to work the farms. There were no labour-saving devices where there was no electricity, and that meant most of rural Ontario. A well-meaning attempt to lend tractors to farmers for the duration of the war floundered when it was realized that the machines of the period worked best on stretches of level ground, and not at all on hills. This limited their effectiveness.

When Sir Robert Borden's Liberal-Conservative "Union Government" was formed in October 1917 it took conscription as its principal objective. An election was scheduled for December. It did not take long for Borden's ministers to realize that they were in some difficulty in rural areas. Newton Rowell, the former Ontario Liberal leader, urged Borden to modify his conscription policy so as to reassure rural voters that essential manpower would be left on the farm. After some hesitation, Borden complied. His Union Government was returned on December 17, election day, and it carried most of Ontario's rural seats. Some farm leaders were concerned, because they feared that the urban-centred attitudes of some of Borden's supporters on issues like a high protective tariff would harm farm interests, but that was nothing compared to their concern when, in April 1918, Borden revoked the exemption his government had given to farm labour. It is true that there was a military crisis on the Western Front in France, but the sense of betrayal among farmers was very strong, and, as it turned out, long-lasting.

One other group besides farmers did not share in the general enthusiasm for conscription and a total war effort. French Canadians in eastern Ontario were alienated from the government and its policies in the aftermath of Regulation XVII. French-language schools resisted the Toronto government's efforts to impose an English standard on their pupils. There were disturbances in Ottawa. The government was obliged to impose its own administration on local schools. A resolution was introduced in the dominion House of Commons condemning the Ontario government's actions, while in Quebec nationalist papers sharply criticized the province's oppression of a minority — an oppression that, it was hinted, was in the same league as German oppression of minorities in Europe.

Ontarians reciprocated. French Canada was not doing its share for the war effort. Too few French Canadians were going to war. Laurier and his Liberal followers were little better than German agents. The dominion election of December 1917 was seen by many in Ontario as a reassertion of majority rights against the near-treasonable resistance of a minority to a policy that, in the hysteria of wartime, was practically Holy Writ.

War hysteria did not outlast the war that generated it. When the German army and government asked for an armistice (a ceasefire) on November 11, 1918, there was an outburst of relief and joy across the province. The troops, those that had survived, would soon be home. With the pressure of war removed, the discontents that had hitherto been concealed surfaced.

The Hearst government was the first victim of the great postwar relaxation. The premier laboured under the delusion that he had done everything possible to please the electorate. Under pressure from temperance societies he had banned bar rooms and liquor shops in 1916; Ontario wines were exempted, but their stay of execution was delayed only until December 31, 1918. Although there were loopholes in the law for medicinal and sacramental purposes, Ontario had acquired effective prohibition. There was, it is true, a sharp increase in the custom of provincial drugstores, and certain doctors were believed to have added substantially to their income through "medical" prescriptions. But this was only the beginning of Ontario's war on liquor, and liquor's war on Ontario.

The government immediately lost two key by-elections. Howard Ferguson, one of Hearst's ministers, attributed the victory of an anti-prohibitionist Liberal (a "wet" as the term went) in Toronto to the revengeful spirit of the liquor interests. Since the liquor interests had just lost their property and livelihood without very much in the way of compensation, this was not an unreasonable conclusion. There followed the disputes over Regulation XVII, conscription, the failure of the premier to replace his departed agriculture minister, and the decline of the Conservative party organization. When Hearst finally called an election, in October 1919, the Conservative government was in much the same political predicament as its Liberal predecessors fourteen years earlier. It suffered a similar fate. For the first time, Ontario's new legislature would be a house of minorities, and the largest minority would be neither of the two old parties. It would be the farmers.

Two Steps Forward, and Two Back: 1919–39

Between 1919 and 1939 Ontario underwent two depressions, a major boom, and a partial recovery. Its people continued to flock to the cities, and its governments, down to 1934, continued to encourage them to go back to the land. The province enjoyed, if that is the word, government by the United Farmers of Ontario, the Conservatives, and the Liberals. Despite the variation in labels, the government throughout the period was firmly conservative, with a small "c," in its outlook.

The trends of the times were already firmly established. Between 1919 and 1939 more Ontarians and immigrants moved to the cities and towns. More farmers and children of farmers left the countryside. The census of 1921 showed that the war had not been kind to the rural part of the rural-urban balance. That year, Ontario's 2.9 million people were 58 percent urban. Toronto was still the largest city, with 522,000 people, and it lagged behind Montreal, remaining Canada's number-two city as it had been since Confederation. Hamilton and Ottawa were far behind Toronto, with just over 100,000 population each, and London and Windsor were further back still.

Ontarians lived spaciously. Over 80 percent of the homes (or dwelling units, in census terms) of the province were detached houses, and another 11 percent were semidetached. There were no more than 8000 apartment units in the whole province, and just under 25,000 row houses. The dwellings were wood or brick, with brick gradually predominating in the years down to 1939. By the outbreak of the Second World War in the latter year Ontario was estimated to be 60 percent brick on the housing front.

The issues that confronted the province changed gradually. Rural depopulation was very much an issue in 1919. A glance down the census lists shows a steady drainage from rural townships after 1901. Where a rural county did not lose population, it was because people were attracted to the local village or town, doubtless because of some jobs available in manufacturing, distribution, or service industries.

The drainage was not yet observable in politics. Urban areas were gaining in population, but they still had fewer seats in the provincial legislature than farmers had. Toronto, with a quarter of the provincial population, had only one-sixth of the seats in the legislature. One urban constituency was home to over 100,000 souls; but it was not unusual for a rural seat to have 15,000. It was doubtful that this disparity would continue indefinitely, and the realization that the trend was against them made the organized farmers of Ontario desperate to act as soon as possible, before something worse happened.

If rural depopulation and the place of the farmer in society were concerns that had surfaced before, so was the perennial question of education. The Catholic church was not about to let separate schools disappear from the political agenda. More money was wanted for the church schools, and that could best be obtained by a reform on the tax base to allow business taxes to flow to separate school boards, instead of into the pockets of the public boards.

Highways were also a familiar concern. "Good roads" appeared every year, in every budget; but good roads cost money, and the better they were, the more expensive. Universities had been around ever since the days of the Family Compact, and every provincial government had to grapple after its own fashion with financing the provincial university in Toronto as well as with the increasing concerns of the two other secular universities, Queen's University at Kingston and the University of Western Ontario at

London. (There were also denominational schools and colleges, but no one suggested that a church-affiliated college should compete for funds with its secular rivals.)

Other problems were more recent. A sharp depression in 1913–14 had placed unemployment on the provincial agenda for the first time, and another depression in 1920–22 returned it there. Governments were not expected to let their people starve or freeze, even if public opinion differed wildly on the causes of, and the responsibilities for, the unemployment of able-bodied workers. Fortunately, the return of good times in 1922 and 1923 rendered the question moot, for the time being; but it would be back.

If the average Ontarian had been asked, at any time during the 1920s, what the great question of politics actually was, he or she would have been bound to reply, "prohibition." The Hearst government, as we have seen, brought in a ban on the sale of alcohol for enjoyment during the First World War. It confirmed its choice in a referendum at the end of the war. Prohibition groups were not satisfied. The United States in 1919 actually amended its constitution to ban, not merely the sale of alcohol in all its forms, but its manufacture, whether for domestic consumption or for export. With that shining example before them, sincere prohibitionists put pressure on the provincial government to ban the importation of alcohol, especially from the wicked province of Quebec, which in 1919 decided to allow the sale of beer and wine, though not liquor. The anti-prohibition forces had been demoralized by the linkage of the war on demon rum with the war to preserve civilization, otherwise known as the Great War and, later, World War I. By 1919 they were recovering their nerve, enough to suspect that prohibition's triumph was temporary and that their opponents had finally over-extended themselves.

What was transitory was the political conjunction that elected the United Farmers of Ontario to power in the election of October 1919. The Farmers themselves helped make it so, and the story of their government is also an object lesson in what can go wrong with a militant, one-issue reform party when it unexpectedly achieves power.

Between 1919 and 1921 farmers' groups elected governments in Alberta, Ontario, and Manitoba, and heavily influenced another, in Saskatchewan. Farm leaders had been proclaiming for years that the two old parties, Liberals and Conservatives, had forgotten, ignored, or opposed outright the true interests of Canada's farm population. The agricultural class ought to send representatives into politics who would not confuse their duty to their constituents with broader (and inevitably compromising and corrupting) considerations. Other classes, such as labour or business, should do the same. Then the various class representatives could sit together in the legislature and debate their interests in the open, rather than behind closed doors or in the smoke-filled party backrooms. Lawyers, doctors, or storekeepers in rural areas were banned from sitting on farmers' platforms at political rallies; let them find somebody else to represent them.

In the legislature elected in 1919, out of a total membership of 111, the farmers had forty-five. With the addition of eleven Labour votes and one independent, they had a bare majority over the combined Liberals (twenty-nine) and Conservatives (twenty-five). The Conservative leader, Hearst, had been personally defeated; but the Conservatives were in better shape than the Farmers, who had no leader. It took the Farmers a month to find one, Ernest C. Drury; after being sworn in as premier, Drury had to find a seat and get elected to the legislature. Drury reflected a farm background, but in more ways than the ideologists of class government would have preferred. He also had a party background, like most farmers; indeed, his father had been Sir Oliver Mowat's minister of agriculture and the great man had once laid a hand on the young Drury's head and wished him well. Drury had even run as an independent Liberal in the 1917 dominion election.

Though he was premier, Drury was just one of several prominent Farmer politicians. Equally as important was J. J. Morrison, the United Farmers' secretary. Morrison had power, if not responsibility, and he used it to lecture the premier and demoralize his followers by pointing out how the Farmers' government was deviating from the true path of class government. Then there was the attorney general. The existence of this post caused the farmers some embarrassment. True to their principles, they had no lawyers in their membership, and so they had to poach an attorney general, learned in the law, from one of the other parties. Drury chose a Liberal, W. E. Raney, who also happened to be a devout prohibitionist and, as it later proved, a foe of vice in its many forms. Raney seems to have believed that in the fight against vice he should act as the strong arm of the law, if possible more vigorously than precedent allowed.

To complete the menagerie, there were the leaders of the opposition. The Liberal leader, Hartley Dewart, was the jovial and anti-prohibitionist chief of a prohibitionist party. Dewart did have the advantage of being a good debater, and he had done rather better than any of his prohibitionist predecessors in getting out the Liberal vote. But he had a fatal handicap, as far as his followers were concerned, and by the end of 1921 he was out and a relative nonentity, Wellington Hay, who was sound on the booze question, was in. The Liberal party followed Hay into the wilderness, where it would languish for another decade and a half. The defeated Conservatives chose as their chieftain Howard Ferguson, minister of lands and forests in the Hearst government. Ferguson hailed from Kemptville on the Rideau River. A Tory to his fingertips, "Fergie" was also an artful and highly skilled manipulator of men. His charm belied his overflowing figure and podgy jowls, and better still, he could deploy the charm on a wide variety of fronts and to very different audiences. Ferguson was a good British Ontarian, firm in his faith in king, empire, and the destiny of the Anglo-Saxon race, but he did not take those attributes to the point of fervent prohibitionism or a determination to resist the wiles of the pope by continuing to ban the use of French in French-language schools. Ferguson rather liked Dewart, who seems to have been a highly sympathetic figure, and together the two men made mincemeat of the UFO government. When Dewart departed, Ferguson was delighted to carry on the fight alone.

The Farmers gave plenty of ground to fight on, and it was possible to select tools both of the fair and of the foul varieties. Fortunately the Farmers spent so much time fighting among themselves that it was sometimes unnecessary for the opposition to lift a finger or raise a voice in protest. On the issue of superannuation (pensions) for the provincial civil service, a normal administrative device, Farmer spokesmen detected a class plot. Let the civil servants save like good farmers for their lean years, the government was told by its erstwhile helpers. The Drury government pointed out, in reply, that at least farmers owned their own farms on which they could, if necessary, grow their own food. The civil servants, in contrast, did not own their own offices, which in any case were unsuitable for cultivation most of the time.

Then there was the question of good roads. Roads were also a class instrument, according to farmer devotees. They took the young away from the farms and benefited everyone other than farmers. The Drury government's highways minister, however, took his department more seriously than the prophets of rural depopulation. Highway mileage increased. The perennial question of the provincial university then resurfaced. The province's secular universities, the government decided, were to receive extra money, as a blue-ribbon committee recommended.

These stands did the Drury government credit and demonstrated its ability to withstand pressures from self-interested and frequently confused special-interest groups. It did not do as well with prohibition. The government's prohibition policy falls into two categories: extension and enforcement. To extend prohibition to imports from outside the province, the government held a plebiscite in 1920. The prohibition forces, "the drys," won. But this time the anti-prohibition forces, operating under the title of the Liberty League, put up a fight. They enlisted the provost of Trinity College, an Anglican foundation in the University of Toronto, to deplore the "lack of moderation" of the "drys," "well-meaning but ill-advised people." Stephen Leacock, a humorist and professor, saw nothing funny about prohibition: "A fanatical minority," he wrote, "has captured the ear of the public and the power of the legislature." It was the "drys' " last substantial victory.

Attorney General Raney had charge of enforcing the law. Finding the ordinary police forces insufficient, he organized a corps of his own. It certainly achieved headlines when one of his inspectors, the Reverend J. O. L. Spracklin in Windsor, was tried for murder. Spracklin was acquitted, but zeal had received a setback.

The Drury government was on sounder grounds when it appointed a two-judge commission to probe the activities of the lands and forests department under Conservative management. The principal target was Howard Ferguson, who had headed the department before the Hearst government's defeat. Certainly Ferguson's reputation was not enhanced by the revelations the commission brought forward. He had ignored the law by granting provincial timber limits without first seeking tenders from bidders. His grantees had been guilty of highly unusual, not to say illegal, practices. But Ferguson, who believed that the best defence was always a good offence, managed to turn the tables on the commissioners, arguing prejudice on their part and simple enthusiasm for development on his own.

Ferguson was not, therefore, destroyed. Instead, he became the next premier of the province. The internal strains in the Drury government finally overcame the Farmers' frail unity in the spring of 1923. Drury dissolved the legislature and called an election for June. Ferguson and the Conservatives swept the polls. Politically they deserved their victory. The Liberal party had committed suicide back in 1921, when it dumped Dewart. The Farmers spent as much time fighting one another as they did fighting the election. The Conservatives were well organized, well financed, and, above all, well led. They won seventy-five seats, an impressive majority.

Ferguson did not interpret his mandate as giving him an entirely free hand. He wanted to reform the Ontario school system by consolidating schools; but he acted cautiously in the face of an economical rural school system, whose trustees preferred to leave well enough alone. He believed that prohibition had had its day, but he acted with extreme circumspection, merely allowing it to be understood that the premier's heart was in the right place, as far as the "wets" were concerned. As for the "drys," another plebiscite showed they were still a majority, though a declining one.

More than his two immediate predecessors, Hearst and Drury, Ferguson was inclined to get into scraps with Ottawa. Ottawa was currently in the hands of another Ontarian, William Lyon Mackenzie King, grandson of the rebel of 1837. King believed that he was his grandfather's true heir, destined to carry the banner of reform forward. It would be truer to say that he resembled his grandfather in almost no respect. Where his grandfather often seemed to inhabit an unreal world populated by persecuting aristocrats, King was very careful to keep a strict division between dreamland and reality. William Lyon Mackenzie loved an audience, and his audiences were usually well entertained from the rebel's boundless store of libellous invective. The rebel's grandson counted a moment lost if it made an enemy. Soft words, he believed, turned away wrath and, better still, won votes. He was right, and was rewarded by becoming Canada's prime minister for a record twenty-two years, off and on, between 1921 and 1948. The fact that in the evenings the prime minister regularly convened a social circle of ghosts ranging from Lorenzo de Medici to William Lyon Mackenzie was not revealed to a public that might not have understood King's idea of a hobby. In any case, it is safe to conclude, the ghosts were kept away from giving King ideas of their own; they were only socially acceptable as long as they agreed with their summoner.

Ferguson did not get on with King, and the two regularly sparred over questions of dominion-provincial jurisdiction. Ferguson, like Mowat before him, sustained the "compact theory" of confederation, and he managed to push it farther and more successfully than any other provincial rights advocate in Canadian history. He could not have done so without allies, however, and for an ally he turned to another Liberal, Premier Alexandre Taschereau of Quebec.

Water power was at the root both of Ferguson's quarrel with King and his soft words to Taschereau. Water power was expensive. Sir Adam Beck's Ontario Hydro Electric Commission was regularly expanding its scope. It wanted its own set of electric railways, and, until they proved too costly, it got them. It wanted its own sources of power, and it got them too, including a costly canal diverting water around the falls of Niagara to Queenston, to the Sir Adam Beck generating station. The canal was useful at a time of high unemployment, but expensive. With the canal built, Beck's eye roved eastwards, to the next great volume of water charging unhindered towards Quebec: the St Lawrence River. The St Lawrence was also a navigational system, under dominion jurisdiction; it was an international boundary water, also federal. Could the Ottawa government move in and seize Ontario's patrimony? It might; and it was as well to be prepared.

To prepare, it would be useful if Quebec helped, and Quebec could help in more ways than one. It could even spare Ontario the expense of developing the St Lawrence River's power for a generation, by exporting its own electricity to its sister province. There were, however, a few minor obstacles in the way of an official collaboration. There was the matter of Regulation XVII. Ferguson had been a member of the government that had fought during the war to resist French Canadian pressures to eliminate the regulation. Could he now reverse himself, in return for electricity with a French accent?

He could. Ontario would import power from Quebec. Taschereau collected brickbats and abuse from Quebec's nationalist press. Then, in 1927, Regulation XVII was gone. Naturally it went only after the best educational advice, and only after it was clearly demonstrated to have failed. In future, French would get the same emphasis as English in eastern Ontario's schools, at least in the French-language variety. The teaching of French to English-language pupils was, it is true, somewhat more advanced in some parts of eastern Ontario than it was in the rest of the province, but to concede that is not to concede much.

There followed an elaborate constitutional minuet. It came to involve virtually all the provinces, the dominion government, and, eventually, the British government as well. Each government wanted something. Ferguson wanted to assert the compact theory dearly beloved of Ontario's several governments. He wanted the rights to St Lawrence water power, and to water power on the Ottawa as well. Quebec's order of priorities was slightly different, but it included the protection of the French-speaking province's rights in Confederation, which could best be advanced by giving the province, or the provinces in general, a great deal to bargain with. The Maritime provinces wanted more attention paid to their local needs, and they wanted the federal government to redress the slow decline in their economic position. The Prairie provinces wanted land, land that the dominion government had withheld from them when they were created, in order to further the settlement of the west as a great national priority. Everyone, or virtually everyone, wanted something more.

What did the dominion government want? Its objectives were both negative and positive. It wanted if possible to avoid spending more money, and it had no great inclination to seek new ways to encroach on expensive areas of provincial jurisdiction. It wanted above all to avoid responsibility for unemployment, relief, and welfare. These were clearly provincial responsibilities, and under the provinces, of the municipalities. The provinces, on the whole, and with the exception of Quebec, would probably have inclined to some sharing of jurisdiction as long as it meant sharing the burden by dipping into the dominion treasury; but that was not to be: not, at least, for the next few years.

On the positive side, the King government wanted to preserve some freedom of action on water power, and it wanted, in the sixtieth year after confederation, to do what the Fathers had failed to do, and bring home the Canadian Constitution by providing an entirely Canadian amending formula. The British, for their part, were reluctantly accepting that imperial jurisdiction over a dominion like Canada — or Australia, New Zealand, or South Africa — was a pointless anachronism. They were ready to negotiate away their legal powers over the rest of the empire.

In 1927, therefore, the King government convened a dominion-provincial conference to consider how to amend the British North America Act. They suggested that certain subjects be reserved for unanimous consent, matters such as language rights that clearly went to the heart of the Canadian constitutional compromise of the 1860s. The provinces let it be known that before they would agree to anything like that, they wished to have their own demands considered. In the end, each supporting the other, they got a great deal. Ontario and Quebec got their water rights. Howard Ferguson wanted more. He wanted the dominion to recognize that it could not amend the Constitution, the ''compact,'' without getting the consent of its true parents, the provinces. Consultation was not enough.

This demand of Ferguson's had a legacy, and it is just as well to advance our story somewhat and consider what it was. In the same year as the dominion-provincial conference, Ferguson attended another convocation, this time of the Conservative party which was choosing a new national leader. Ferguson took a strong part in the proceedings, torpedoing the former leader, Arthur Meighen, and promoting the chances of R. B. Bennett, a corporation lawyer from Calgary. Bennett defeated Mackenzie King and the Liberals in 1930 and became prime minister just in time to wrap up the constitutional negotiations between Canada and Great Britain. In defining what Canada wanted, Bennett reserved the position of the provinces. That is, matters of dominion-provincial relations were excluded from the constitutional agreement, and the amendment of the British North America Act was left precisely where it had been since 1867, in the hands of the British Parliament, acting on the request of the Canadian government. The Canadian government, Bennett promised, would not act without the consent of the provinces. This was more, much more, than any previous government had conceded, and it gave Ferguson and enthusiasts for the compact theory their clearest and most significant victory in the long history of federal-provincial relations in Canada. In the future, the balance of the British North America Act could be altered only after a long and cumbersome constitutional process; what had been flexible now became rigid; and the provinces had a great deal more to bargain with in their relations with Ottawa.

The constitutional struggle was merely the superstructure of a much more complicated and largely invisible relationship. During the 1920s the dominion government took in less money, and spent less money, than it had before. Its revenues actually declined by over 5 percent. The municipalities, however, raised almost 38 percent more revenue, and the provinces an extraordinary 105 percent. These figures may seem ordinary enough, but what they disclose is a major change in the way provincial governments saw themselves and their role in society. Government would never be minimal again. With a vengeance, and without entirely recognizing the fact, Canadians had entered the era of the interventionist state.

A glance at the provincial budget during the 1920s shows what the government was spending money on. The highway system was being expanded. County roads were being built, and sometimes given hard surfaces. Hospitals were rising across the province, some provincial, some municipal. Schools had to be built. Teachers had to be paid, and they had to be paid more. The Drury government had started a trend, and the Ferguson government continued it. For example, we can compare Ontario's spending on schools of all kinds in 1916 and 1925. In the first year, the province spent, in total, some $16 million. In 1925 the corresponding figure was $45.6 million, an increase of almost 200 percent. Teachers' salaries accounted for much of the increase, but much of it was for new school buildings or for improvements of existing plant. (Salaries, however, varied considerably by locality and, it goes without saying, they varied according to sex.) There were also almost 500,000 pupils and students in Ontario schools in 1925, compared to 355,000 in 1916. This reflected an extension of compulsory education, passed in 1919, as well as a high birth rate.

The province was not the only big spender during the 1920s. The cities and towns of Ontario had to spend money, and had money to spend. Suburbs were being built at a rapid rate as cities extended outwards. Streetcar lines snaked out to the suburbs, running usually along paved streets on which suburbanites drove their new cars, manufactured in factory assembly lines in Windsor, Oakville, or Oshawa. Cities like Toronto relied not only on property taxes, but on a municipal income tax, levied on their citizens. For the province, there were amusement taxes (the Farmers' government had a special attraction to taxes on vice, such as a tax on cabarets) and a gasoline tax.

There was also a liquor tax. Howard Ferguson moved slowly, but he moved exceedingly surely. A plebiscite there had to be, in 1924, and it showed that a narrow majority of Ontarians were still against the sale of liquor, beer, or wine, even in sealed packages "under Government control." The next year the government revealed that its own experiments had shown that beer up to a certain percentage of alcohol was, truly, unintoxicating. The magic figure was 4.4%. "Fergie's Foam," as it was called, had arrived. To the Foam (available from 1925 on) must be added native wines (1.9 million gallons produced in 1924) and home brew, which could be had for the price of a permit and brewers' yeast. There were 30,000 permit-holders in Ontario at the height of prohibition.

The next step came in 1926. Ferguson decided to run for re-election on a platform of government control. The government would take over the distribution and sale of liquor. It would control access to alcohol, and thereby prevent a return to the high days of the open bar. It would save a great deal of money uselessly spent on enforcing the anti-drink laws — more, as Ferguson liked to point out, than on enforcing all other laws combined. It would, instead, make money by allowing the government to set the price and collect the profit.

Ferguson's position was endorsed, and in 1927 the last vestige of prohibition came to an end, at least as far as the availability of alcohol for personal consumption, at home, in ostensibly limited quantities, was concerned. For men there were "beverage rooms," evil-smelling dimly lit beer halls. For those who wished to flout the law, there were teacups at fashionable restaurants that could afford to practise a bottle-under-the-table policy. Liquor had not entirely disappeared as a political issue, but it would never be *the* political issue again.

The return of liquor marked the end of an important era in Ontario, and not just in politics. The 1920s were a watershed decade. The decade brought short skirts, Model-T Fords to drive the new highways, jazz, smoking for women in public, and, as moralists did not hesitate to argue, a general decline in standards. One person's decline is another person's liberation, but we need not quarrel with the virtually universal feeling of the time that things were different and would never be the same again. The start of the decade saw an attempt to turn the clock back, to an era when the country ruled the city, but also to an era when life was simpler but harder, more precarious and definitely worse-paid. Canadians in the 1920s were, generally, making more money than they ever had before, and Ontario was leading the way.

In business as in other things it was a decade of advance. Investment flowed in, from abroad, meaning usually the United States, or from untapped domestic sources. The pulp and paper industry boomed, and it was expanded. Automobiles boomed, and the Canadian automobile industry, a branch of the American industry on the other side of the Great Lakes, grew. In Toronto, companies turned to making the domestic products that the new era demanded: electric stoves, refrigerators, and vacuum cleaners. They were still a luxury item, but they did exist, and they were getting relatively cheaper. There were radios, usually tuned to American programs, but there were Canadian radio stations too. A royal commission under a bank president was examining them, and it would presently recommend a government broadcasting system. Needless to say, in a decade of dominion-provincial disputes, the question of who actually controlled or regulated radio was before the courts; before that question was resolved there would be a new decade, and different circumstances. By then Howard Ferguson would be a dominion civil servant, working for Canada in London, England. R. B. Bennett would be prime minister of Canada. And there would be an economic depression.

The Great Depression of the 1930s was a world-wide phenomenon. It was characterized by over-capitalization, over-production, and deflation. World trade sank. In response, virtually all countries retreated from competition in international trade. Tariff walls went up, and behind the walls politicians and bankers fiddled with their currencies to bestow a transitory advantage in terms of trade on their own country's products.

Different countries suffered in different ways. Britain and France suffered less than Germany, the United States, or Canada. That is, there were fewer unemployed, and the average standard of living fell less far. In North America, national income fell by almost half between 1929 and 1933, in both the United States and Canada. Export prices fell, sometimes a little and sometimes, as with the price of wheat, a lot. Farmers on the prairies were exceedingly badly off, and their troubles were compounded by the worst drought of the century.

Ontario was severely hit by the Great Depression. In the worst year, 1933, half a million people depended on local governments for relief. Those who could not find relief had to go begging. Small businesses went bankrupt. Layoffs were common from factories and offices. Governments saw the number of taxpayers shrinking, and with it their ability to finance relief. Property taxes went up, and where they could not, a city or a town had to consider whether it could afford to pay off the bonds it had sold in order to build roads, hospitals, and schools back in the 1920s. Some cities, such as Windsor, decided that the burden was too much to bear. On a higher level, Ontario discovered the provincial income tax, a resource which has remained with the province ever since.

The dominion government, headed by the Conservative R. B. Bennett between 1930 and 1935, helped out. It paid one-third of the cost of relief, even while it pointed out that welfare was a provincial responsibility. Ontario and the other provinces paid another third, and the rest was made up by the municipalities.

The man doing the paying out in Ontario was the premier, George Henry. Howard Ferguson had retired in 1930 and became Canada's high commissioner in London and occasional delegate to the League of Nations in Geneva. "Fergie" was missed for the vivacity and charm he had brought to provincial politics. Conservatives missed his decisiveness and his negotiating skills, and it was certainly true that his combination of political skill and administrative ability would not be seen for another generation. His political machine was now put to its severest test, and, lacking the hand and judgement of its creator, it failed.

Of course, the circumstances in which the Conservative party sank towards oblivion were among the most unfavourable that any Ontario government had ever faced. The government drifted from crisis to crisis, hoping each time that Ottawa would hand over more dollars to pay for relief. Though it got the necessary funds, they were never enough to be generous to the unemployed. The extent of unemployment made it impossible to assume, as Ontarians preferred to do, that joblessness was somehow the fault of the jobless, but it was nevertheless true that the unemployed were feared as well as pitied and that the authorities oversaw the dole with a mistrustful and grudging eye.

Partial solutions were unveiled from time to time. There were airports to be built across northern Ontario, and drafts of unemployed were shipped off to the north to work on them. There were highways to be built, such as the new Highway 7 north of Lake

Ontario, and towns shipped off their contingents of the able-bodied unemployed to work on them too. Tariffs protected some of the Canadian market, and Ontario factory hands were not in as great difficulties as farmers, or workers in construction or certain primary industries such as pulp and paper. With construction running at about one-third of its level in the 1920s, the great suburban sprawl of the previous decade came to an end.

It was not all bad. Those who kept their jobs might, like teachers and civil servants, be forced to take a pay cut. Frequently, however, the pay cuts were less than the actual fall in prices that also characterized the 1930s. And, given the economic circumstances of the time, families with quite modest incomes were able to hire servants, or buy some of the new luxury items that were appearing. Certain industries, after falling to a low level of activity, revived as early as 1932 or 1933. Gold mining proved to be the great boom in northern Ontario. Gold rose in price internationally, and as it rose more mines, and more gold miners, went into production. The miners had jobs, and the mining promoters made fortunes. Bay Street, which by now was accustomed to think of itself as the capitalist centre of Canada, sported a new breed of speculator whose fortunes soared. It was the decade of E. P. Taylor, of J. P. Bickell, of "Sell 'em Ben" Smith. To commemorate the fact, a new art deco Stock Exchange building in the contemporary fluted grey style went up on Toronto's Bay Street. It was not the largest building in the city, but it was the first air-conditioned one, another sign of modern times and rising expectations.

The 1930s were not, therefore, a consistent decade. If the country doctor was taking his pay in chickens or milk, his civil servant cousin might be experimenting with hiring a maid, while his son might be signing on at one of Ontario's expanding automobile factories. Automobiles, thanks to trade agreements with the British empire, were selling as far afield as Australia and India, even if American tariffs made it difficult to sell them sixty miles away in Rochester or Toledo. And if the son were working in Windsor or Oshawa, he might well be joining a union.

Unions had existed in Ontario far back in the nineteenth century. Ontario history in the late nineteenth century is punctuated by labour disputes and disturbances. If the strikes got out of hand, the militia might be called out to assist the civil power. When a strike occurred at Stratford, and the authorities called in the soldiers, Ontarians were treated to the unusual spectacle of seeing armoured cars on streetcorners. Labour unions rose and fell. There were Knights of Labour in the late nineteenth century. They vanished and were succeeded by craft unions, variants of the American Federation of Labor (AFL). These unions tended to be socially conservative, and resistant to independent political action by or on behalf of labour.

Traditionally, periods of depression are periods of accommodation in labour-management relations. The 1930s, with their patchwork of gloom and occasional prosperity, were an exception. It is certainly true that the worst part of the Depression, between 1930 and 1933, did not see a great deal of activity. It was only when the province began to climb out of the trough, in the middle of the decade, that a change occurred.

Politically, Ontario grew all kinds of parties and movements during the 1930s. On the left there was the Communist party, which enjoyed an active and rather appealing leadership, and which had some strength in the Toronto area and among some (but not all) recent immigrants in northern Ontario. The Communist party never achieved mass appeal, despite its hope that it would speak for "the masses" or "the people." The people looked elsewhere.

They looked, for example, at a new social democratic organization that travelled under the cumbersome name of the Co-operative Commonwealth Federation, or CCF. The CCF, whose leader, James Shaver Woodsworth, was Ontario-born and Methodist-bred, achieved some modest success among urban intellectuals, whose support gave the new party more respectability than the Communists ever had. During the 1930s, however, the CCF was an exotic taste.

The real competition to the Conservative party was the Liberal party. The Farmers' movement was gradually slipping below the political water line. Farmer politicians were either retiring, or seeking alliances with the Liberals. Harry Nixon, from Brant County, a man with Conservative roots and service in the Drury cabinet, drifted towards the Liberals. So did Farquhar Oliver, once the youngest Farmer member of the Assembly. The Liberals, thoroughly drubbed by Ferguson in three elections, were for their part looking for somebody new: somebody colourful, somebody who could shake off the mossbound image of the party and give it a sense of direction. It hardly mattered which direction, as long as it was towards power.

In December 1930, the same month that saw Ferguson make way for George Henry, the Liberals chose a new leader — Mitchell F. Hepburn. "Mitch" Hepburn was the Liberal member of the federal Parliament for Elgin, the county around St Thomas along the north shore of Lake Erie. He was young, and he certainly was active. As a member of the federal liberal caucus he attracted the attention of Mackenzie King. King did not support Hepburn for the Liberal leadership, but he did remain discreetly in the background as the Liberals made their choice. King's views, then and later, were probably best summed up by a disgruntled St Thomas Liberal, who wrote to the federal leader (who was then experiencing a spell in opposition) that Hepburn was "a very foolish young man," "entirely unfitted by nature and by training for the difficult task he has undertaken .... I regard the selection as a supreme act of folly." This was the authentic voice of old Ontario, of the older generation of the Liberal party that had guided the party on a path of prohibition, economy, and political failure. Hepburn was not a prohibitionist, to put it mildly, and he did not take his cue from Ontario's rural heartland, despite the fact that he himself represented a rural constituency. Hepburn liked to cut a swath. He liked fast cars, fast music, and, some said, fast women. Most important for the Liberals, Hepburn was a fighter, with a natural gift of the gab that made him a spectacular performer on the election platform. Nor was the new leader ill-natured. Reflecting on his career, a former supporter mused: "Mitch was a sinner. But he wasn't what you'd call a bad man."

Bad man or not, Hepburn was a good organizer. When the election bells tolled for George Henry, in June 1934, Hepburn was ready with as impressive an array of candidates as the Ontario Liberals had seen since the hey-day of Oliver Mowat. There were stalwarts like Harry Nixon. There was Robert Laurier, Sir Wilfrid's nephew, to add the lustre of a great name and help carry French Ontario. There was the left-leaning labour lawyer, Arthur Roebuck; and the reform mayor of Windsor, David Croll, who had not feared to let his city pass on its bond payments rather than reduce its services to its needy citizens.

Hepburn's team had issues — familiar issues, but Hepburn gave them a new life and clothed them in earthy language. There was economy, used by every opposition party since Mackenzie's reformers to tar a sitting government, and the related issue of corruption. Where there was extravagance there must be corruption of some kind: high living by Ontario cabinet ministers at the people's expense was roundly condemned, as was the fleet of official limousines. "Toll-gating" in the Conservative government's new Liquor Control Board, the Liberals charged, collected tolls for the Tory party or the party faithful from companies wanting to place their brands on its lists. Even George Henry, the safe, honest, dull premier, was transformed by Hepburn into a caricature of a stuffed shirt, too prosperous and insulated to know or care what people were experiencing in the Depression. Then there were separate schools. Hepburn would give the Catholic schools a fair assessment and a fair share of tax money. Other politicians had promised the same thing, but Hepburn was confident that he could deliver. This was a local, even regional issue, but it would count heavily in French-speaking areas. Finally, there were Ferguson's hydro contracts. They had been signed in the days of prosperity and expansion. Now they were unnecessary, an extravagance.

Hepburn was successful. The Henry government was defeated in the election of June 1934, sixty-six Liberals to seventeen Conservatives. There were also three Progressives and one solitary UFO, who could be counted on to support the Liberals.

The Hepburn government never had a dull moment. The new premier picked a quarrel with the lieutenant-governor on grounds that William Lyon Mackenzie would have approved. The lieutenant-governor, appointed by Bennett, was of course a Conservative and symbolized the extravagant outgoing regime. His mansion, Chorley Park, maintained by Ontario taxpayers, was another useful symbol. Hepburn forthwith began to snipe away at both the office and its incumbent, and was rewarded with a political firework that sputtered on for over three years at virtually no cost to the government in terms of legislation or money.

There was also the federal government (the term dominion was gradually giving way). It was Conservative, too, and it was deeply unpopular. Hepburn blazed away at Ottawa and at R. B. Bennett, whom he dubbed ''Lord Gopher of Calgary.'' In Hepburn's view, Ottawa refused to give his province its due in terms of relief. Under the circumstances, it was easy for Ontarians to believe the worst of Bennett, whose government bore the stigma of being in office during the worst depression in the country's history.

There were the power contracts. The Hepburn government, spurred on by Attorney General Arthur Roebuck, repudiated them. Nothing else Hepburn ever did provoked so much wrath and political steam as this gesture. Very few things Hepburn ever did were as pointless, for the contracts furnished power that would soon be needed again, as the province's economy recovered from the worst of the slump and industrial production rebounded.

There were other things too. Croll introduced a minimum wage. Hepburn tried to deal with the separate school question only to find his best efforts defeated by a campaign of good, old-fashioned bigotry. He was stigmatized as a tool of the Catholics. In a by-election in East Hastings, his candidate was badly beaten. A rising Conservative star, George Drew, travelled to East Hastings, where he was reported to have appealed to the electors' most delicate feelings. The French, as Catholics, were supporting Hepburn, everyone knew. "It is not unfair," Drew stated, "to remind the French that they are a defeated race, and that their rights are rights only by tolerance by the English element who, with all respect to the minority, must be regarded as the dominant race." By the spring of 1937 Hepburn's attempt to improve Catholic schools' financial position had been stymied.

Fortunately, the government's policy in other areas was more persevering. Hepburn's most lasting contribution to his province was pasteurization. Opposed by farm groups because of the costs it would impose, pasteurization was the key to defeating bovine tuberculosis, spread through infected milk. Hepburn's judgement, that tuberculosis could be defeated, eventually proved correct, and his determination to prevent what could be prevented was a major factor in the conquest of the disease.

Hepburn was more traditional in theme, if less customary in practice, when he tackled the issue of economy. We have seen economy as a stick with which to beat incumbent governments. Hepburn used the stick on George Henry, and when he achieved office he did not desist. The government's fleet of limousines was auctioned off at Toronto's Varsity Stadium. Hepburn then proceeded to rid the province of another form of Tory waste: he fired every civil servant hired since the fall of 1933, including every game warden in the province and every bee-keeper (183 of them). Ontario House in London, the province's overseas agency, was closed.

It was only to be expected that Hepburn would quarrel with the Conservatives' national chieftain, Prime Minister Bennett. Ontario wanted more money from Ottawa for relief, and Bennett wanted if possible to give it less. There were fruitful possibilities here to condemn the hard-hearted anti-Ontario stance of the federal government, and Hepburn was not the man to let such an opportunity slip. The premier did more: he campaigned vigorously, even frantically, for the federal Liberals in by-elections and in the general election of October 1935 that turned Bennett out of office and put Mackenzie King back in.

Hepburn's feelings towards his old leader were affectionate. They were also almost feudal. He had done his lord some service, and it was time for Mackenzie King to reciprocate. He might, for example, appoint a Hepburn ally, just elected a federal MP, to the cabinet. King did not. Instead, he drew a sharp line between the provincial and federal spheres and let Hepburn know that his advice on federal issues was unnecessary. The Ontario premier, in turn, was wounded. Similar incidents followed. Most were trivial or accidental; others showed that Ottawa's basic position on expenditure and on subsidies to the provinces had not altered very much from Bennett's time. Hepburn began to vocalize his discontent. Soon the sounds out of Queen's Park took a shrill, sharp note. King's Ontario ally was a friend no longer. "I am a Reformer," Hepburn told an audience in June 1937. "But I am not a Mackenzie King Liberal any longer. I will tell the world that, and I hope he hears me."

There were two main theatres of war between the King Liberals and the Hepburn clan. The first was over hydro-electricity and related problems. The hydro contracts, it turned out, were valid after all. The courts so ruled. Ontario now had surplus power. To get rid of it, Hepburn wanted to export it to the United States. But the American government, and the government in Ottawa too, wanted to develop the St Lawrence River for both electricity and navigation—the St Lawrence Seaway project, as it became. Hepburn demanded a permit to export power — a permit that only Ottawa, with control over exports, could give. He enlisted the support of an unlikely ally, Maurice Duplessis, the former Conservative leader in Quebec, who had formed a Tory-Nationalist alliance and taken power in 1936 from the provincial Liberals. Mitch and Maurice soon discovered that they agreed on more than power and the St Lawrence; they agreed on relations with Ottawa (bad) and in their personal lifestyles (if possible worse). Summits between the two leaders were among the most convivial ever known, and the distillers of Ontario and Quebec must have derived a considerable profit from the occasions.

The Hepburn-Duplessis alliance was bothersome for King, and the power contracts threatened to be a nearly perpetual issue. But in the long run its political significance was less than that of another event that seemed more limited in time and space. In 1937 there was a strike in the General Motors factory at Oshawa. The strikers belonged, not to a limited craft union, but to the new Congress of Industrial Organizations, or CIO, an industrial union movement based in the United States, which drew its strength from its willingness to organize everybody in a company, rather than sticking to traditional craft-based divisions.

The CIO's principal opponents were the automobile companies. Its confrontations with Ford and General Motors on the south side of the Great Lakes were sensational. Canadian industrialists took note. An infestation of the CIO would deprive them of their ability to run their factories, mills, or mines as they pleased. The CIO was communist-infiltrated, they charged. The accusation was true, but only partially true. What was really at stake was the ability of workers in Ontario industries to organize a union of their own, and to bargain with management.

Those who believed that the Red tide was lapping Lake Ontario's shores had the ear of the premier. One of Hepburn's intimates was George McCullagh, the publisher of the *Globe and Mail*, a promoter of strong causes and a believer in leadership with a capital L. Others included Bay Street promoters of greater or lesser notoriety, who had a strong interest in keeping unions out of the northern Ontario mines. These men helped to persuade Hepburn, but it must be admitted that the premier did not need much persuading. His perspective on the world was that of small-town Ontario, deeply traditional and mistrustful of novel approaches and, especially, strange and foreign institutions. When it was learned that the CIO had taken root in Oshawa, Hepburn immediately assumed the worst.

By April 1937 it was known that a confrontation was building. General Motors declined to have anything to do with any CIO members; it would negotiate only with its in-house, company union. On April 8 a strike began, and the heavens descended. Hepburn, vacationing in Florida, returned to Queen's Park. He was briefed on the situation, and concluded that the strike would lead to violence and illegality, as had occasionally happened in the United States. He wired the justice minister in Ottawa to ask for reinforcements from the Royal Canadian Mounted Police. The police were quartered in Toronto's University Avenue armouries pending developments, and the first development was not long in coming. The premier issued a statement calling for a "showdown" with the CIO.

The showdown was postponed for several days, but soon Hepburn grew agitated once more. He demanded more police (there had been no need to commit the first batch) from Ottawa. Ottawa declined to send any more. Hepburn thereupon sent back the first batch, which was just as well since there was no call on their services. Instead, he recruited special constables among university students and war veterans: "Hepburn's Hussars" or, more simply, the "Sons of Mitch." They were not needed either, but the appearance of action had a temporarily calming effect on the premier and his supporters. The strike went on; there was no violence, and eventually a settlement was reached. The settlement was in fact between General Motors and the United Auto Workers Union, a part of the CIO. The actual names of the union signatory, CIO or UAW, were omitted, allowing the premier to pretend that it was really a pact between General Motors and its own employees. The subterfuge achieved, the premier proclaimed victory.

This farcical episode was the prelude to two other events. Hepburn's bitterness towards the federal government increased. His estrangement from King and, equally important, from King liberalism also grew. Liberalism, Ontario-style, would be more rural, more conservative, and less cautious than its federal variant. This tendency became more pronounced with the departure of Hepburn's two left-leaning ministers, Arthur Roebuck and David Croll, from his cabinet. Both eventually found solace in Ottawa, where their talents received appreciation and a modest reward. Their talents would have been better displayed at the provincial level, however, for both men took with them organizational ability as well as an appeal to specific constituencies. Ontario liberalism was narrowed by the conjunction of events around Hepburn.

In the short term this did not matter. As Hepburn's biographer, Neil McKenty, concludes, the premier undoubtedly had the support of most of the province. He initially considered forming a coalition with the provincial Conservatives, a union government to confront the Reds, but although that project commended itself to a few Conservatives, such as the Guelph lawyer George Drew, it did not win the approval of the Tory leader, Earl Rowe. Hepburn therefore called a provincial election instead, in October 1937. It was another triumph. The Liberals lost a few seats but actually increased their percentage of the popular vote. Hepburn's political perception seemed to be confirmed.

In the long run, however, it was Mackenzie King who controlled the rules of the political game — and of federal-provincial relations. It was King who acted, and Hepburn who reacted. Again and again Hepburn found himself rushing onto ground not of his own choosing. Increasingly he found himself speaking out of turn, becoming more and more isolated in the face of Canadian public opinion. A case in point was the federally appointed Royal Commission on Dominion-Provincial Relations, usually known as the Rowell-Sirois Commission from its two chairmen.

The Royal Commission was appointed in the face of the collapsing finances of the three Prairie provinces. None could stand without federal aid, which was always forthcoming because the credit of Canada as a whole would suffer if one or another of the provinces went bankrupt. The Royal Commission was told to go away and examine the problem, to listen to the opinions of Canadians, and in particular to collect the viewpoints of the various provincial governments. It perambulated across Canada in search of enlightenment, and it found it, in the shape of briefs from groups ranging from the Chamber of Commerce to the Canadian Communist Party.

Six provinces co-operated with the commission. Three — Alberta, Quebec, and Ontario — did not. (It must not be forgotten that there were only nine provinces in 1937.) Two of the six consenting provinces, British Columbia and New Brunswick, proved difficult in the kinds of arguments they made. But Ontario was almost in a class by itself. When the commissioners arrived in Toronto, the premier set aside the legislative building for their hearings. He appeared before them himself; he complimented Newton Rowell; and then he began his argument. It proved to be a shrill concoction of misstatements and half-truths, founded on a fixed conviction that Ontario was being put upon by the federal government and by improvident provinces, especially in the west. It was by any standards a poor performance, but its effect was augmented by a drunken party Hepburn gave for the commissioners to show that there were no hard feelings. The public relations effect was little short of disastrous. The commissioners, it goes without saying, were embarrassed and unimpressed. So was the press, which had a field day with Hepburn's ungenerous attitudes to the impoverished western provinces.

What Hepburn failed to sense — and along with Hepburn there were the members of his cabinet and his senior advisers drawn from Ontario's somewhat rudimentary civil service — was that opinion in Canada was shifting under the stress of the Depression. The Depression had shown that the provinces had suffered each in its constitutionally watertight compartment. Oliver Mowat, when he devised the compact theory, or Howard Ferguson when he preached it, or, especially, Hepburn when he used provincial rights as a bludgeon against Mackenzie King, had not envisaged the universal misery that economic chaos had brought about. The movement in Canadian opinion was towards the centre. Against that movement Hepburn's defence of provincial autonomy as the bulwark of Canadian democracy rang hollow. It would soon ring hollower still.

It is not to be thought that Ontarians dwelt on the intricacies of dominion-provincial relations or shaped their political preferences on the basis of some abstract theory. It is most probable that what the province's citizens wanted or expected was that their governments resolve their differences and somehow get on with the job. The important issue of the decade was the economy; the preferred solution of Ontarians, as we have seen, was essentially conservative, whether it was Bennett, King, or Hepburn. There were signs that this was changing, but the change had not as yet achieved any kind of official political recognition.

Life in the Depression was punctuated by the intrusion of extraneous events. These were brought to Ontarians through the traditional form of the newspaper, and if reading habits and distribution are any guide, there was a tendency to the warm-hearted sensationalism practised by Toronto's and the province's largest newspaper, *The Toronto Star*. There were other means. There was radio, both private and public. Radio brought news as well as plays, music, and comedy. Much of the last three categories came direct from the United States, either on Canadian stations or American ones. There were movies, and movie houses to see them in. The movies themselves might be educational or escapist, but with them came newsreels, making foreign events truly vivid in a way that the newspapers could not quite manage.

Over their radios Ontarians, like other Canadians, learned that their own province was the host of a family of quintuplets — near North Bay. The Dionne Quintuplets eventually became wards of the provincial government in another of Hepburn's spectacular gestures, and their residence a place of pilgrimage for the curious. The story of the Dionnes was essentially domestic and unthreatening. It was a great event, but it harmed nobody in particular outside the family. Another great event, in the year 1936, was more ambiguous.

In the fall of 1936 Ontarians learned that King Edward VIII had formed a connection with an American divorcée. Divorce, in 1936, was a relatively rare event. In Ontario, in 1936, there were 507 divorces for a population of 3.7 million; churches frowned on the practice where they did not absolutely prohibit it. Divorce was held to be a kind of social stigma, evidence of a moral failing, and for the monarch to be involved in the fringes of a divorce (his fiancée was in the throes of getting a divorce from her husband) was both fascinating and at the same time contrary to the established moral tone of the province. When the King abdicated the throne rather than give up "the woman I love," he announced the fact to his empire, including Ontario, on the radio. Ontarians were thrilled at the novelty; they gave Edward their sympathy, but not their support.

Fortunately his successor was made of sterner stuff. King George VI and his wife Queen Elizabeth were, it seemed, a stable couple with two attractive daughters. The King and Queen visited Ontario in the spring of 1939, and were rewarded by the bestowal of the Queen's name on Ontario's first four-lane road, the Queen Elizabeth Way, from Toronto to Niagara. People flocked in droves to see their sovereign, the first reigning British monarch to touch Canadian shores. Canada's and Ontario's British loyalty and British identity were reaffirmed. And beside the King and Queen, Mackenzie King, escorting them as prime minister, beamed.

Within three months of the royal visit, Canada's British identity was tested again. On September 1, 1939, the German dictator Adolf Hitler sent his army across the frontier of Poland. Great Britain and France, which had guaranteed the Polish border, declared war on Germany on September 3. The Canadian Parliament was called into session to pass a resolution approving a declaration of war on Germany by Canada; and on September 10 it took effect. Canada, and Ontario, were at war. The whole agenda of provincial politics suddenly was turned upside down.

The miracles of the age: electric appliances — from a circular saw to a washing machine — in a Hydro travelling display, circa 1914.

A festival of lights as hydro-electric transmission comes to Berlin (Kitchener), Ontario, 1910.

The martial spirit: recruiting office in Acton, outside Toronto, 1916.

The United Farmers come to town: satirical placard placed on the doors of the legislature, the day after the 1919 election.

Prohibition in action: a raid on a "blind pig" in a northern Ontario mining town, 1920s.

Archives of Ontario, S-15000

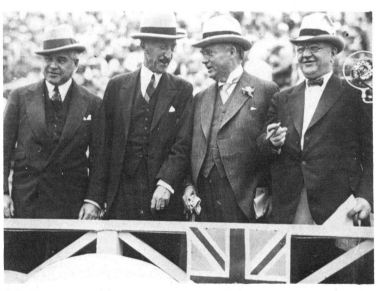

R.B. Bennett (second from right), Howard Ferguson (right), and other dignitaries, late 1920s.

Archives of Ontario, S-797

Mitchell Hepburn enjoying a good time.   Archives of Ontario, S-304

The new consumerism: electric ranges in 1944 in a Hydro Shop in London, Ontario.

Royalty and politics: Premier Leslie Frost and Queen Elizabeth II open a power station on the St. Lawrence, 1959.

Courtesy Ontario Hydro

A nuclear Ontario: Premier William G. Davis at the Darlington nuclear plant, 1984.

The Search for Security

7 The province that went to war in 1939 had
changed drastically from the province that went
into World War I. The Great War had been
greeted with anticipation and excitement as a
novel adventure. In 1939 there were too many
people who knew what war was for them to be
excited. There was no panic, but there were few
of the effusions of the earlier generation.

The structure of the province had changed along with its mood.
In 1914 the only reliable way to get from place to place in Ontario
was by train. Road journeys were lengthy and sometimes, de-
pending on the direction one took or the weather one braved,
actually risky. In 1939 the road system had been greatly extended,
and it would grow still more as planners in the provincial Department of Highways contemplated the possibility of a four-lane
super-highway across the length of the province. By 1943 paved
roads in Ontario totalled over 4000 miles, leaving, however, another 68,000 miles covered in gravel or sporting "other surfaces."

Travelling the roads in 1939 were 704,000 motor vehicles,
including trucks and buses. That year, 682 people were killed on
Ontario highways in accidents. Roads did not extend everywhere,
but where they did not it was still possible to take ferries to
destinations where it was difficult to transport a car. Boats plied
regular routes between Toronto and Niagara-on-the-Lake, or between Toronto and Queenston. Other ferries loaded cars in Sault
Ste Marie and took them (and their riders) over to Port Arthur and

Fort William, the twin grain ports at the head of the lakes. While it was possible to get to those cities by land, through the province, it was difficult and not especially recommended.

Travellers were more likely than not to live in cities. We have already noted Ontarians' tendency to dwell in cities or towns in increasing numbers. By the 1940s the cities were getting bigger, and almost 47 percent of Ontarians lived in cities boasting over 100,000 people, while another 11.5 percent lived in cities between 30,000 and 100,000. How did they live, and in what? To answer the last question first, the 1941 census still indicates an overwhelming majority (two-thirds) of Ontarians lived in single houses. But in contrast to previous decades, apartments were gaining in favour (15 percent). That was appropriate, because Ontarians were restless: almost 30 percent had moved since 1939. In cities, 90 percent of the people had indoor flush toilets; but in the countryside the percentage was almost reversed: 87 percent still trekked to an outdoor privy. At the same time, 62 percent of farm households relied on kerosene lamps, while in cities electric lighting was virtually universal.

In 1941 there were roughly 1.2 million men over fourteen at work, including 120,000 on active service, and 315,000 working women, with about 500 on active service. Twenty-one percent of working men were listed in agriculture, and almost exactly the same number in manufacturing. The rest were divided among trade and service, construction, and transport. Women, not surprisingly, were under-represented in agriculture (only 5000), while 17 percent were engaged in manufacturing, 10 percent in trade, 23 percent in clerical occupations, and 43 percent in service.

The numbers and percentages would change over the next few years. Overall, people were moving to Ontario. War cut off overseas immigration, but then immigration had been almost negligible since the beginning of the Depression in 1929. It was migration from other provinces and from the countryside that swelled the cities. At the same time, service in the army and jobs in new war industries virtually eliminated unemployment.

By and large, as one might expect, living standards improved during the war. With more people at work, and with wage rates rising, there was more money to go around. The government, however, took its bite, since the war had to be paid for and the government decided that it would be paid for, as much as possible, out of taxation.

Which government? The answer is the government of Canada, and thereby hangs a tale. As we have seen for the period 1914-18, in time of war the federal government assumes as much power as it wishes for the purpose of prosecuting the war. Sir Robert Borden's government left behind a statute, the War Measures Act, which allowed the federal cabinet to govern, as long as the state of war existed, by passing cabinet orders, called orders-in-council, which had the same effect as laws passed by Parliament. The cabinet of Mackenzie King, in September 1939, found that it had all the authority it wanted, or needed, to prosecute the conflict.

Or did it? Law rests on the consent of public opinion. It is always possible to pass a law on one subject or another, but unless it enjoys popular support it remains a dead letter or, like prohibition, a subject of conflict and evasion. The King government needed, and it knew that it needed, the support of public opinion. That support was registered in two ways. It was reflected in the government's parliamentary majority, which was substantial, though based on an election back in 1935. And it was registered in the official, vocal support that the King government received from prominent, and not-so-prominent, Canadians.

There were very few Canadians who were opposed to the war: some pro-German, Nazi sympathizers and the Communist Party of Canada, whose patron, the Soviet Union, had decided to stay out of the war and to divide up eastern Europe with Germany. Some French Canadians were unhappy, but the King government had succeeded in muting their opposition by promising not to impose conscription on the model of the First World War. Instead, the government (and the Conservative opposition too) promised that there would be no conscription for overseas service, and that meant that any Canadian soldiers who crossed the Atlantic to fight would be volunteers.

Canada set about raising an army, a navy, and, for the first time at the beginning of a war, an air force. The federal government also started to organize the Canadian economy to produce supplies that Canada and its allies might need. At first there was some dispute, and even doubt, as to what Canada could or should produce, which meant that the war effort in the winter of 1939-40 was not as vigorous as some thought it should have been. Among those who thought that the war was not being run as it should was the premier of Ontario, Mitchell Hepburn.

Hepburn had seemed curiously adrift in 1939, a politician in search of an issue or, in Hepburn's case, a cause. At the beginning of 1940 he thought he had found it. The King government was slacking off. Mackenzie King, that peaceful man, had no idea how to mobilize Canada's resources for war. Hepburn started to talk to people about the inadequacies of the government of Canada. And in January 1940 he got together with the leader of the opposition in the legislature, George Drew, to pass a resolution condemning Ottawa's war effort.

It was considered, at the time, an incredible thing to do. The spectacle of a Liberal provincial government combining with its hereditary enemies, the Conservatives, to abuse the national Liberal government was seen as a direct assault on the credibility of the latter government. Some provincial Liberals voted against their leader's motion, while others took refuge behind the curtains of the legislative chamber. But the resolution passed nevertheless. What would Mackenzie King do now?

King understood that he could not let this challenge go unanswered. The more he thought about it, the more fortunate the challenge seemed to be. The prime minister knew that he needed to renew his mandate, but he knew too that the electorate frowned on politics in wartime. But if the challenge came from somebody else, then it became necessary to respond, and to let the other fellow take the blame for playing politics. King suddenly dissolved the federal Parliament on the day it convened in January 1940 and called a general election for the end of March. Before he sent his MPs into battle, King called them together for instruction. Any Liberal who ran in the approaching election would be a Mackenzie King Liberal and nothing else, he told them. Anyone who had doubts about his leader should leave the room, now. Nobody left.

King won the general election. He won overwhelmingly, in fact, and decimated the opposition. He made his opponents, including Hepburn, look ridiculous. He firmed up his own party support, and demonstrated to Ontario Liberals that their provincial leader had very short political coat-tails. And he made certain that Ottawa would face no serious and convincing opposition from the province of Ontario for the duration of the war.

The Second World War, then, was a period in which the federal government had undoubted legal dominance in the Canadian Constitution. But it had more than that: it held the political initiative as well, through the defeat of Hepburn and the demolition of the federal opposition. That Ottawa would need that political initiative was demonstrated during the rest of 1940.

1940 was a disastrous year, militarily, for the allies. In the spring, Hitler's armies conquered Western Europe, including France. In the summer and fall his air force bombarded Great Britain. His navy was becoming continually stronger, and German submarines were sending a large number of ships to the bottom of the Atlantic. Canada was now the number two nation on the allied side (the Russians and the Americans were abstaining from the war), behind Great Britain itself. The British needed all the guns and ammunition that Canada could make and ship, and more besides. The British also could not pay for what they wished to buy.

This circumstance created a crisis in Canadian finance in the summer and fall of 1940. The federal government had to find the money to buy raw materials for conversion to war supplies in factories that in many cases had been unplanned and even undreamt-of in the fall of 1939. Everything had to be built or converted, and to pay for it the government had to find money. Taxes rose, but it was obvious that they could only go up so far before they ran into the competing taxing jurisdictions of the provinces. Moreover, some provinces were still, in the summer of 1940, on the verge of financial collapse: British Columbia, Alberta, Saskatchewan, Manitoba, and New Brunswick all faced serious difficulties. And if New Brunswick failed to meet interest payments on its debt, it was likely that Nova Scotia would default as well. Like a row of dominoes, the finances of Canada's provinces, and of the dominion itself, were inextricably linked. It did not take a great deal of imagination to foresee a situation in which the federal government itself would have difficulties borrowing money.

Mackenzie King reluctantly decided to act. He called a dominion-provincial conference for Ottawa in January 1941 to consider the proposals for reform of the federal-provincial system made by the Rowell-Sirois commission, which had finally reported in May 1940. The commission envisaged the restructuring of the division of powers between the dominion and the provinces. The commission preferred a plan (Plan I) whereby the federal government took over responsibility for unemployment insurance and all provincial debts, and in return received all the proceeds from income, corporation, and succession taxes. For the poorer provinces there would be "national adjustment grants" to bring the level of services provided by local governments up to a national Canadian average. The commissioners knew that some provinces, particularly Ontario, would not like what they had to recommend, and in case the federal government could not secure agreement, they suggested a milder alternative whereby the federal government would simply take over responsibility for the unemployed, and pay for it out of increased taxes (many of them naturally from Ontario).

The commissioners were not mistaken. Mitchell Hepburn and his advisers believed that Ontario could pay its own way — with a little help from Ottawa, as during the 1930s — and should not be expected to contribute to the solution of other people's misfortunes. When the conference convened, Hepburn attended in full patriotic garb. He would not agree to revamp the Constitution. It was scandalous, he alleged, that the federal government was attempting to foist a constitutional revolution off on the country in the midst of the greatest war Canada had ever known. The connection between the conference and the war Hepburn preferred to ignore. In a series of violent speeches Ontario's premier denounced Mackenzie King. What he wanted, Hepburn proclaimed, was a conference on how the provinces could aid in the war effort.

It was a shabby, shallow, and demagogic performance, and it delivered Hepburn into the hands of Mackenzie King. For the federal government had very precise ideas on what the provinces could do to help the war effort, as the federal minister of finance, J. L. Ilsley, explained to the assembled premiers. There was no escaping the fact that the federal government had to find more money somewhere. If there could be no agreement with the provinces, then Ottawa would proceed on its own, as it had the right to do. It would reduce its contributions to the provinces' deficits, and it would go ahead and raise as much money as it needed through taxation, regardless of whether the provinces were attempting to tax the same money. Let the provinces explain to their citizens why this was so.

Naturally this statement provoked further rage from Ontario's representatives. Hepburn jumped up to exclaim that the Rowell-Sirois report was "the product of the minds of a few college professors and a Winnipeg newspaperman [one commissioner, Newton Rowell, having died in the interim], who has had his knife into Ontario ever since he was able to write newspaper articles." Supporters of Rowell-Sirois were "wreckers of Confederation." King adjourned the conference, and Ilsley and his officials began planning a new federal budget that would reform the tax system and revamp the distribution of revenue among the dominion and the provinces.

When the budget came down, at the end of April 1941, it

offered the various provinces the same revenue they had had in 1940. In return, the provinces were to concede to Ottawa all tax powers over income, corporation, and succession taxes. All the provinces promptly agreed, except, of course, Ontario. It took Hepburn the best part of a year to concede defeat and announce that he would, after all, accept Ottawa's terms. A Wartime Tax Agreement was finally concluded and ratified by the provincial legislature in the spring of 1942. For the first time Ontario's taxation and revenue priorities were integrated into those of the Canadian nation as a whole.

Why had Hepburn conceded? He had little choice. Canadians, including Canadians resident in Ontario, placed their national obligations first, in time of war. Hepburn's own arguments attacking King over the war effort said it all: nothing should be allowed to interfere with the efficient prosecution of the war, and that included the priorities or sensitivities of provincial governments. Hepburn did not help his case by his oafish and offensive behaviour at the Ottawa conference, which caused one observer to call the dominion-provincial gathering ''the god damnedest exhibition and circus you ever saw.'' For Hepburn a dominion-provincial conference was a forum for confrontation, for carrying on his war of words with the federal government or, as many people were beginning to suspect, simply for carrying on. Newspapers back in Toronto — indeed, newspapers around the province — did not approve of the manner in which the premier had purported to represent his province. Hepburn's buffoonery marked a further stage in the decline of the provincial Liberal party, for it would take a great deal of time for Ontarians to forget, or forgive, the premier's increasingly erratic behaviour.

The dominion-provincial conference therefore set the stage for relations between Ontario and the federal government for the duration of the war, just as Hepburn's public behaviour had helped to tilt the political balance, finally, in favour of Mackenzie King and the Ottawa government. Ottawa's spending soared, as the federal government put billions into defence and defence production.

A great deal of the money was spent in Ontario. There are two salient facts to remember about the shape of war production in Canada. First, there was very considerable new investment in plants, machinery, and other equipment — capital goods. Second, the investment tended to go where there was already an established industrial strength or tendency. For example, Canada's largest single war industry, producing the country's most significant economic contribution to the allied war effort, was automobile products. Factories in Oshawa, Windsor, and Oakville turned out first thousands, and then hundreds of thousands of vehicles, trucks, cars, and other wheeled products for Canada's army, as well as those of Canada's other allies, Britain, the United States (since December 1941), and the Soviet Union (which, having been attacked by Hitler in June 1941, was no longer neutral). Mills at Sault Ste Marie and Hamilton made steel for automobile production, and also for ships, guns, shells, and aircraft. The federal government gave the steel companies money for extensions to their plants, extensions which would still be there when the war was over. More federal funds, and, just as important, permission to use scarce wartime goods, went into establishing a new iron ore mine at Steep Rock in northwestern Ontario. The existing mines in northern Ontario went into full production: nickel at Sudbury was especially desirable, although the industry was handicapped by a growing shortage of miners as the war went on.

In other areas Ontario acquired new technology. The province was already the centre of Canada's rubber industry, but the production of rubber was threatened by the Japanese conquest of the rubber-producing East Indies in 1942. To substitute, the Canadian government established a crown corporation, Polymer, at Sarnia, the most concentrated chemical-producing area in the country. Polymer was to make artificial rubber and within a year it was operating successfully. Another crown corporation, Research Enterprises Limited, was more specialized, working in high technology such as optics and radar.

Aircraft production had been at a low ebb in prewar Canada. It was necessary in 1940 to design and construct entire assembly lines for aircraft production. Frames only were built in Canada; engines were imported from outside. A large variety of firms participated in building aircraft, from Fort William to Fort Erie, but the best known was probably the National Steel Car Company in Malton, near Toronto's principal airport. When labour disputes and uncertain management threatened to paralyze National Steel Car, the federal minister of munitions and supply, C. D. Howe, sent in a controller appointed by himself to take over the enterprise. Renamed Victory Aircraft, the Malton plant operated as a crown company producing Lancaster bombers for the Royal Canadian Air Force and the Royal Air Force.

It was fortunate that central Canada, and especially Ontario, had a surplus of electricity when the war began, but even the surplus did not last long. The central government instituted power control, limiting the amount of power available for non-essential purposes, and banning certain uses of electricity (for electric space heaters, for example) altogether. There followed gas rationing, which put the brakes on the fleets of private automobiles that cruised the province's improved highways. Transportation took a step backwards, as railways and buses took up the slack. Ontario Hydro gave consideration to supplementing its power supply by resorting to thermal power stations, burning coal. But even coal was scarce, and in the middle of the war, in 1943, there was nearly a crisis in supply. The problems of dependence on a foreign source of energy, in this case the United States, were underlined, and thoughtful Ontarians took note. It goes without saying that certain programs designed to extend electricity into rural Ontario ground to a halt; and only the most vital repairs were made to facilities designed to serve the civilian public.

Shortages affected everybody. Men were told that they would have to get by with fewer suits of clothes, and those suits were to be made according to strict federal specifications. For example, there would be no cuffs on pants, or flaps for covering pockets. The cloth saved went to the armed services. At Christmas 1943 the manager of Simpson's, one of Toronto's two largest department stores, announced that his store would not keep extended hours for the season. For one thing, the manager admitted, "there is not sufficient merchandise to permit it." Eaton's, Simpson's great rival, had found that it could not get its usual supplies of imported clothes, and so it was having its Hamilton factory make them. Unfortunately, the production line at Christmas was turning out men's underwear, creating a shortage for children which an official observer labelled "severe." There were no pyjamas at all, and for Christmas Eaton's had no more than a single day's supply of men's shirts.

The vagaries of clothing purchases were nothing compared to the ins and outs of gasoline rationing. Gas rationing was administered from Toronto, by a crusty executive from a gas company, George Cottrelle. Cottrelle took his duties very seriously, and he made sure that the police took them seriously too. Gas was doled out in small quantities according to how important someone might be to the war effort, and strictly for vocational or professional purposes. Informers set to work, and cars that seemed to cruise too frequently along city streets could be stopped and their occupants hauled in for questioning to the nearest police station.

Complaints were surprisingly few, but that is not to say that there were none, or that the rationing system worked perfectly. One Liberal politician from Wentworth County complained that in 1944 "there are four different prices on every variety of fruit which our fruit farmers sell." A farmer had to turn into the rationing authority (the Wartime Prices and Trade Board) a bill of sale for every basket of fruit he sold. But it could be worse. There was sugar rationing, and Canadians were being urged to conserve. In practice, in some restaurants, this meant that "It is illegal to shake sugar on your own porridge." If a farmer had to use his truck (which had specially coloured gas) for his business, the gas controllers frowned on his wife riding with him. That extreme position was modified, but it was only one of many.

To create war industry was one thing, and to regulate it another.

Despite imperfections, capital flowed and scarce goods were, on the whole, conserved. The government's labour policy was considerably more controversial. Labour policy falls into two jurisdictions, with the federal government controlling such industries as railways and shipping, and the province all the rest. In time of war, with war production dominating the scene, federal jurisdiction was extended. It was Ottawa, not Queen's Park, that would regulate labour during the war.

Ottawa's touch in dealing with labour was somewhat uncertain. The government was anxious to secure a steady labour supply, but it was unable to co-ordinate the demands of the armed forces for manpower (and womanpower) with those of industries such as logging and mining. Too many skilled workers went into the army, in part because the army offered better working and living conditions than some of the jobs they left. Nor was this war free of labour troubles: strikes at Kirkland Lake, in Hamilton, and in St Catharines punctuated Ontario's production history. It is true that Ottawa's labour regulations showed a consistent tendency towards the recognition of union rights, culminating in an order-in-council in 1944 that established compulsory collective bargaining and compulsory arbitration. The provincial government made its own labour legislation conform to the model established by the federal government, thus ensuring universal coverage for labour. Liberal politicians appreciated it: as one of them remarked, the King government's position "has helped our position with labour."

It is also true, however, that others felt differently. Certain sectors of the trade union movement thought the King government had moved too slowly and that its industrial policy was too favourable to management. This sentiment encouraged socialists and trade unionists to flock together, a tendency which became an important factor in the politics of the province during 1942 and 1943. The CCF was the natural receptacle for this surge of union feeling, although it is true that the CCF's totalitarian rival, the Communist Party, had considerable influence over certain unions such as the United Electrical Workers or the Canadian Seamen's Union on the Great Lakes.

The first sign that the CCF was having an impact on Ontario politics came in a federal by-election in February 1942, in the suburban Toronto riding of York South. There the national Conservative leader, Arthur Meighen, a former prime minister who had once represented a constituency in Manitoba, was trying to enter Parliament and at the same time promote the cause of conscription for overseas military service. Mackenzie King dreaded Meighen's reappearance, both for its symbolism and for the former prime minister's skill in debate. Liberal organizers were more practical than their leader. While King sat in Ottawa and quaked, the Liberals decided to enter no candidate in opposition to Meighen but to donate money to the CCF instead. To most people's surprise, the CCF beat Meighen, who disappeared from Canadian politics as a consequence.

King may later have wondered whether, in defeating his immediate and pressing enemy, he had not created an equally formidable force in time for the next federal election. The public opinion polls (first taken in Canada in the fall of 1941) began to show that the CCF was rising in favour with the voters. It was rising just in time for Ontario's next provincial election.

By the time of the election the premier and Liberal leader was no longer Mitchell Hepburn. Mitch had suddenly resigned in October 1942 as premier, although he remained as provincial treasurer in the cabinet of his successor, the former attorney general, Gordon Conant. Hepburn carried on as usual over the next six months, repeating his attacks on the Ottawa government, which he now customarily compared to the Nazis. When the former premier's language became too much even for his hand-picked successor, Conant dismissed him at the beginning of March 1943.

Conant had almost no alternative. His political position, and that of the provincial Liberals, was desperate. He needed cooperation from Ottawa. By 1943 the federal government's impact on all aspects of Ontario life was so pervasive that provincial politics, except for personalities, were becoming a pale reflection of the main events in Ottawa. Conant believed he had to have concessions from the federal government, and one of the concessions he sought was on the control of liquor sales, restricted during wartime as a rationing measure. Mackenzie King met Conant's delegation, and recorded his impressions on January 28, 1943: "As I looked at the faces of the men from Ontario ... it made me sad to see the change that had taken place in the countenance of every one of them. Every man of them looked harassed and I must confess that they looked like a bad lot. It made me sad to think that a province like Ontario could be governed by such men. Conant quite the best of the lot though quite reactionary." King was unyielding in his opposition to the Ontario government's requests for an easing of liquor and beer regulations, and in this stand he was truer to the Ontario Liberal faith than the hapless Conant and his associates.

Conant had to face opposition from within his party as well. Harry Nixon, the veteran of both the Drury and Hepburn cabinets, refused to accept Conant as leader. A convention was called, at which Nixon prevailed over Conant, and Nixon became premier in April 1943. He was far less tainted with the Hepburn miasma than his predecessor; he got on better with the federal Liberals and had openly preferred Mackenzie King to Hepburn on several occasions. This said much for Nixon's good sense and good taste, but unfortunately these qualities were combined with a proverbially colourless personality. He had to face an election. Hepburn had prolonged the life of the legislature, which should have expired in 1942, but by 1943 there was no way to avoid going to the polls. Election day was set for August 4, 1943.

Three main parties contested the election. The Liberals we have already met. The Conservatives fielded a full slate of candidates under their leader, George A. Drew of Guelph. Drew was a lawyer, soldier, and publicist. He had had a distinguished record as an officer in the First World War (hence the "Colonel Drew" that he was often called). He had been Ontario securities commissioner from 1929 to 1934, and had made a name for himself as a writer of magazine articles that alternately denounced munitions manufacturers as the roots of war and called for increased British-style patriotism. The contradictory quality of Drew's writing did not bother him much, although it did offend some Conservatives including Prime Minister R. B. Bennett. (Bennett later forgave Drew.) Like Hepburn, Drew practised extreme language, in public and in private. The two men had flirted with one another in contemplation of a Liberal-Conservative coalition, but their negotiations had come to nothing. Drew finally became Conservative leader in 1939, and used his platform to fight a war on two very different fronts: against the provincial Liberals under Hepburn, on the one hand, and against the federal government under Mackenzie King on the other.

Drew's assaults on Hepburn were the more successful of the two campaigns. He was even able to transfer his repertoire of Hepburn stories to Nixon, who strangely enough decided that he had no choice but to run on the "colourful" record of his predecessor. Drew had his ammunition ready, both of the negative and the positive variety. The negative kind included attacks on Hepburn's extravagance and his well-known patronage habits. The positive included a twenty-two point program unveiled with great fanfare on July 8, 1943. Drew promised reforms in health, lands and forests, prisons, and liquor control, among other things. He was confident of success, as indeed he should have been, given the Liberals' record and the state of the party in the public opinion polls. There was, however, one thing that the polls showed that came as a surprise. The CCF was also in contention.

The CCF party's success during the war has often been a subject for learned comment. Two features of CCF success should be noted. First, its popularity peaked, according to the polls, in September 1943, a month after the Ontario election. Thereafter it slowly declined, while the two old parties gradually re-established their political positions. Second, voters who preferred the CCF did so for a variety of reasons. Some were looking for the kind of security they believed they had not found, and could not hope to find, under capitalism. Others were looking for change, and did not think that Drew was the man to bring it about.

When election results came in, the Liberals had dropped from sixty-three seats to fifteen. The Conservatives had gained, but only to thirty-eight seats. And the CCF, under their scholarly leader Edward Jolliffe, had taken thirty-four. Nixon resigned, and George Drew was sworn in as Ontario's fourteenth premier.

Drew's first government was one of the most active in Ontario history. The new premier and his associates were aware that the public mood demanded action, but action of a certain kind. It was well known that Ontarians were affected by an international mood in favour of the rationalization of the economic system. Thus the Conservatives promised ''planning,'' the magic political word of the mid-1940s. It was unfortunate that, for the time being, all planning was in the hands of the federal government in Ottawa, and the province, with its limited resources based on its 1940 revenue, was in no position to offer industry the same kinds of incentives as the Ottawa government.

This fact deserves to be underlined. The economic role of the provincial government was secondary in respect of most of Ontario's economy, not just during the Second World War but for some years thereafter. In discussing the policies and principles of the government of Ontario we are dealing with a secondary actor with restricted responsibilities. Drew was conscious of what was to him a problem, and the ideology of his government, an ideology that he lost no opportunity to promote, reflected a desire to recapture a lost initiative from the federal government and to place it back where it belonged, in Queen's Park.

Drew's chosen instrument was confrontation. He was in this respect similar to Hepburn, although, unlike his Liberal predecessor, Drew did not rule out co-operation over minor programs. Confrontation, it must not be forgotten, was to be applied against a Liberal administration in Ottawa. Drew was a profoundly partisan man, who deeply distrusted Mackenzie King and his ilk, and was ready at all times to suspect the worst of the Liberals. He suspected the worst of other people too. One of the premier's first acts on taking office was to re-establish a special branch of the Ontario Provincial Police (Ontario had since 1909 its own force of gendarmerie) whose mandate it was to search out and identify communists, or, better yet, people with communist leanings.

It was certainly not hard to find a communist in Ontario in 1943. Two of them were members of the legislature. Some prominent union leaders were communists, including the secretary of the Canadian Trades and Labour Congress. The Soviet Union was Canada's honoured ally, and ex-premier Hepburn had even conquered his repugnance for the Reds by appearing on the same platform with far-left, but pro-war, agitators. There was a sense that the Communist Party would never conquer power by its own efforts, unaided. There was still the CCF, which was by then the official opposition in the Ontario legislature and in three other provinces. Would not the CCF open the political door to socialist enslavement, or pave the way for a period of political confusion during which the wily Bolsheviks would seize power just as they had in Russia in 1917?

These propositions now seem fantastic, but they were common political currency in some circles in 1943 and 1944, and were offered up to the premier of Ontario as models of political analysis by his "special branch" and its ally, the professional anti-socialist publicist Gladstone Murray. Murray was a friend of Drew's and a regular correspondent of the premier, as well as a familiar of the special branch. The special branch regularly sent in reports on suspicious personalities, including many in the CCF, but also including sinister figures like B. K. Sandwell, the editor of *Saturday Night*, and the principal of Queen's University.

The reports are of less significance than the fact that Drew tolerated them and even seems to have found their analysis profitable. The premier was, of course, very concerned about communism, which would for many years remain a preoccupation with him, and there is no reason to believe that his concern was a cynical political ploy. At the same time, there is no denying that his preoccupation would eventually prove politically beneficial.

Drew lost no time shoring up links with Ontario's motherland. Ontario House in London, closed by Hepburn, was reopened by Drew. More money was made available to local educational authorities. Those authorities were also instructed to bring religion back to the public school classroom, and in the fall of 1944 they did so, using a "non-sectarian" manual approved by the provincial Department of Education. A mining institute was established at Haileybury. The "manufacturing condition," which Hepburn had removed, was restored on pulpwood exports.

What Drew was truly anxious to do was to reconquer control over Ontario's finances. This he could not do as long as the war lasted and he began to fear that even then his hands would be tied. The federal government was embarking on a program of social expenditures which greatly expanded its role in Canadian life. The first, the family allowance or baby bonus, was passed by the federal Parliament in the summer of 1944. It offered a monthly payment for each Canadian child to each Canadian family, direct from the federal treasury. To Drew this initiative was intolerable. Ontario taxpayers would have to fund the baby bonus, and where would it be spent? Outside the province, and particularly in Quebec which as everybody knew was Catholic, opposed to contraception, and blessed with a high birth rate and many children. Drew's federal Conservative allies doubtless would have preferred that Ontario's premier keep silent, for they either voted for the baby bonus or were discreetly absent when the vote was taken.

Before Drew could finally engage Mackenzie King in constitutional and political battle, he had one local political task. The Liberals and the CCF in the legislature foolishly combined to defeat the Drew government on a vote of confidence in March 1945. Drew called a provincial election for June 11; when the federal government announced that it too would have an election on June 11, Drew advanced his date to June 4. The Conservative campaign went smoothly until, with ten days to go before the poll, the CCF leader, Edward Jolliffe, announced to a startled radio audience that Premier Drew had established his own provincial Gestapo (a reference to Hitler's political police). The charge was true, as we have seen, but its truth was not immediately apparent. It looked, rather, like an overheated and discreditable attempt to smear Drew's integrity. Drew announced a royal commission to investigate the charges, but meanwhile won the election with a crushing majority. The Conservatives took sixty-eight seats, the Liberals eleven, the CCF eight, and the Communists two. Drew had a secure majority.*

So, unluckily for Drew, did Mackenzie King. The federal Liberals won the June 11 election. They had fewer seats than they had before, and they did not do very well in Ontario. But they still had a majority in Parliament, and Mackenzie King was still prime minister. As a footnote to history, the CCF did badly federally, too. Provincially and federally the CCF was a dead issue. Socialism had been halted, as it turned out for good, and it would be representatives of the two old parties, Conservatives from Queen's Park and Liberals from Ottawa, who would refashion Canada's, and Ontario's, economic and social destiny.

The forum for the reshaping was a dominion-provincial conference summoned to Ottawa on August 6, 1945. The war with Germany was over, but the war with Japan, Germany's ally since 1941, was still on, and everyone expected it to last for months, if not years. It came as a considerable surprise for the assembled premiers to learn from Mackenzie King that an atomic bomb had been dropped that day on Japan. They were more surprised still to learn that Canada had had a role in developing the allies' atomic

---

*The Royal Commission, under Mr. Justice LeBel, confirmed the accuracy of some of Jolliffe's charges, but on the main issue both Drew and Gladstone Murray swore that the CCF leader's charges were false. Many years later David Lewis, with the assistance of Allan Whitehorn, showed that Drew's evidence, taken under oath, was misleading. See David Lewis, *The Good Fight* (Toronto, 1981), chapter 12.

weapon. King did not stress that two key atomic facilities were located in Ontario—a uranium refinery at Port Hope and a reactor under construction at Chalk River, on the Ottawa River. These features of the atomic program would become important in the future; for the moment they were the highest level of military secret.

The atomic news was sensational, but the more immediately pressing news for the premiers was that Ottawa had evolved a comprehensive plan for the redirection of Canadian government and, with it, of Canadian society. It would be possible, the premiers learned, to establish a comprehensive social security program that would include child support, old-age pensions, unemployment and health insurance. Some of these areas were already covered by legislation (unemployment insurance, the most recent, dated from 1941). These programs would be run, coherently and comprehensively, by the federal government according to a national standard. In addition, and perhaps more crucially, the federal government spoke in the accents of modern economic planning. It was highly desirable that the federal government possess sufficient economic power — the power to tax and the power to spend when and where appropriate — to serve as the balance wheel of the economy. This meant that in economic slumps the federal government would prime the pump of the economy, spending to restore purchasing power. During booms, the federal government could work to cool down the economy through taxation, guiding it through successive cycles of boom and bust in the hope that there would be no more overheated booms or bottomless busts as there had been during the Depression.

Prime Minister King, in presenting this program, had secret misgivings. His ambitious and optimistic civil servants and ministers could well have overstated their case. Even if they had not, King believed that they had underestimated the obstinacy and political force of the potential opposition. The opposition centred on two men. George Drew was instinctively opposed to any formula that would take away from Ontario's financial autonomy and, by the same token, opposed to any scheme that would add to Ottawa's economic power. Viewing relations with Ottawa as a struggle or a contest, he did not wish to subtract from his strength or add to that of the enemy. Maurice Duplessis, premier of Quebec, took essentially the same point of view, although it is doubtful that he worked out his opposition as carefully as Drew had. Quebec's government believed that it had a mandate for provincial rights and cultural autonomy, and such a mandate was difficult to square with Mackenzie King's quest for economic rationalization.

Drew, as we have seen, touted "planning" as the modern way to run an economy. It is notable, therefore, that he arrived in Ottawa without any concrete proposals of his own. That did not prevent the Ontario premier from reacting negatively. Speaking in response to King, Drew read a lecture in classical federalism, praising decentralization and financial autonomy, and proclaiming that a government that could not tax could not govern. That was precisely the federal point, reversed.

Drew never reversed his stand. He stood for fiscal autonomy. He did not want to see Ontario taxes transferred to federal control. He was willing to consider certain mechanisms that might dilute federal control over the sums to be raised, but he was fundamentally unwilling to abridge Ontario's own financial powers. Although the dominion-provincial conference of August 1945 did not finally conclude its labours until April 1946, after several recesses, it proved impossible to reconcile the Ontario and Canadian points of view.

The immediate effect of Drew's stand was clear. When the Wartime Tax Agreements expired, in 1947, Ontario revived all its prewar taxes, except for the personal income tax. It collected its taxes too, for the centralized tax collection authority established in 1942 also lapsed, as far as Ontario was concerned. Ontario had refused its consent to a revision of the balance established in the Constitution between provincial and federal economic powers, and the federal government respected its refusal. There is no question that the Ontario government was more autonomous than it would otherwise have been had it accepted the federal government's 1945 proposals.

At the same time, the Ontario government did not succeed in turning back the clock. Ottawa refused to abandon its own principal revenue sources such as the personal income tax. The federal government continued to spend more money than it had before the war: much more, indeed, so that the balance between federal and provincial expenditures leaned heavily towards the federal side throughout the 1940s and into the 1950s. From this perspective it was the federal government, not Queen's Park, that prevailed in 1945-46. The dominion-provincial conference of 1945-46 left one other legacy. It set a social policy agenda for all Canadian governments for the next generation. What had been proposed in 1945 may well have been too ambitious for its time: the political results of the conference demonstrated that all too clearly. But what had been opened for discussion was not forgotten, and it would result in a change in priorities, not just for the federal government, but for Ontario too. A government which, like Drew's, was primarily concerned with developing provincial resources would be forced to reconsider its priorities. In this sense Drew spoke for the past, not the future. By linking provincial autonomy with a reactionary style of politics, and by failing to show much imagination or interest in effective social policies, Drew gave his successors a doubtful heritage.

Ironically, it was nature and not the Constitution that highlighted Drew's last year in office. Ontario was again facing an energy crisis in 1947. This was, in part, the legacy of Sir Adam Beck, who had bequeathed to the province two distinct electrical systems. Those parts of the province that got their power from Niagara Falls got twenty-five-cycle power. Those that got it elsewhere were on sixty cycles, as was the rest of North America. Inhabitants of what was called "the Golden Horseshoe," the province's industrial heartland, enjoyed the use of machines and appliances that were entirely useless anywhere else. This problem would take a great deal of money ($200 million) to correct, and it was only in the late 1940s that the Ontario government felt capable of tackling it.

The controversy over twenty-five cycles coincided with bad weather. Bad weather meant, in this case, insufficient rain and falling water levels. Low water meant not enough water flow around Ontario Hydro's turbines. That in turn meant a shortage of electricity. Brownouts and electrical shortages occurred. Drew fumed. The chairman of Ontario Hydro, tainted in Drew's eyes by too close a friendship with C. D. Howe, one of the detested Ottawa Liberals, suddenly departed. A new Tory chairman, innocent of engineering, was appointed. Meanwhile, conversion to sixty cycle proceeded, a conversion that touched every urban home in south-central Ontario. Thermal plants, burning coal, were planned and then built. Agreement was reached with Quebec on a new power development on the Upper Ottawa River, around Des Joachims (forever called Deswisha on the Ontario side of the river).

Most of this was sound policy, and nobody disagreed with it. Drew nevertheless discovered that he had a need for a mandate and he called a general election for June 7. It was an election the Conservatives won, and Drew lost. He was, strangely enough, defeated on a traditional issue, liquor. The government had passed legislation expanding the public's opportunities for drinking in public places. There would in future be cocktail lounges where it was possible to buy liquor by the glass, and wine with dinner. The "drys" took their revenge, defeating Drew in Toronto-High Park where the premier had bravely decided to run. Drew never again sat in an Ontario legislature.

The premier had by now other ambitions, larger ones, more appropriate to someone who had given Ontario vigorous and dynamic government. He wanted to be leader of the federal Conservative party. The resignation of the federal leader, John Bracken, gave Drew his chance, and when a national convention was held, Ontario's handsome premier was the run-away winner.

Drew's legacy to his province is, like the man himself, contradictory. He was the last Ontario premier to espouse the traditional issues of autonomy, isolationism, and competition with the federal government. He was the last one to focus his primary attention on provincial development, and even in this area there are clear signs in his rhetoric that he recognized, although he might not accept, the reordering of political issues brought about by the new mood of the Canadian people after the Second World War.

Drew's political style was, like that of Mitchell Hepburn before him, unfortunate. Lacking Hepburn's vulgarity, he may be said to have overcompensated for it by affecting a cool reserve and a pompous public manner, treating every gathering of more than three people as a full-blown public meeting. Some of Drew's preoccupations, such as his interest in the largely imaginary Red menace, or his belligerent attacks on federal schemes to farm out Ontario's money to other less fortunate provinces, made far more enemies than friends, and helped caricature Ontarians in the eyes of the rest of the country as selfish, parochial, and, just possibly, un-Canadian.

That judgement was, however, excessively harsh. Drew thought of himself not as un-Canadian but as the best kind of Canadian, preserving the country's essential heritage of conservatism, locality, and decentralization. There had been a time, when Drew was young, when most Ontarians thought as he did — of a society that was mostly Anglo-Saxon, that tolerated others, such as French Canadians, but that had rights superior to those of the minorities who had come to live in the province. Drew was no bigot in terms of his time or his province, and he left behind evidence (Ontario's first anti-discrimination act, for example) that showed he was willing to legislate to counter traditional abuses.

Drew's later years were a disappointment. His utterances as an Ontario politician came back to haunt him when he tried to project himself on a national stage. Disastrously defeated in two federal elections, he was pensioned off into the diplomatic service, like Howard Ferguson, as Canada's high commissioner to the United

Kingdom. He returned eventually to Ontario and died in 1973. His rival, Mitchell Hepburn, was by then long dead. Hepburn was retired by his electors in Elgin in the 1945 provincial election, after a brief revival as Ontario Liberal leader. His legacy was rather less enduring than Drew's. Drew built a political machine that first defeated the Liberals and then entrenched the Conservatives in a majority across the province. But Hepburn may be said to have contributed his mite as well. If it is true that governments defeat themselves, Hepburn's contribution to Ontario's political tradition was to undermine the strength of the Liberal party and to leave it vulnerable to its replacement. The true father of Ontario's Conservative dynasty was not George Drew, but Mitchell F. Hepburn.

The Golden Horseshoe
and Beyond

8 The years that followed Drew were kind to Ontario. Citizens of the province grew accustomed to reading about their wealth, their industry, their abundance of everything that the modern world considered best for the good life. Many of the products that Ontarians consumed were made right at home, in the province's "Golden Horseshoe" of industry that stretched around the western end of Lake Ontario from Niagara Falls to Oshawa and Peterborough. If an investor wanted to invest, he would most probably choose Ontario, and the province boomed on a surge of investment — much of it from the United States — in the years after 1948.

Boom times were reflected in a population surge, the "baby boom," that began in the final years of the war and accelerated thereafter. By the late 1950s Ontarians were producing children at three times the rate that had obtained in the Depression of the 1930s. Observers caustically claimed that every woman in sight was pregnant, but even if we discount for exaggeration, it proved to be an era of babies, children, and, as the children grew, youth. The cities of the province, stalled by the Depression and the war, outgrew their boundaries. Cow pastures were replaced by houses, and orchards by factories, roads, and schools.

The crude figures tell the story. Ontario in 1941 had 3,787,655 residents. In 1951 the figure had grown to 4,600,000, up by 800,000 in ten years. It took only five years to generate the next 800,000, either domestically or by immigration, and by 1961 the sum of

Ontario people was 6,236,000. Where were these people located? The short answer is that they were not, by and large, on farms. Just over 8 percent of Ontario's population lived on farms in 1961, at a time when many people, including the premier, could remember when the province was predominantly rural. It was less than forty years since the farmers' last stand had produced Ernest Drury and his UFO government, a government that probably seemed to contemporary Ontarians as distant as Mars from their actual concerns.

The UFOs would have had trouble recognizing the province they had left behind. For one thing, the people were changing. Just under 60 percent of the population hailed from the British Isles; the rest were, in descending order, French, German, Italian, Dutch, Polish, Ukrainian, and various groups leading down to "other." Toronto, proud repository of the province's British heritage, was becoming less British; in the metropolitan census district just over 60 percent claimed British ancestry, and the proportion was going down. But we must remember that ancestry was one thing, and place of birth quite another. Even under this heading the proportion of immigrants was quite impressive: 22 percent of the population of Ontario claimed a birthplace outside Canada (another 9 percent were born elsewhere in Canada). The largest immigrant group, not quite half the total of immigrants, was British — men, women, and children who came to Canada after the end of the Second World War, attracted by higher living standards and greater opportunities.

The immigrant totals indicate that Ontario was considered to be a good place to live: good enough for two million people not born there to make it their home. It was not that Ontario alone was desirable. All of Canada was booming to varying degrees, and it was by and large the policies of the national government, rather than of the province, that shaped the prosperity that drew the immigrants, and caused native-born Ontarians to stay at home and enjoy life.

It was not that life in the province was trouble-free. Some

sectors of the economy, and some areas of the province, did better than others. Farmers on marginal land were left behind in a rural slum. It was true that almost everywhere the slum could be lighted with electricity, as the rural electrification project finally approached completion after fifty years. Almost everyone, the census reported, had "refrigeration facilities" and the humble and traditional ice box was finally on the way out. Eighty percent of Ontario homes had at least one television set; some had two. When one considers that television was unknown, except in magazine articles, in the province before 1948, and that Canadian television broadcasting had begun only in 1952, this was a notable advance.

If we look across the province, it is obvious that some districts were less than prosperous. A home-owner or renter in Manitoulin Island or Bruce County was more likely to live in an older house than someone in Toronto or Ottawa. The house was more likely to need repair. The income of the householder would be much lower. Of course, it would be easier, proportionally, to live in a picturesque old dwelling. In the county of Lennox and Addington, near Kingston, no fewer than 63 percent of the houses dated back to World War I or beyond, compared to 35 percent for the province as a whole. In fact, 43 percent of Ontario's homes had been built in the twenty-five years since World War II.

Between the houses there were streets, and beside the streets, in the newer districts, there were ditches; where civilization had gone one step further, there were storm as well as sanitary sewers. In most neighbourhoods there were new schools (red and occasionally yellow brick were much in fashion, and one and two stories were the rule). The long, narrow schools matched the ranch houses that sprawled alongside them, or the newly fashionable "split level" dwellings that some contractors loved to create. All of this added up to sizeable suburbs, and almost every Ontario city or town had one. Between the suburbs there were main roads (arterial roads, as the planners liked to call them) and trunk sewers and water mains. As cities got bigger so did streets, from two lanes to four, and in the mid-1950s urban expressways, like Ottawa's Queensway or Toronto's Don Valley Parkway, began to make their appearance. Simultaneously, railway lines began to contract and disappear. Rural lines dried up and withered away with the blessing of governments that no longer viewed them as the modern miracle.

Instead of trains there were buses for people and trucks for goods. The railway workers advanced the process slightly by holding a Canada-wide strike in 1950, but at best they accelerated it by only a couple of years. The provincial highway system now reached everywhere in southern Ontario, and even to the remoter corners of the north. The federal government conveniently provided a subsidy — a large subsidy — for a Trans-Canada Highway built up to a national specification, and Ontario was able to convert miles of existing road as well as to build a brand-new asphalt section north of Lake Superior between Sault Ste Marie and Nipigon where no road had gone before.

Most people in Ontario, if asked about highways during the 1950s, would have thought first about the province's brand-new expressway, stretching for 500 toll-free miles from Windsor to the Quebec border, from Lake St Clair almost to Montreal. At least, it would eventually, for the new highway, designated as number 401, took more than a decade to complete. Where it existed, the speed limit was raised, from the old fifty miles per hour, to sixty, and eventually, in the faster decade of the 1960s, to seventy.

Schools, roads, hospitals, and highways all cost money, a great deal of money. They took time to design and expertise to administer. Money meant taxes, or if not taxes then subsidies from the federal government, which meant more taxes. Administration meant the civil service, and experts meant a better civil service than Ontario had wished to employ in the past.

Fortunately the money was there, because people were earning more of it. Tax rates could go down, and still more money rolled in. From the point of view of the Treasury there was never quite enough, but it is clear that there was sufficient to go on with. Budgets were geared to expansion, because expansion meant jobs. Jobs meant security, and security was what people wanted. What they wanted, the politicians meant to give them, or at least to seem to be giving.

There were three main policy areas in Ontario government during the late 1940s and the 1950s. There was expansion, generally of social services and of the infrastructure of the provincial economy, such as roads. There was development, a more traditional concern. And there was finance. Finance at the beginning of this period was the concern of the provincial treasurer, Leslie Frost. Frost, as Drew's financial agent, had sat in on the various dominion-provincial wars that had been started up by the coming of peace in 1945. Frost, some people noticed, was tranquil when Drew was excited, and concerned when Drew was belligerent. It was whispered that he had travelled to far-off Winnipeg, far from his leader's eye, to be briefed on the dominion's reconstruction proposals, and on Manitoba's Liberal-Progessive view of them. It was even said that Frost did not like Drew.

That was Drew's bad fortune, for Frost, after a brief interregnum (Colonel Tom Kennedy, premier, 1948-49), became Ontario's premier. Frost would remain premier for the rest of Drew's tenure as national Conservative leader, and beyond, until 1961, and during that period Canadians were treated to the unusual spectacle of an arm's length relationship between Canada's most senior Conservative in office, Frost, and his national leader. Cooperation was not entirely lacking, but closeness and cordiality were not much in evidence.

That was just as well, because the federal Liberal party was firmly entrenched in office. Mackenzie King, its leader for twenty-nine years, finally retired in 1948, and was succeeded by a Quebec City lawyer, the former minister of justice and external affairs minister, Louis St Laurent. St Laurent was a Canadian nationalist and a believer in both strong national direction and equal opportunity for Canadians in all parts of the country. The prime minister had been one of the counsel for the Rowell-Sirois commission back in the 1930s, and the experience had told on him.

Frost too showed a firm sense of Canadian identification. He understood that, since 1939, Ottawa had come to occupy large unchartered areas where no federal government had ever penetrated before — areas like the direction of a national tax policy, or the establishment of national minimum standards in government services. Unlike Drew, Frost understood the federal government's agenda, and believed that it was better to participate through co-operation rather than belligerent grandstanding. It was not that Frost shared in all the federal government's objectives, but he shared enough of them to make the 1950s a generally sunny decade in the relations between Ottawa and Queen's Park.

It was in the field of energy that the government of Ontario and the federal government most often, and most fruitfully, agreed. There were three facets: first, the old issue of the St Lawrence power development; second, the question of uranium and atomic power; and third, the establishment of a national policy to bring Canadian natural gas from Alberta to central Canada. All three policies were associated, on the federal side, with C. D. Howe, St Laurent's minister of trade and commerce from 1948 to 1957. All three commended themselves to Leslie Frost.

Energy was important because Ontario had run out of sources of water power to fuel more electrical generation. Niagara could be tapped for more power, and it was, but there would be no more from that source. The St Lawrence River was the last big untapped source of water power, and Frost was determined to secure it. He had the agreement of the federal government, as well as that of the government of neighbouring New York State, which also wanted the power. Only the American Congress, packed with the representatives of railways and rival shipping interests, stood in the way. It would take threats by both the federal government and that of Ontario, to the effect that Canada would go it alone on a seaway linking Lake Ontario and the Gulf of St Lawrence, as well as powerful persuasions by American interests that stood to benefit from the seaway's completion, for the American government to give way. The St Lawrence Seaway treaty was signed in 1954, and construction began immediately.

In Ontario there was some disruption as the seaway proceeded. A series of obsolescent canals along the St Lawrence were closed down. Riverside communities disappeared under the river, either in whole or in part. Relocated historic buildings eventually formed an artificial settlement, turned into an outdoor museum as Upper Canada Village. In 1959 construction was complete. Ontario got its hydro power, and large ocean-going ships sailed for the first time up the St Lawrence, along the lakes, as far as the lakehead at Thunder Bay. In 1960, as a result, Ontario Hydro generated over 99 percent of its electricity by hydraulic means.

Hydro planners knew this situation would not last. They had coal and oil-fired thermal plants in reserve, and during the 1960s more and more electricity was generated from these plants (37.8 percent in 1970). Coal and oil had to be imported, either from the United States or western Canada. (Although Ontario has coal and oil reserves of its own, they are insufficient and costly.) Once the sources of water were used up there seemed to be no question that Ontario would import its energy.

Two developments changed that eventually. The first was the discovery in 1952 of large quantities of uranium in central Ontario, in the Algoma district between Sudbury and Sault Ste Marie. Uranium in 1952 was a highly strategic mineral, whose principal use was to make nuclear weapons. Because of its military importance, the federal government had assumed jurisdiction over uranium mining and it was through and with the federal government that the Algoma uranium fields were developed. There were hundreds of millions of dollars at stake, even, as it turned out, billions, and there followed a stampede of prospectors and mining promoters to Algoma. A city in the bush, Elliot Lake, was created, and by 1959, 25,000 people were living there.

There hopes were almost entirely pinned to the future of uranium, but just as Elliott Lake assumed a finished form, the bottom dropped out of the world uranium market. The Americans had found more than enough uranium in their own country, and they refused to import any more once their existing contracts ran out. The contracts, after renegotiation, would expire in 1966. The federal government, which negotiated and then renegotiated the contracts that breathed life into Algoma, hoped that by then there would be demand from another source: nuclear power.

The possibility of nuclear power had been considered as far back as the 1930s. Uranium generated power, and if a proper reactor were designed it would do it more efficiently than coal. Engineers in the late 1940s believed that such a reactor was decades away from perfection. It was surprising, therefore, to learn that a United Nations conference in Geneva, Switzerland, had shown reactors far closer to feasibility than had been believed.

The conference took place in 1955. By then, however, Ontario Hydro had had a team of engineers at work at the federal government's nuclear laboratory at Chalk River on the Ottawa River for some time. Their mandate was to help design a nuclear reactor that would solve Ontario's long-term electricity shortage. And, within a measurable time, they were successful. A demonstration power reactor was built at Rolphton, near Chalk River, and Frost and C. D. Howe ceremonially turned the sod, sod that had been specially flown up to cover the native rocks.

The third development in Ontario's energy policy also involved digging. It had occurred to Howe that a Trans-Canada pipeline would give Canada security of supply for energy. The discovery of large deposits of oil and gas in Alberta and the development of long-distance pipeline technology suggested that in principle such a pipeline was feasible. It remained to find the necessary money to build one, a task which took Howe several years. When his project was ready, or nearly so, it still needed parliamentary financing, but the trade and commerce minister believed that with Leslie Frost's support he would run into no serious obstacles in getting the necessary legislation passed.

Howe proved to be wrong. A ferocious battle developed over

the pipeline in May and June 1956, with Ontario Conservative members of parliament leading the charge against Howe's dictatorial tactics in demanding parliamentary approval of his projects. Eventually, using the parliamentary device of closure to limit debate, Howe and his Liberal colleagues prevailed. The effort left them exhausted, and George Drew considered taking the next step, by blocking necessary legislation, to force an election. But Drew and his federal friends were told that there would be no money forthcoming from Toronto to run any such campaign, and their hopes fizzled.

It is not, of course, surprising that Frost could not greatly influence his Conservative counterparts in Ottawa. They owed him little, and they knew, uncomfortably, that he owed them nothing. The pipeline went ahead anyway. It outlasted the Ottawa Liberals, as we shall see, and it snaked down to Toronto and Montreal in the fall of 1958. Toronto, which had converted from twenty-five cycles to sixty cycles barely a decade before, now converted from artificial gas, manufactured locally, to natural gas, from Alberta.

Energy supply was important for the Ontario economy. Just as important, in the short term, were the several measures designed by Ottawa for industrial expansion. Industry was duly encouraged, as were foreign investors. So was the Ontario economy, which expanded its energy demands at the rate of 4 percent per year, with the results that we have already seen in energy policy.

The economy, or at least the industrial side of the economy, therefore occasioned little dispute. The same was not the case with the other, social-policy side of federal-provincial relations. On that side of affairs there was potential for disagreement, and, with the best will in the world, disagreement was not long in coming.

Under Frost, Ontario entered Ottawa's umbrella tax-rental agreement in 1952. The federal government collected taxes and remitted a "rent" to the province. The rent was agreed in advance, in five-year cycles. The trouble was that in the mid-1950s Frost wanted more than Ottawa was willing to offer. Discussions between the two levels of government proved unsatisfactory to the Ontario premier, and the discussions took both parties towards the next general election. Unluckily for the Liberals in Ottawa, Frost no longer had to put up with George Drew. Drew had retired, and John Diefenbaker, a fire-breathing orator from Prince Albert, Saskatchewan, had taken his place. Frost had no trouble putting his political expertise, and his political machine, at Diefenbaker's service.

Diefenbaker arrived in power just in time to implement a reform that Frost had once been inclined to resist. Health insurance had been among the programs Ottawa had proposed as part of its social security package back in 1945. Drew had rejected it, and it had stayed rejected on the federal level. Despite the lack of a federal program, Saskatchewan and British Columbia had gone ahead with their own programs, in Saskatchewan's case a very successful hospital insurance plan. Frost and St Laurent, both socially conservative men, did not like the idea of state intervention in a new field; oddly, it proved to be Frost who was the first to break ranks. It was probably Frost's sensitive political antennae that suggested that hospital insurance was an idea whose time had come, but he was assisted in his conversion by the cancellation of his own private insurance when he moved into a high-risk actuarial category on his sixtieth birthday. Without Frost's support and facing pressure inside his own cabinet, St Laurent capitulated. Ontario would have hospital insurance, and so, eventually, would the rest of the country. A new national program was born.

We have said little in this chapter about electoral politics. That is because electoral politics invariably produced the same result. Frost won provincial elections in 1951, 1955, and 1959. He won the elections, in part, because he was the proud owner of an alert, powerful, and well-fuelled political machine. He was assisted by the Conservatives' chief provincial organizer, from 1942 to 1960, A. D. McKenzie, with whom the premier conferred on an almost daily basis. McKenzie not only stimulated the premier with his advice; it was a commonplace that deserving Conservatives with problems needed to consult McKenzie in his haunts in Toronto's Royal York Hotel. It was a measure of their, and McKenzie's, discretion that the results seldom reached the public eye.

Frost also won elections because there was no other party capable of defeating him. The opposition in Ontario was divided into two. There were the Liberals, operating out of a shrinking but on the whole faithful electoral base in southwestern Ontario, with a very few outposts elsewhere. And there was the CCF, still surviving, with which the Liberals disputed the title of official opposition. From time to time the opposition uncovered a scandal. There was a scandal in the provincial highways department. The relevant minister resigned. Frost called an election. The former minister was re-elected, and the issue was forgotten. There was another, later, scandal involving natural gas. Frost called another election and, despite the heavy publicity given to the "Northern Ontario Natural Gas" (NONG) affair, he was re-elected. He could count on it, because the opposition vote cancelled itself out.

Frost's ability to seize control of issues whose time had, in his judgement, finally, come, combined with the inherent political fragmentation of the opposition parties, mixed in with a healthy dose of Conservative party elixir, ensured that he would remain Ontario's unchallenged political chief until he chose to retire. "Old Man Ontario," "the Silver Fox," beamed on his public as he perambulated the province. His reassuring countenance concealed the fact that a deeply Conservative government had in fact presided over substantial changes in the province, and had taken major steps to bring it into a competitive position in the last half of the twentieth century.

Frost set his retirement for the fall of 1961. His cabinet immediately scrambled for the succession, but strangely it was one of the most recent recruits who was able to seize the glittering prize. John Robarts, from London, Ontario, was best known among his colleagues for his hard-drinking night life. Despite some misgivings, Frost appointed Robarts minister of education and then, barely two years later, saw him run for the Conservative leader-ship. The very fact that Robarts was a recent appointee, and a man with relatively few enemies, made him everybody's second choice, and as the more senior and more probable candidates dropped away, the man from London was left holding the field.

Robarts was to remain premier for not quite ten years, from November 1961 to February 1971. His small city background, his war service, and his old-fashioned choice of stimulants made him in some respects a peculiar leader for Ontario in a decade of social change and unrest. Robarts, however, demonstrated more flexibility in government than might have been anticipated, and that feature, combined with a strong commitment to the preserva-tion of Canada, made him a natural political leader during the turbulent 1960s.

The turbulence was in some respects a natural continuation of the prosperity of the baby boom decade of the 1950s. Affluent (or at least comfortable) parents produced a revolution in expecta-tions. Where the previous generation prided itself on the achieve-ment of good roads, universal flush toilets, and rural electrification, the newer generation wanted better cars, better jobs, and higher incomes. To a remarkable extent they got them. Ontarians' in-come rose substantially in the 1960s, whether we measure it in current (inflated) dollars or constant, uninflated ones. Unemploy-ment, bothersome at the beginning of the decade, virtually disap-peared in the middle years of the 1960s. Although these phenomena were remarked on at the time, especially in the provincial treasur-er's annual budget speech, it seems doubtful that Ontarians en-tirely appreciated just how well off they were in fact becoming.

The provincial government took the point. The 1960s were another decade of development. The road system naturally con-tinued to grow. Four lanes became six lanes, and then eight, as superhighways snaked around and through the province's cities. New high schools opened, especially at the beginning of the de-cade, to hold the baby boom as it surged through grades nine to thirteen. The Catholics reliably asked for money for their upper grades, and the provincial government as reliably refused them. Few people seemed to care.

Beyond high school there was university. There were new universities too, some beautiful, like Trent University in Peterborough, placed on a fast-flowing river in parkland, and some not, like York University on the plains of Downsview. York was built in an interesting combination of totalitarian and feudal architecture, but both kinds were dwarfed by the monotony of Downsview's geography. Every year there was a new university. Old sectarian schools changed their spots so as to qualify for government grants, and the province generously adopted them and opened its purse. To the universities flocked students in their thousands, and then in their tens of thousands. The first entrants tended, like their predecessors of the 1940s and 1950s, to be job- or career-oriented, but by the mid-1960s there were signs that the mood on campuses was changing. The Youth Culture had arrived.

So had what the 1960s learned to think of as the Quebec Question. Ontarians did not think very much, or very often, of their sister province. Those who considered the problem of Quebec might have reflected that the two central provinces had a great deal more joining them together — tradition, economic interchange, and, possibly, political interest — than separating them. But as Quebec asserted itself inside and outside Canada's federal framework under first the Lesage Liberal government (1960–66) and then the Johnson Union Nationale government (1966–68), only a few pointed out that Quebec had traditionally been less assertive than Ontario in demanding provincial rights.

Quebec in the 1960s did not stop at provincial rights, however. That province's governments made increasingly pressing demands for the expansion of their jurisdiction, and for a rollback of federal initiatives. Occasionally the interests of the Quebec and Ontario governments directly coincided. In 1963, when the federal government, under Lester Pearson's newly elected Liberals, urged a comprehensive pension plan on the provinces, Ontario lent support to Quebec at a crucial moment. Ontario's support, as it proved, was largely tactical and, in the end, with the very reluctant acquiescence of Premier Robarts, the province joined the national Canada Pension Plan.

Ontario was also a reluctant convert to a universal health insurance scheme — medicare — and the province's relations with Ottawa over the division of finances were anything but happy through the 1960s. The other provinces for the most part fared no better in securing concessions from the federal government, at a time when it seemed that agreement and federal concessions were virtually synonymous in the minds of most provincial governments. The Pearson government, which prided itself on its program of "co-operative federalism," found itself driven into a corner from which it believed it could not move without damaging the fabric of Canada's constitutional balance.

Robarts's attitude under the circumstances was highly ambivalent. He pressed for concessions, but never at the cost of what he perceived to be national unity. And if national unity happened to be a factor in the frequently bitter federal-provincial disputes of the period, Robarts would direct Ontario's support towards compromise and the "national interest." Although it would be fair to say that relations between Toronto Conservatives and Ottawa Liberals were less cordial than they had been in the days of Frost, St Laurent, and Howe, the Ontario government nevertheless believed that the country's interest demanded compromises rather than confrontations.

It was in this spirit that Robarts hosted a Confederation of Tomorrow conference in Toronto in 1967, Canada's and Ontario's centennial year. The conference brought the premiers of the ten provinces together in a downtown Toronto skyscraper to discuss the future of Canada's federation, and to discover whether a political and personal basis existed for settlement of differences. No final agreement emerged from the discussions, but the fact that they were held at all signalled Robarts's intense concern for the future of the country.

That concern continued to be expressed over the next decade

and a half of constitutional discussions between the eleven governments of Canada — Ottawa and the ten provinces. The short-lived Bertrand government in Quebec (1968–70) and the Liberal and pro-federalist Bourassa government (1970–76) posed less of a direct challenge to the existing federal regime than had the Lesage and Johnson administrations, but support for the separation of Quebec inside that province became both more vocal and more organized. When separatist agitation briefly erupted in terrorism in 1970, the federal government invoked its emergency powers to crush the terrorists; Premier Robarts was once again one of Ottawa's firmest supporters during the crisis.

By 1970 Robarts had been in power in Ontario for nine years. He had won two elections, in 1963 and 1967, and in the nature of things another election would be due in 1971. The premier was still a relatively young man, able, apparently, to go on indefinitely, but instead he decided to retire. A new leader would be chosen at a convention in Toronto in February 1971. The post was fiercely contested by various Robarts ministers, but the winner was William G. Davis of Brampton. Robarts retired to practise law, occasionally re-entering the public arena in pursuit of his elusive goal of national unity. Dogged by a tragic personal life, the former premier committed suicide in 1982.

The new premier, like his predecessor, a lawyer, had been in the provincial legislature since 1959. He had held one of the most prominent and important cabinet posts during the 1960s, that of education. Under Davis, Ontario's traditional high school practices were revolutionized. Provincial school-leaving exams were abolished in 1967. New curricula were examined and new and daring educational theories were propounded. Ontario's Hall-Dennis committee (chaired by Emmett Hall, a judge, and Lloyd Dennis, an educator), proclaimed a brave and destructured educational system for the province. The results of the Hall-Dennis experiments are still in dispute among experts, but as the 1970s proceeded it was apparent that public opinion was beginning to tilt more and more firmly against their process and their product.

Having destructured schools in the early 1970s, the provincial government restructured them later in the decade, and still more in the early 1980s.

By then, of course, education was becoming both less popular and less prominent than it had once been. The crude basis for this development was a sharp fall in the provincial birth rate (mirroring a national and international trend) or, more properly, in the province's reproduction rate. This fell by about one-half between 1961 and 1971. The results were startling. From bulging schools, the province went to empty academies. Junior schools, high schools, and to a much lesser extent universities all felt the pinch. Teachers lost their jobs as their pupils vanished. In universities, retirees were not replaced. Education ceased to be the wave of the future and became more of a holding action, as educational planners contemplated what to do next.

If the 1970s were the end of boom times for the birth rate, 1971 marked a milestone in the ideology of civic expansion of the 1950s and 1960s. The Ontario expressway system by 1971 was highly advanced. Planners studied traffic patterns and plotted how to channel the maximum number of automobiles to the optimum number of workplaces. Obstacles in the way, whether man-made or natural, were simply plowed under. This tendency gradually created or even excited an opposite and eventually equal reaction. When Toronto, in 1971, contemplated putting a new expressway through the city's ravine and urban core, opposition became extremely vocal. In June 1971 the Conservative government stepped in and, to the general surprise, stopped the expressway. Having got people's attention, the Davis government called an election for the fall, which it won very handily.

It was the Davis govenment's first creative application of its careful study of public opinion. Polls and samples were commissioned by the provincial government on a large scale, so that at any given point Queen's Park, more than anyone else, would have its collective thumb on the people's pulse. Combined with an increasingly elaborate and sophisticated political apparatus, and bolstered by judicious patronage, Ontario's "Big Blue Machine" became one of the most powerful in the country.

Political machinery is not all in politics. The Davis government suffered two setbacks at the polls, in 1975, when it was returned in a minority position, and in 1977, when an attempt to reverse the earlier verdict failed. The two elections saw the two opposition parties, the Liberals and the New Democratic Party, trade positions. In 1975 the Liberals gained votes (coming less than 2 percent behind the leading Conservatives) after a vigorous campaign by their leader Robert Nixon, the son of former premier Harry Nixon. Paradoxically, the Liberals lost the position of official opposition to the NDP (the successor to the old CCF), which by an electoral fluke gained more seats with 6 percent less of the total vote. In 1977 the Liberals lost both votes and seats, but not as many as the NDP, which thereupon returned to its position as third party. Its leader, Stephen Lewis, shortly retired to journalism and, later, diplomacy. The Davis government demonstrated its affinity for seizing popular or potentially popular causes when it enacted a system of rent controls. Rent controls alleviated the problem of surging rents in a time of high inflation, but as elsewhere they helped to create other problems: a dearth of rental accommodation as builders converted their efforts to other and more profitable lines, and an aging stock of rental housing.

The Davis government did not recover its majority in the legislature until 1981, when the Liberals remained as the official but perennially unsuccessful opposition, and the New Democrats suffered further losses. The Davis government showed considerable skill in maintaining itself for six years as a minority administration, but it was helped as always by the fact that the Liberals and the NDP had less in common with one another than either did with the ruling Conservatives.

Although provincial politics were anything but tame during the 1970s, and although the Davis government, as with rent controls, made a number of significant excursions into the economy, the issues that preoccupied Ontarians during the decade tended to be national rather than provincial in scope. This preoccupation was reflected in voting patterns in federal elections. During the period 1962 to 1984, Ontario showed a marked tendency to vote Liberal on the federal level. The support was not consistent, but it was strong enough to keep the federal Liberals in office in 1972 and to bring them back to power in 1980.

Rightly or wrongly, the federal Liberal Party was seen as responding to Ontario's interest in a strong and united national economy. Equally, the Liberal government in Ottawa stood for security of energy supply and for a Canadian (lower) price for oil and gas during a time of skyrocketing world energy prices. Less prominently, a federal crown corporation (Atomic Energy of Canada Limited) and Ontario Hydro continued to work on the development of a network of nuclear electrical generating stations. At the same time, the federal government's preference for marketing boards as a mechanism for directing and abating market fluctuations in agricultural products meshed with that of the Ontario government. Sometimes, of course, the marketing boards could go too far, as they did when a chicken and egg war broke out over which province had the right to sell what, where, and to whom.

The great Canadian question of the 1970s, as of the 1960s, continued to be that of Quebec. The Canadian electorate hoped that Pierre Elliott Trudeau, federal Liberal leader and prime minister for all but eight months between 1968 and 1984, would be able to discover a solution to the Quebec government's desire for greater autonomy within confederation. When a separatist government was actually elected in Quebec in 1976, Canadians gave their trust to Trudeau as the country's last and best hope to defeat separatism.

Trudeau succeeded, although the extent of his success was not at first apparent. The Quebec government called for a referendum on ''sovereignty-association'' (independence inside an economic union with the remaining parts of Canada) in May 1980. Ontario left no doubt where it stood on the matter: the provincial government would have no truck nor trade with the Quebec government's implausible scheme of sovereignty-association. When the Quebec electorate decided that the province should not withdraw from Canada, Trudeau's position was greatly strengthened. Quebec's government could hardly claim to enjoy any kind of mandate to determine the French-language province's constitutional destiny, and as time passed it became obvious that even in Quebec the citizenry was fatigued by a decade and a half of constitutional impasse.

Trudeau therefore took the initiative. In September 1980 he tried, and failed, to obtain the agreement of the provinces to bring the Canadian Constitution, the British North America Act, entirely within Canadian jursidiction, thereby abrogating the extreme position that Howard Ferguson and company had forced on the country back in 1930. Premier Davis showed no disposition to follow in the footsteps of the departed Ferguson; instead, he backed Trudeau's effort to bring the Constitution back to Canada (the term used was "patriation," the act of giving an existing constitution to a country it had governed for over a century). Davis went further. He supported the federal government's entire constitutional package, including a Charter of Rights and Freedoms and restrictions on the rights of provinces to legislate against education in either of the country's two official languages and to bar another province's citizens from gainful employment.

The only other province to follow Trudeau's lead was New Brunswick. The other eight, spearheaded by Alberta and Quebec, fought the Trudeau scheme root and branch. From September 1980 until April 1982 Canadian politics were dominated by the struggle between the federal Liberal government, which had no elected MPs from the three westernmost provinces but was supported by the Conservative governments of New Brunswick and Ontario, and the remaining eight provinces. The war was waged in newspapers, classrooms, television studios, and even in dining-rooms in London, where the eleven Canadian governments competed in offering hospitality and propaganda to bewildered British

MPs who had to vote on the return of the British North America Act to Canada.

A compromise was eventually struck. The Trudeau government abated some of its demands, and the provinces conceded that Canada could, after all, have a constitution that could be amended in Canada, as well as some restrictions on the rights of provinces over official languages and interprovincial migration. Canada also acquired a Charter of Rights and Freedoms, subject to a number of significant qualifications including the right of a province to exclude its legislation from the charter's operations. The province of Quebec, the only province to refuse its consent, was isolated and impotent in the face of Trudeau and the other nine provinces. In April 1982 Queen Elizabeth II journeyed to Ottawa to sign and proclaim the new constitutional accord.

The fact of a patriated constitution met with general satisfaction in Ontario. There were many who worried that the province had isolated itself too much from the other provinces, particularly in the west, and there is no doubt that the 1970s and early 1980s marked a low point in the relations between Ontarians and their western fellow-citizens.

The differences were only partly constitutional. Westerners generally believed that their region was adversely affected by national economic policies designed in fact if not in theory to benefit the two central provinces. Although some economists disputed the reasonableness of this view, it was virtually an article of faith in the western provinces. Interestingly enough, the view of Ontario held in the west — industrialized and full of highly paid, highly skilled workers — was coming unstuck.

Ontario's industries had boomed during the 1950s and 1960s. In 1965 the federal government negotiated an Autopact, providing for a modified kind of free trade in automotive parts and vehicles between Canada and the United States. As a result, Ontario's automobile industry grew rapidly in the early and mid-1970s. It suffered a setback in the last part of the decade because

Ontario car factories were largely making obsolete models, and in the early 1980s the automobile industry passed into a major recession.

There were a great many causes for the setback. For one, there was increasing foreign competition, particularly but not exclusively from Japan. Japanese competition was not confined to automobiles, but affected other established industries, such as electronics. These industries passed under a cloud, as did others. For example, factories making appliances had to cope with the fact that most people in Ontario and elsewhere in North America had a full range of stoves, refrigerators, vacuum cleaners, and the like. What the appliance industry had to face now was replacement, a much slower process than the happy days when family after family had proudly boasted of its first refrigerator.

Statistics showed that the manufacturing sector of Ontario's economy was declining in importance. Iron and steel, cars, televisions, all were down. Up were white collar jobs and service occupations. There was nothing unusual about this. It happened elsewhere in Canada, and it also happened in the United States and in other developed economies overseas. Where all this would lead no one knew. Some worried darkly about the ''deindustrialization'' of Ontario and argued that Canada could not afford to become dependent on outside suppliers for so many vital products. The government studied the situation and tried to encourage the combination of what was coming to be called ''high tech'' with industry, for example in urban transportation, where the Ontario government vigorously promoted its own brands of subway and other rapid transit systems.

Observers of the economic scene generally agreed that the great postwar economic spurt had finally run its course by the late 1970s. Ontarians were, by the early 1980s, much more prosperous than their parents and grandparents had been back in 1945. They had electricity and a galaxy of gadgets to show for it. They had cars, and expressways to drive them on. They had large cities still remarkably clean and free of the urban warfare that disfigured some large American cities in the years after 1945. They had many more people, and many more different people than an earlier generation could have imagined. Large cities blossomed with Italian, Portuguese, Chinese, and West Indian immigrants. Immigration placed a strain on some Ontarians' tolerance, and the provincial government responded by persuasion and, where persuasion failed, by legislation to enforce equality of opportunity and treatment among racial groups.

Presiding over it all was the same Conservative government first elected in 1943. That government's tenure was, as we have seen, virtually guaranteed by the division of the opposition vote between the Liberals and the NDP. It appeared to be reinforced by a strong anti-Liberal trend that replaced the Liberals in every province where they had once held power and that culminated in the crushing defeat of the federal Liberals in the national election of September 1984. In Ontario the federal Conservatives, under Brian Mulroney, scored a particularly impressive victory, with the encouragement and support of Premier Davis and his Big Blue Machine.

Polls showed that the provincial Conservatives could count on re-election whenever they chose to run. Premier Davis, after almost fourteen years in power, looked well-nigh unbeatable. A measure of Davis's confidence was his sudden decision, in 1984, to solve the interminable problem of funding separate schools. Already public funds had been furnished to finance grades nine and ten in the Catholic schools, and, it was argued, it was both inevitable and entirely natural that funds should cover the rest. A poll was taken, and it appeared to show that Ontarians would back their premier's decision. Even sophisticated observers believed that it was just another example of Davis's political savoir-faire, and just another monument to the premier's uncanny sense of political timing. In any case, both opposition parties were committed to extending funding; now they once again had no issue to appeal to in the next provincial election.

If Davis's initiative took people by surprise, observers were almost as astonished by the premier's next move. In the fall of 1984 Davis told the province that he had decided to retire. A leadership convention, called as always in Toronto, met in January 1985 to select a new leader and premier, and in a close-run fight the delegates picked the provincial treasurer, Frank Miller, a veteran of the political wars. Miller had suffered a serious heart attack some years before, but had fought his way back, acquiring on the way a considerable reputation for competence as well as for unusual frankness. Miller, in the context of internal Conservative politics, represented an older and more traditional element in the party — the delegates over fifty who preferred to see someone from the hinterland prevail over later-model Tories from Toronto or its suburbs.

With Miller at the helm the polls continued to look up. The economy was doing reasonably well, even if there never seemed to be enough money to go round to satisfy the clients that the government had acquired for itself: hospitals, day-care centres, school boards, universities, and the like. There were worries over what the next federal budget, the first federal Conservative budget, might bring to Ontario. It seemed like a good time to appeal to the electorate, and Miller did just that, announcing a provincial election for May 2, 1985.

The election campaign did not go quite as expected. It was true that all parties agreed on funding for separate schools, but the issue, instead of remaining buried, took on a life of its own. There were many Ontarians who did not want extra funding extended to Catholic schools. Leaders of other sects protested. Teachers worried about their jobs, traditional Tories worried over the abandonment of their party's stand on principle, while Catholic voters — who after all could get the same result from the two opposition parties — did not flock to Miller's standard. The polls began to look down while the Conservative campaign went into a kind of free-fall. The Big Blue Machine ground to a halt.

On May 2nd, Ontario elected a legislature of minorities: 52 Conservatives, 48 Liberals, and 25 NDPers. The Liberals received 1 percent more in popular vote than the Conservatives. After some hesitation the NDP decided to throw its support to the Liberals, in return for a mutually agreed package of legislation, and an agreement to keep the legislature in being for two years. Miller was defeated on a vote of confidence when the legislature convened, and in June the Liberal leader, David Peterson, became premier.

Peterson did not face an easy future. The economy was not doing badly, but after the buffetings of the early 1980s it was difficult to maintain an unalloyed confidence in Ontario's industrial future. Rumours of a federal free-trade agreement with the United States frightened some observers while pleasing others; it remained to be seen whether any such agreement would help or harm, or whether it would, in fact, make any measurable difference. Separate schools would, Peterson proclaimed, get their funds, just as Davis had promised, only it seemed that the cost was going to be rather greater than the Conservatives had estimated: double, in fact, at a time when the provincial government was having trouble finding funds for some of its other struggling enterprises.

The issues therefore remained much the same as they had been, and government's approach to them varied less than some political partisans would have imagined. But if problems abounded, so did opportunities: the potential of nine million citizens, the wealth of the province's farms and forests, and the richness of its mines, not to mention the variety and viability of its manufacturing and service industries. With that backdrop, Ontarians could contemplate the approach of the twenty-first century with genuine, if guarded, optimism.

Further Reading

Additional explorations in Ontario history must begin with the massive *Bibliography of Ontario History*, edited by Olga B. Bishop, Barbara I. Irwin, and Clara G. Miller (2 volumes, Toronto, 1980), covering virtually every aspect of Canadian history and society that can be related to Ontario. The collection emphasizes the local nature of works on the subject of Ontario: the vast majority of its citations pertain to local (city, town, village, county, or township histories) or sectoral matters (the history of an industry or a school board, for example). Although general histories of Ontario are cited, the last truly comprehensive one is J. E. Middleton (with Fred Landon), *The Province of Ontario: A History, 1615-1927*, in five volumes (Toronto, 1927–28). To these should be added the book edited by F. H. Armstrong, H. A. Stevenson, and J. D. Wilson, *Aspects of Nineteenth-Century Ontario*, a collection of essays on a wide variety of Ontario historical topics (Toronto, 1974), and the Ontario Historical Society's *Profiles of a Province*, its centennial publication (Toronto, 1967).

Ontario History, the publication of the Ontario Historical Society, presents its readers with the results of many years of worthy labouring in the historical vineyard and is an essential source for the reader seriously concerned with following developments in the history of the province. Besides Ontario history, searchers can rely on virtually every county, and many townships, having a specialized history. Some of these are by professional or semi-professional historians; many, however, are enthusiastically amateur in nature.

The Champlain Society has for some years been presenting volumes of documents on Ontario history: two volumes on York (later Toronto), for example, or a collection of Loyalist narratives from Upper Canada. Its efforts, encouraged by government subsidy, have now been supplemented by the Ontario Historical Studies Series, edited by Goldwin French and Peter Oliver. The series has been sponsoring a collection of biographies of Ontario premiers, two of which, *Howard Ferguson, Ontario Tory*, by Peter Oliver (Toronto, 1977), and *The Pre-Confederation Premiers*, edited by J. M. S. Careless (Toronto, 1980), have appeared. Both books are extremely useful, as is another OHSS-sponsored book, *Ontario since 1867* by Joseph Schull. The biography of Sir James Pliny Whitney, originally an exceptionally able Ph D thesis by Charles Humphries, appeared during 1985. Other volumes seem to be farther off in terms of completion, but the series, when finished, will form the basis for a new synthesis of the history of the province.

The prehistory of the province is generally covered in very small monographs on particular sites, or in small parts of much larger studies. Very convenient, however, are the works of J. V. Wright of the National Museum of Man in Ottawa: *Ontario Prehistory* (Toronto, 1972) and *Six Chapters of Canadian Prehistory* (Toronto, 1976). Those with a special interest in the history of the Huron will find the books of Conrad Heidenreich and Bruce Trigger useful, while the wars are covered in many of the standard works of Canadian and American history. The life of Joseph Brant has been written up many times, from the mid-nineteenth century onwards, but the recent study by Isabel Thompson Kelsay, *Joseph Brant* (Syracuse, 1984) has much merit.

Every study of pre-Confederation Canada must at some point pay tribute to Gerald Craig's *Upper Canada 1784-1841* (Toronto, 1963), a magisterial summary of the province's early settlement. H. V. Nelles's *The Politics of Development* (Toronto, 1974) still stands as one of the best studies of the development of natural resources in North America, and is a pleasure to read because of its fluent style and comprehensive vision. Nelles's work must be supplemented by Christopher Armstrong's study, originally a Ph D thesis, *The Politics of Federalism* (Toronto, 1981), exploring Ontario's federal-provincial role. More specialized is Barbara Wilson's *Ontario and the First World War* (Toronto, 1977), a documentary collection with extensive and illuminating commentary.

Outside the OHSS series, Premier Mitchell Hepburn has received a vivid biography from Neil McKenty, *Mitch Hepburn* (Toronto, 1967). Portraits of other Ontario politicians between 1880 and 1930 may be found in Hector Charlesworth, *Candid Chronicles* (Toronto, 1925) and *More Candid Chronicles* (Toronto, 1928). Leslie Frost left an autobiography covering his overseas service during the First World War, *Fighting Men* (Toronto, 1967).

There is a great deal written on the subject of education in Upper Canada and Ontario; of special interest are Franklin A. Walker's *Catholic Education and Politics in Upper Canada* (Toronto, 1955) and his *Catholic Education and Politics in Ontario* (Toronto, 1964).

Lastly, we must pay tribute to the Canadian census and the *Canada Yearbook*, which until recently was published every year, on time. In default of a proper Ontario yearbook (a curious lack), these two federal publications remain an essential source for readily available statistics on Ontario, its population and economy.

Appendix

Lieutenant-Governors of Ontario, *1867–1985*

Henry William Stisted	*1867–68*
William Pearce Howland	*1868–73*
John Willoughby Crawford	*1873–75*
Donald Alexander Macdonald	*1875–80*
John Beverley Robinson	*1880–87*
Alexander Campbell	*1887–92*
George Airey Kirkpatrick	*1892–97*
Oliver Mowat	*1897–1903*
William Mortimer Clark	*1903–08*
John Morison Gibson	*1908–14*
John Strathearn Hendrie	*1914–19*
Lionel Herbert Clarke	*1919–21*
Henry Cockshutt	*1921–27*
William Donald Ross	*1927–32*
Herbert Alexander Bruce	*1932–37*
Albert Matthews	*1937–46*
Ray Lawson	*1946–52*
Louis Orville Breithaupt	*1952–57*
John Keiller MacKay	*1957–63*
William Earl Rowe	*1963–68*
William Ross Macdonald	*1968–74*
Pauline Emily McGibbon	*1974–80*
John Black Aird	*1980–85*
Lincoln Alexander	*1985–*

Premiers of Ontario, *1867–1985*

John Sandfield Macdonald	Liberal-Conservative	*1867–71*
Edward Blake	Liberal	*1871–72*
Oliver Mowat	Liberal	*1872–96*
Arthur Sturgis Hardy	Liberal	*1896–99*
George William Ross	Liberal	*1899–1905*
James Pliny Whitney	Conservative	*1905–14*
William Howard Hearst	Conservative	*1914–19*
Ernest Charles Drury	United Farmers of Ontario	*1919–23*
George Howard Ferguson	Conservative	*1923–30*
George Stewart Henry	Conservative	*1930–34*
Mitchell Frederick Hepburn	Conservative	*1934–42*
Gordon Daniel Conant	Liberal	*1942–43*
Harry Corwin Nixon	Liberal	*1943*
George Alexander Drew	Conservative	*1943–48*
Thomas Laird Kennedy	Conservative	*1948–49*
Leslie Miscampbell Frost	Conservative	*1949–61*
John Parmenter Robarts	Conservative	*1961–71*
William Grenville Davis	Conservative	*1971–85*
Frank Miller	Conservative	*1985*
David Peterson	Liberal	*1985–*

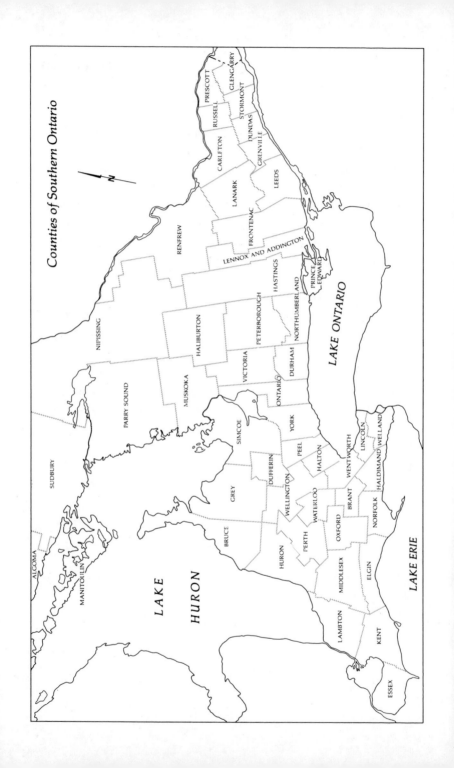

Counties of Southern Ontario

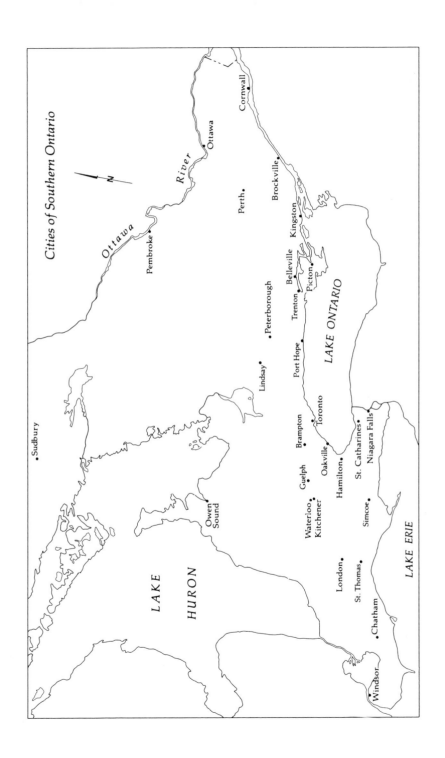

Cities of Southern Ontario

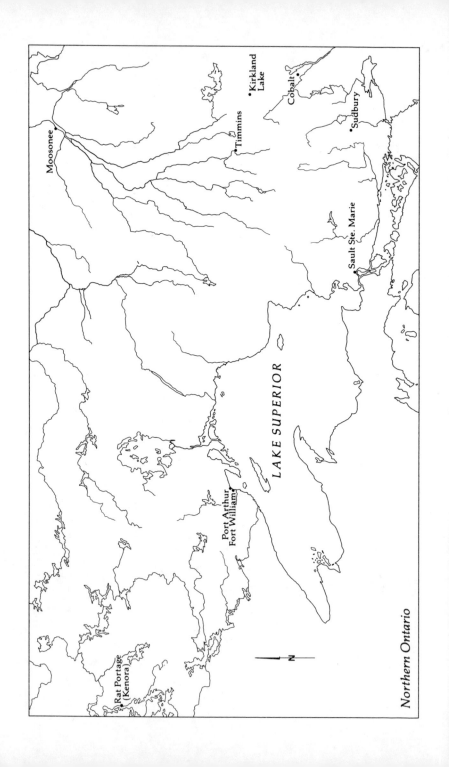

Kirkland
Lake

Cobalt

Sudbury

Timmins

Moosonee

Sault Ste. Marie

LAKE SUPERIOR

Port Arthur
Fort William

Rat Portage
(Kenora)

N

Northern Ontario

Index

agriculture, 5, 35–37, 50, 68, 79; in eastern Ontario, 72–73; drainage, 73; in southern Ontario, 73–74; dairying, 74; in northern Ontario, 84; agricultural education, 107; and World War I, 116; and World War II, 159; on marginal land, 175; marketing boards, 191
Ahearn, Thomas, 103–4
aircraft industry, 157
Albany, New York, 8
Alberta, 123, 146, 154, 179, 181
Algoma, 180
Algonkian tribes, 5, 19
"alien question," 39
Allan, William, 40
American Revolution, 12–17; invasion of Canada, 12–13; Loyalists in, 13–17; frontier warfare, 14–16; effect on Great Lakes region, 17, 19; effect on Canadian institutions, 23
Americans, as settlers, 24; loyalty of, 27–28, 30, 32–33, 39–40
Amherstburg, 33
Ancaster, 33
Anglicans (Church of England), 25–26, 40, 45
architecture, 74–75, 120–21, 136, 176
Army, Canadian: and World War I, 113; Ontario enlistments in, 112; and World War II, 150, 157
automobiles and automobile industry, 131, 133, 143, 149, 157

baby boom, 174–75, 185, 186, 188
Baldwin, Robert, 41, 42, 43, 55, 56
Baldwin, William Warren, 41, 43, 75
Bank of Montreal, 78
Bank of Upper Canada, 58–59
banks, 110
Baptists, 25
barley, 73
beaver, 6–7
Beaver Dam, battle of, 32
Beck, Sir Adam, 104, 128, 170
Bell, Alexander Graham, 92
Belleville, 73, 77
Bennett, R.B., 130–31, 134, 135, 140, 141–42, 147, 163
Bertrand, Jean-Jacques, 188
Bickell, J.P., 136
blacks, 36–37, 63

Blake, Edward, 78–80, 81, 82
"Bloody Assizes," 33
Bond Head, Sir Francis, 42–43, 46
Borden, Sir Robert, 112, 114, 117
Boulton, D'Arcy, 40
Bourassa, Robert, 188
Bracken, John, 171
Bradstreet, Colonel John, 11
Brant, Joseph, 14–15, 19–20, 27
Brantford, 92, 99, 100
brewing, 73
British Columbia, 66, 82, 146, 154, 183
British North America Act, 68–69, 82
Brock, General Sir Isaac, 29–30, 34
Brown, George, 56, 59–60, 63, 67–68, 70, 72, 78
Bruce County, 52, 176
Brûlé, Etienne, 6
Buchanan, Isaac, 61
buffalo, 32, 93
Burlington Bay, 21, 31
Burlington Heights, 33
Butler, Colonel John, 15
Butler's Rangers, 15–16
By, Colonel John, 38
Bytown; *see* Ottawa

Cadillac, Lamothe de, 5
Canada Company, 49
Canada, Dominion of, constitution, 67–69, 81–86, 128–31, 146–47, 155–56, 192–93
Canada, Province of: established, 46; politics in, 54–55, 66–68; government of, 55–56; population of, 63; and us Civil War, 63–64; tariff, 61, 66; and Confederation, 66–70
Canadian Pacific Railway, 83, 91
Canadian Shield, 4, 7, 52, 71, 73, 91
canals, 38, 47–49, 179
Carleton, Sir Guy (later Lord Dorchester), 13–14
Caroline, 44
Cartier, Jacques, 5–6
Catholicism; *see* Roman Catholics
Cayuga, 8

Chalk River, 6, 181
Champlain, Samuel de, 6
Charlottetown, 67
cheese, 74
Chippewa, 19
Civil War (us), 63–64
Clear Grits, 56, 59
clergy reserves, 25, 61
Cobalt, 109
Collingwood, 111
colonization, 7
Communist Party, 137, 143, 146, 160–61, 165
compact theory, 81–82, 130–31
Conant, Gordon, 161–62
Confederation, 66–70
Confederation of Tomorrow Conference, 187
Congress of Industrial Organizations (cio), 143
Conservatives, 67, 75–76, 87, 93–94, 98, 99–100, 102, 119, 120, 123, 124,
    126–27, 139, 162–64, 166–67, 173, 183–84, 189–90
Constitution, 67–69, 81–86, 114, 128–31, 146–47, 154–56, 168–70, 192–93
Constitutional Act (1791), 22–24
Co-operative Commonwealth Federation (ccf), 137–38, 160–61, 163–64, 165,
    166–67, 184, 190; see also New Democratic Party
Cornwall, 64, 76
Cornwall Canal, 48
Cottrelle, George, 159
Craig, Gerald, 39
Croll, David, 139, 140, 145
Crooks, Adam, 89

Davis, William G., 188–92, 195
Deseronto, John, 20
Detroit, 29, 30, 33
Dewar, Ken, 103
Dewart, Hartley, 124–25, 126
Diefenbaker, John G., 183
Dionne Quintuplets, 148
distilling, 74
Drainage Act (1879), 73
Draper, W.H., 46
Drew, Colonel George, 141, 145, 152, 162–73, 178, 182, 183

Drury, Ernest C., 123–24
Ducharme, Captain Dominique, 32
Dufferin County, 73
Dundas Street, 35
Duplessis, Maurice L., 142–43
Durham, Earl of, 46

Eaton's, 110, 159
Eddy, E.B., 51
Edison, T.A., 92
Edward VIII, 148
Egan Company, 51
elections: 1836: 42–43; 1867: 76; 1871: 79; 1905: 102; 1919: 119; 1923: 126;
    1934: 140; 1937: 145; 1943: 162–64; 1945: 166–67; 1948: 171; 1951: 183;
    1955: 183; 1959: 183–84; 1963: 188; 1967: 188; 1971: 189; 1975: 190;
    1977: 190; 1981: 190; 1985: 196
electricity, 92–93, 100, 103–5, 110, 118, 128–29, 140, 142, 158, 170–71,
    176, 179, 180
Elgin County, 49, 138
Elizabeth II, 193
Elliot Lake, 180
energy, 92, 10, 103–5, 128–29, 158, 170–72, 179, 180–82, 191
English (ethnic group), 99
Erie, 5
Erie Canal, 48
Erie, Lake, 4, 19, 30, 48
Essex County, 49
Etobicoke, 21
Executive Council, 23

Fallen Timbers, battle of, 26
Fallon, Bishop M.F., 106
Family Compact, 40–42
farmers: in politics, 58–59, 87–88, 119, 121, 138; decline in strength, 98, 121,
    138, 175; prosperity of, 107; and World War I, 116–18
federal-provincial relations, 76–77, 81–86, 105, 129–31, 140, 141–47,
    152–56, 164–66, 167–70, 172, 179, 180–82, 182–83, 186–88
Fenians, 64–65
Ferguson, G. Howard, 119, 124–34, 135
Fitzgibbon, Lieutenant James, 32
Five Nations; see Iroquois

Ford Motor Company, 143
forest, 4, 5, 108, 126; *see also* timber, lumber, pulp and paper
Fort Cataraqui; *see* Kingston
Fort Detroit, 10, 12, 13, 20, 26, 29; *see also* Detroit
Fort Duquesne, 10
Fort Frontenac, 10–11; *see also* Kingston
Fort Frances, 71, 83, 108
Fort George, 31, 32
Fort Henry, 37
Fort Malden, 29
Fort Michilimackinac, 10, 12, 26, 29
Fort Niagara, 10, 11, 12, 16, 17, 20, 26, 31, 32, 34
Fort Orange; *see* Albany
Fort Oswego, 10, 26
Fort William, 71, 83, 111
France, 5–11
French Canadians: in Province of Canada, 52–53; immigration to Ontario, 72;
    as proportion of Ontario population, 99; as political factor, 105, 139–40, 172
French language, as political issue, 22, 52–53, 60, 75, 93–95, 99, 105–6, 118,
    124, 141
Frenchtown, 30
Frontenac, comte de, 9
Frost, Leslie, 178–79, 181, 182–85
fur trade, 6–7

Galt, John, 49
Gamey, R.R., 101–2
gas and oil, 159, 180; *see also* natural gas
General Motors, 143, 144
George III, 17
George VI, 148
Georgetown, 92
Georgian Bay, 6, 108, 111
Germans (ethnic group), 99, 175
Ghent, Treaty of (1814), 34
Glengarry County, 172
Globe (newspaper), 56, 70, 72
Globe and Mail, 143
Goderich, 49
Gourlay, Robert, 40–41
grain elevators, 111

Grand River, 20-21, 26-27
Grand Trunk Railway, 57-58, 59, 66
Great Britain: colonial system of, 22-24, 37-38, 53-54, 83-84, 112, 130-31; army in Canada, 28-35, 64, 65; expenditures in Upper Canada, 37-38; immigration from, 38-39, 52, 175; and Upper Canadian politics, 42, 46; exports to, 50, 51; Ontarians' attachment to, 111-12; and outbreak of World War I, 112; and World War II, 153
Great Depression, 134-37
Great Lakes, 3-5, 6, 11-12, 19-20, 71
Great Western Railway, 57
Grenville Canal, 38, 47
Grenville, William, 22
Grey County, 52
Groseilliers, Medard Chouart des, 9
Guelph, 107, 162

Haileybury, 109
Haldimand, General Frederick, 20
Haliburton County, 52
Hall-Dennis Committee, 188
Hamilton, 75, 77, 99, 120, 157, 160
Hardy, Arthur S., 100
Harrison, General William Henry, 30
health, 107, 131, 141, 163, 183
Hearst, Sir William, 113-14, 118-19, 123, 127
Henry, George, 135, 138, 139-40
Hepburn, Mitchell F., 138-47, 152-53, 161, 162, 163, 164, 165, 172, 173
Highway 401, 149, 177
highways, 35, 111, 121, 131, 135-36, 148, 149, 176-77, 178, 184, 189
Hincks, Sir Francis, 54, 56-57
housing, 74-75, 120-21, 150, 176-77
Howe, C.D., 158, 171, 179, 181-82
Hudson Bay, 4, 71, 97
Hull, General William, 29
Huron, 5, 6-8
Huron, Lake, 5, 9, 49, 73
Huron County, 49
Huron Tract, 49

Ilsley, J.L., 155
immigration, 5, 20-21, 38-39, 107, 174, 175, 194-95; *see also* settlement

Indian policy, 20-21, 34, 71
Indians; *see* under individual tribes
Ireland, 64-65, 75
Irish, 99
Iroquois Confederacy, 5, 6, 11, 12, 14-17; as settlers in Ontario, 20
Italians, 175

James Bay, 4, 83
Jay's Treaty (1794), 26
Jesuits (Society of Jesus), 8
Johnson, Daniel, 186
Johnson, Sir John, 15, 16
Johnson, J.K., 68
Johnson, Sir William, 11, 12, 13
Jolliffe, Edward, 164, 167
Jones, R.L., 74
Judicial Committee of the Privy Council (British), 82-85

Kennedy, Brig.-Gen. ("Colonel") Thomas, 178
Kenora (Rat Portage), 71, 83-84
King, William Lyon Mackenzie, 127, 130, 138, 142-43, 144-45, 146, 147, 148, 152-53, 161-62, 165, 166, 167-68, 178
Kingston, 9, 19, 29, 31, 38, 47, 54, 73, 75, 99, 176
Kirkland Lake, 109, 160

labour, 115–16, 136–37, 150, 160
Lachine Canal, 47
LaFontaine, Louis-Hippolyte, 55
Lake Erie and Northern Railway, 110
Lanark County, 38, 71
land, as political factor, 24–25
Laurier, Robert, 139
Laurier, Sir Wilfrid, 87, 95, 112, 114
Leacock, Stephen, 109, 126
Legislative Assembly: origins of, 22–23; quarrels with governor and council, 39; disappears, 46; revival of, 1867, 69, 76; location, 77
Legislative Council, 22–23; quarrels with Assembly, 39
Lennox and Addington County, 176
Lesage, Jean, 186
Lewis, David, 167n
Lewis, Stephen, 190

liberalism, 60, 96, 97–98, 138, 144–45
Liberal Party (Ontario), 67, 79, 83, 87–89, 93, 95, 96, 97–98, 99–102, 120, 124–25, 126, 138–39, 142, 144–45, 153, 161–62, 173, 184, 190
lieutenant-governor, 24, 81, 97, 140
London, 35, 45, 57, 75, 99, 100, 184
Lount, Samuel, 45
Lower Canada, 22, 44–45, 61, 68
Loyalists, 13–17; refugees, 18–20; settlement of in Ontario, 20–21, 24
lumber, 50–51; in Ottawa Valley, 72
Lynch, Archbishop, 89

Macdonald, Sir John A., 55, 59, 61, 64, 67-68, 76, 78, 81, 83-86, 87, 93-94
Macdonald, John Sandfield, 64, 76-77, 78
Macdonnel, Bishop, 106
Mackenzie, Alexander, 78, 83, 86
Mackenzie, William Lyon, 41-45, 48, 98
Macleod, Alexander, 44
MacNab, Sir Allan, 55, 59
Madison, Dolly, 33
Madison, James, 33
Maitland, General Sir Peregrine, 39-40
Manitoba, 83-85, 94-95, 123, 154, 178
Manitoulin Island, 71, 176
manufacturing, 50-52, 86-87, 115, 133-34, 157-58, 174
Massachusetts, 12
Matthews, Peter, 45
McCaul, John, 62
McCullagh, George, 143
McKenty, Neil, 145
McKenzie, A.D., 183-84
McNab settlement, 50
Meighen, Arthur, 161
Merritt, W.H., 48
Methodists, 25, 99
Midland, 111
mines and mining, 90-91, 109, 136, 143, 157
Missisauga, 19-20
Mohawk, 8, 32
Mohawk River, 9, 12, 14
Montcalm, marquis de, 10-11
Montgomery's Tavern, 44

Montreal, 6, 7, 8, 9, 11, 13, 38, 47, 48, 50, 52, 57, 65, 78, 120, 177
Morrison, J.J., 123-24
Morton, W.L., 69
Mowat, Sir Oliver, 80-82, 83-86, 93-94, 95-96, 97, 123
Murray, Gladstone, 165
Muskoka, 112

"National Policy," 87
natural gas, 179, 181-82, 184
Nelles, H.V., 108
Neutral, 5
New Brunswick, 18, 66, 85, 146, 154
New Democratic Party (NDP), 190, 197
New France, 6-11
New Liskeard, 84
New Orleans, 10
New York City, 51
New York State, 179
Newark; see Niagara-on-the-Lake
Newfoundland, 18
Niagara-on-the-Lake, 32, 149
Niagara Falls, 48, 92-93, 100, 128, 170, 174
Niagara Peninsula, 73
Niagara River, 48, 65
Nipissing, Lake, 4, 9
Nixon, Harry, 138, 139, 162, 164, 190
Nixon, Robert, 190
Nova Scotia, 18, 66, 78, 82, 85
nuclear technology and power, 168, 179, 181, 191

Oakville, 132, 157
Ojibwa, 5, 71
Oliver, Farquhar, 138
Oneida, 8, 16
Onondaga, 8
Ontario Agricultural College, 107
Ontario Hydro, 103, 110, 118, 128-29, 140, 142, 158, 170-71, 179-80, 191
Ontario, Lake, 31, 38, 179
Ontario, Province of: origin of name, 69; founded, 69-70; politics in, 75-81,
    122-24, 139-41, 161-64, 165-67; dominion-provincial (federal-provincial)

relations, 81–86, 105, 127–31, 141–47, 153–55, 164–65, 166, 167–70, 178, 179, 181, 182–83, 186–88; boundary dispute, 83–85; boundaries extended, 97; population of, 98, 120–21; resource management in, 108–9, 126, 163; British imperial patriotism in, 111–12
Orange Lodge, 43, 75–76, 78, 89–90
Orillia, 109
Oriskany, battle of, 14
Oshawa, 69, 132, 143–44, 157, 174
Ottawa (tribe), 5, 71
Ottawa (city), 51, 57, 60, 62, 72, 75, 92, 98, 103–4, 120
Ottawa Electric Company, 103–4
Ottawa River, 4, 5, 6, 7, 9, 38, 72, 108, 171
Owram, Doug, 72

"Patent Combination," 76, 78
Patrons of Industry, 88
Pearson, Lester B., 186
Perth, 71
Peterborough, 38–39, 51, 92, 174, 186
Peterson, David, 197
Petun, 5
Pickering, Joseph, 36
pine, red, 4-5
pine, white, 4-5, 50
Plattsburg, battle of, 33
Pleistocene period, 4
politicians, characteristics of, 75; and Ontario politics, 86; and scandals, 101
Pontiac, 12
population, 28, 52-53, 63, 72, 98, 120, 150, 174-75
Port Arthur, 111, 149
Port Hope, 75
Presbyterians, 25, 99
Prescott, 44, 57, 111
Prescott County, 72
Prevost, General Sir George, 27–28
Prince Edward Island, 18, 66
Procter, General Henry, 30–31
prohibition, 101, 118–19, 122, 124–27, 132–33
Protestants, 7–8, 25–26, 45, 61, 75–76, 88–90, 99
pulp and paper, 108

Quebec Act, 12-13
Quebec City, 6, 11, 14-15, 50
Quebec Province, 13-14, 18-19, 85, 94, 122, 128-30, 142-43, 146, 166, 186-88, 191-94; division of, 22; reconstituted, 69
Queen Elizabeth Way, 148
Queen's University, 121-22, 165
Queenston, 27, 32, 149
Queenston Heights, battle of, 29-30
Quinte, Bay of, 20, 73

radio, 133-34, 147-48
Radisson, Pierre, 9
railways, 57-58, 77, 79-80, 83, 109; electric railways (radials), 110, 179
Rainy River, 84
Raney, W.E., 124
Rat Portage (Kenora), 71
Read, Colin, 44
Rebellions of 1837, 43-46
Reciprocity Treaty (1854), 66
Red River, 71, 78, 83
Reform Party, 41, 54, 59, 78; see also Liberals
Regulation xvii, 106, 118, 128-29
religion: as factor in colonization, 7; and origins of Upper Canada, 22; in Upper Canadian politics, 25, 40, 45, 61; in Ontario politics, 75-76, 86, 94-95, 99, 121, 140-41, 166, 185-86
Renfrew County, 50
"Responsible Government," 43
Rideau Canal, 38, 47
Rideau River, 38
Ridgeway, battle of, 65
Riel, Louis, 78, 79.
Robarts, John P., 184-85, 186-88
Robinson, John Beverley, 40
Roebuck, Arthur, 139, 140, 145
Rolph, John, 42
Rolphton, 181
Roman Catholics, 7-8, 13, 22, 61-62, 75-76, 88-90, 94-95, 99, 140-41, 166
Ross, Sir George, 98, 100-2
Rowe, Earl, 145
Rowell, Newton Wesley, 114, 117, 145-46
Rowell-Sirois Commission, 145-47, 153-55, 179

Rush-Bagot Agreement (1817), 34
Russell County, 72
Ryerson, Egerton, 43, 61, 88

Sackets Harbor, 31
St Catharines, 160
St Laurent, Louis, 178-79
St Lawrence River, 4, 6, 7, 9, 38, 47, 111; canals on, 47; power source, 128, 142-43, 179-80
St Thomas, 45, 138
Ste Marie Among the Hurons, 8
Sandwell, B.K., 165
Sarnia, 57, 78, 157
Saskatchewan, 154, 183
Sault Ste Marie, 48, 71, 101, 149, 157, 177, 180
schools and schooling, 61-62, 68, 79-80, 88-90, 105, 106, 114-15, 128-29, 131-32, 140-41, 166, 177, 188-89
Scott Act, 62
Scott, Sir Richard, 62
Scott, Thomas, 78
Scott, Sir Walter, 88-89
Secord, Laura, 32
Seneca, 8
settlement: first, 9; across the Appalachians, 11-12; in old province of Quebec, 18-19; by Iroquois, 20; by Loyalists, 20-21; in Upper Canada, 35-36; Talbot settlement, 49; Canada Company, 49-50; Ottawa Valley, 50
Seven Years' War, 10-11
Sheaffe, General Roger, 30
Simcoe, John Graves, 24-25, 35, 49
Simcoe, Lake, 35
Simpson's, 110, 159
Six Nations; see Iroquois
Smith, "Sell 'em Ben," 136
Stacey, C.P., 34
steamships, 47, 48
Stisted, Major-General, 69
Stoney Creek, battle of, 31-32
Strachan, Bishop John, 34, 40
Stratford, 74
Stratton, J.R., 102
Sudbury, 91, 157, 180

Superior, Lake, 4, 177
Susquehannock, 5, 8
Sydenham, Lord (Charles Poulett Thomson), 46, 53-54

Talbot, Colonel Thomas, 49, 57
Talbot Settlement, 49
tariff, 60-61, 66, 68, 86-87, 136
Taschereau, Louis-Alexandre, 128-29
taxation, 68, 90-91, 131, 134-35, 151, 155-56, 168-70, 177-78
Taylor, E.P., 136
Tecumseh, 31
Temiskaming and Northern Ontario Railway, 109
temperance, 101, 118-19, 162, 163, 171
Thames, battle of the, 31
Thomson, Charles Poulett; see Sydenham, Lord
Thorold, 108
Thunder Bay, 180
timber trade, 50
Toronto (formerly York), 43, 98-99, 120, 181; ambitions of, 60, 72, 78; economic importance of, 60, 75, 109-10; capital of Ontario, 69; municipal revenue, 132; ethnic composition of, 175
Toronto Star, 147
Tory Party, 45-46, 54, 55, 59; see also Conservatives
Trades and Labour Congress, 165
Trans-Canada Highway, 177
Trans-Canada Pipeline, 181-82
transportation, 35, 47-49, 56-57, 77, 79-80, 83, 109, 111, 148, 149, 158, 177-78, 179-80, 181-82
Trent University, 186
Trent incident (1861), 64
Trinity College, 125
Trudeau, Pierre Elliott, 191-93
Tupper, Sir Charles, 95
Tuscarora, 11

unemployment, 122
unions, 137, 143-44
United Auto Workers, 144
United Farmers of Ontario (UFO), 120, 122-26
United States: independence of, 14, 17; Indian policy of, 21, 26-27; relations

with Great Britain, 26–27, 64–65; and War of 1812, 26–34; and rebellions of 1837, 44, 45; lumber exports to, 50–51; railway connections to, 57; Civil War in, 63–64; emigration to, 71–72; investment from, 109, 133–34; cultural influences, 133–34; Ontario's dependence on for energy, 158, 180; uranium sales to, 180–81

universities, funding of, 121–22, 186, 189

University of Toronto: established, 56; faculty politics, 62; reformed, 103; in 1920s, 121

University of Western Ontario, 121–22

Upper Canada: creation of, 22; government of, 22–24; and War of 1812, 26–34; loyalty of population, 27–28, 29–30, 32–33; politics in, 28, 39–46; merged with Lower Canada, 46; British immigration to, 52; population of, 52–53; education in, 56, 61–62

Upper Canada Village, 180

uranium, 168, 179, 180–81

Versailles, Treaty of (1783), 16–17

Victoria, Queen, 97

vineyards, 73–74

Walker's Distillery, 73

War of 1812, 26–34; effect of, on Upper Canada, 34–35

Washington, DC, 33

Waterloo, 110

Welland Canal, 48, 108

Wentworth County, 159

wheat, 37, 50–52, 73

whisky, 73

Whitney, Sir James P., 98, 102–7, 113

Willcocks, Joseph, 32

Wilson, Sir Daniel, 62

Windsor, 110, 120, 132, 135, 157, 177

wine (Ontario), 73–74, 118

women's suffrage, 115–16

women in labour force, 132, 150

Woodsworth, James S., 137

World War I: outbreak, 112; Canadian response, 112–13; chauvinism during, 114; constitution during, 114; politics of, 114, 116–18; war industry, 115; effects on society, 115–16

World War II: outbreak of, 148; constitution during, 151; politics during, 151–53;

war industry, 156–58, 160; rationing, 158–59
Wyandotte (Wendat), 8
Wyoming Valley, 15

Yonge Street, 35
York (later Toronto), 28, 31, 35
York County, 42
York University, 186